Mutual Integration in Immigration Society

Bodi Wang is a postdoc researcher in Department of Humanities, Social and Political Science at ETH Zurich.

Bodi Wang

Mutual Integration in Immigration Society

An Epistemic Argument

Campus Verlag
Frankfurt/New York

The open access publication of this book has been published with the support of the Swiss National Science Foundation.

The work, including all its parts, is subject to copyright protection. The text of this publication is published under the "Creative Commons Attribution-NonCommercial-NoDerivatives 4.0 International" (CC BY-NC-ND 4.0) licence.
The full licence text can be found at:
https://creativecommons.org/licenses/by-nc-nd/4.0/deed.en

Any use that exceeds the scope of the CC BY-NC-ND 4.0 licence is not permitted without the publisher's consent. This applies in particular to adaptations and translations of the work.

The images and other third-party material contained in this work are also subject to the aforementioned Creative Commons licence, unless otherwise stated under references / illustration index. Insofar as the material in question is not subject to the aforementioned Creative Commons licence and the usage in question is not permitted under statutory provisions, the consent of the respective rightsholder must be obtained.

ISBN 978-3-593-51788-9 Print
ISBN 978-3-593-45530-3 E-Book (PDF)
DOI 10.12907/978-3-593-45530-3

Copyright © 2023. Campus Verlag GmbH, Frankfurt am Main.
Some rights reserved
Coverdesign: Campus Verlag GmbH, Frankfurt am Main
Typesetting: le-tex xerif
Printed in the United States of America

www.campus.de
www.press.uchicago.edu

For all those who try to make a life elsewhere

我想：希望是本无所谓有，无所谓无的。
正如这地上的路
其实地上本没有路，走的人多了，也便成了路。
——鲁迅

I thought: hope cannot be said to exist, nor can it be said not to exist.
It is just like roads across the earth.
For actually the earth had no roads to begin with, but when many pass one way, a road is made.
——Lu Xun

Contents

Acknowledgements 9

Introduction – Integration Beyond Formal Equality 11

One – The (Im)Possibility of Integration 21
    The Assimilation-like Integration 22
    The Muhammad Cartoon Controversy and the Generalized Other . 28
    The Problem of Moral Generalism 34
    Segregation and Perpetual Foreignness 42
    When is Integration Possible? 49

Two – Identity-based Thinking 55
    Social Orders and Necessary Identity 56
    Apparent Necessity, (Un)Justifiable Necessity, and the Identity of "Immigrant" 63
    Identity-based Thinking and How It Excludes 73

Three – The Epistemology of Identity-based Thinking 81
    The Model of Assumed Objectivity 82
    Epistemic Irresponsibility 89
    Epistemic Injustice 98

Four – Knowing People 111
    Why Take Subjectivity into Consideration? 112
    Narrative Knowledge and the Concrete Other 123
    Ethics of Difference and the Moral Significance of Self-Cultivation 134

Five – Making Sense of "Strangers" 145
    Who are "Strangers" in Our Midst? 146
    Structural Injustice and Two Structures That Make "Strangers" 152
    "Not-Self": The Self-Centered Model of Strangeness 160
    The "Stranger" and the Need for the Third Element 167

Six – History and Structural Transformation 177
    Alienation: the Interactional, the Structural and the Existential ... 179
    Why History? 186
    History as a Social Connection Model of Responsibility 192
    History as the Site of "Possibility" 201
    Structural Transformation 211

Conclusion – Integration as Integration of People 215

Works Cited 227

Index 237

Acknowledgements

This book originates from my PhD dissertation, which was originally titled "Mutual Integration. A Study of Integration Beyond Formal Equality." Undertaking the PhD, writing the thesis, and finally handing it in and defending it has been a valuable learning process for me, throughout which I have received a great deal of support.

First, I would like to thank Prof. Dr. Christian Neuhäuser, Prof. Dr. Robin Celikates, and Dr. Johann Siebers for their supervision, help and support for the research project. Their encouragement and insights have meant a great deal to me as someone who has just started to learn how to conduct research independently.

My sincere thanks also go to TU Dortmund University for offering me a comfortable and supportive place to work as well as allowing me to teach during my PhD. In the same way, I also want to thank Prof. Dr. Dr. Nadia Mazouz, Prof. Dr. Michael Hampe and ETH Zürich. They took me in as a researcher after I moved to Switzerland. With the peace and security that my current job provides, I was able to proceed with and complete the publication of this book.

I would like to express my gratitude to Prof. Dr. Christine Bratu, Dr. Felix Bender, Dr. Anna Welpinghus, Prof. Dr. Antonio Calcagno, Prof. Dr. Kristina Lepold, and Leire Urricelqui. I would like to thank them for their comments and insights. I also would like to thank Samuel Cloake for proofreading the early drafts, Sean Winkler for proofreading the later version of my dissertation, and Maren Barton for the final proofreading.

I greatly appreciate the discussions I had with colleagues from TU Dortmund University, School of Advanced Study (University of London) and Ruhr-University Bochum in colloquiums and conferences. I also would like to thank Mr Malte Schefer from the Campus Verlag publishing house for his assistance.

Of course, the research project would not have gone so smoothly and so far without finance support. For this matter, I am grateful for the PhD scholarship I received from Heinrich Böll Stiftung and the open access fund from SNF (Schweizerischer Nationalfonds).

I am indebted to my family and friends, who offered me comfort when I was feeling down or drowning in self-doubt. I especially want to thank my mother for believing in me unconditionally. I would not have got this far without her trust and support. I also want to thank my husband Nils Eling for his support and for the joy he brings into my life.

Introduction –
Integration Beyond Formal Equality

Contemporary debates about integration focus primarily on the distribution of rights; that is, on how to ensure immigrants' participation in their receiving society and to improve social solidarity through securing the (quasi) formal equality of immigrants. For example, Will Kymlicka's theory of minority rights offers a new conception of rights as such that accommodates minority cultures within liberal democracy, and Ayelet Shahar's *jus nexi* ("earned citizenship") suggests a new category of citizenship transfer that eases cases of injustice faced by individuals who do not have a traditional claim to citizenship, such as via blood and birth. However, despite the flourishing literature about improving formal equality, integration is also concerned with problems that are beyond the distribution of rights.

The widely shared conception of integration still places the onus to integrate only on immigrants. But this one-sided conception misunderstands the actual dynamic of integration and who are involved in this process. One may emphasize that when talking about integration, what is meant is the integration of immigrants, so it is only natural to think that it is immigrants who should integrate. However, just as the abovementioned rights discourse shows, it is in fact clear that immigrants cannot really integrate – that is, generally speaking, sufficiently participating in and interacting with the receiving society – if they are left completely on their own. The receiving society also needs to provide them with some things that ensure their capability of participation and interaction. That means, even if integration only refers to the integration of immigrants, integration still incorporates more than just immigrants or people with migration background. As I shall introduce in what follows, the conceptual problem of integration goes further.

First, although it is assumed that only immigrants need to integrate, the standard of a successful integration remains unclear, sometimes even assimilationist. When is an immigrant successfully integrated into the receiving society and who should decide it? Does what appear to be a so-called parallel society, such as Chinatown, Little Italy and Koreatown, necessarily mean that integration fails, because people with migration background start their own community? Or do protests, especially when they involve a large number of people with migration background, necessarily denote an integration failure? But why not an integration success, since they clearly show that immigrants have mastered the local language(s) and know their rights very well.[1] If a successful integration implies that immigrants should adopt the mainstream lifestyle of the receiving society as well as a certain interpretation and way of values, then isn't integration just another name for assimilation?

Second, the expectation about what integration should bring seems to be a conflict-free society. Whenever immigrants are involved in social problems, calls for more integration will ensue. Consequently, after the Oldham riots in 2001, two official reports – the Cantle Report and the Ritchie Report – either attributed the cause to the lack of a common identity or to immigrants' poor knowledge of English, although both reports also recognized that there had been a long-term and deep-seated segregation problem in Oldham, for which the local government and pre-existing problems like racial discrimination were responsible. David Miller also describes the riots as an integration failure of the immigrants and calls for more and better integration of this group. However, immigrants that took part in the riots were mostly third or even fourth-generation immigrants, who neither lacked knowledge of the English language nor a common identity, be it British or Oldhamer. As other discussions point out, their rage was "the violence of the violated," who had been denied as part of society for generations.[2] Similar combinations can be also found in incidents elsewhere such as the Muhammad cartoon contro-

---

1 For a discussion about successful integration leading to more conflicts, see Aladin El-Mafaalani (2018), *Das Integrationsparadox. Warum gelungene Integration zu mehr Konflikten führt*. Cologne: Kiepenheuer & Witsch.
2 Chapter Five will deal with David Miller's analysis about immigrants and his analysis of the riots in his book *Strangers in Our Midst*. For a thorough discussion about the riots see for reference Ash Amin (2003), "Unruly Strangers? The 2001 Urban Riots in Britain," *International Journal of Urban and Regional Research* 27 (2): 460–463; Arun Kundnani, "From Oldham to Bradford: the Violence of the Violated," *Race & Class* 43(2)(2001): 105–110. Also see Bodi Wang (2021), "Imagine Strangers in Our Midst," in Corinna Mieth and Wolfram Cremer (eds.), *Migration, Stability and Solidarity*, 59–80. Baden-Baden: Nomos.

versy in 2005, which will be dealt with in Chapter One, and the 2018 Chemnitz protests.³

These further observations reveal an important but underexplored aspect of integration, namely the epistemic aspect. On the one hand, without a clear, justifiable and feasible concept of integration, there will be confusions and contradictions in practice. On the other hand, as mentioned above, since integration involves more than just immigrants, an epistemic analysis also concerns what epistemic efforts or contributions can be expected from the receiving society. In the case of immigrants, such epistemic effort is not only obvious but also treated as a basic standard, for example knowledge of the local language(s) and about the law, order, institutions as well as important historical events of the society where they live. And when it comes to what the receiving society can do for integration, there seems to be nothing but giving rights. But won't wrong or at least inappropriate knowledge about immigrants, social problems, political membership and so on in general affect integration? I think the answer is positive.

In reality, actual people cannot be reduced to right holders, otherwise rights will greatly simplify the complexity of a person's life. Having (the same) legal status does not mean that rights will also be real and effective. The social status of a group is subject to many more factors than the rights discourse can cover. Despite rights, it is still probable that some people do not enjoy an equal social status due to the identities they bear. Immigrants may try their best to participate in the receiving society by learning everything they can and by being as active as they can, but if they keep being rejected by landlords, employers or neighbors because they are immigrants – or even more specific, because of their origin, race or cultural background – they probably have to eventually turn to what they consider to be their own community. In their eyes, they are successfully integrated, because they possess the necessary knowledge for legal and appropriate social participation, and they also interact regularly with the receiving society. But in the eyes of the locals, they may not have tried hard enough to integrate. And regarding the community

---

3 See Johannes Grunert (2018), "Der Abend, an dem der Rechtsstaat aufgab," *Die Zeit*, August, https://www.zeit.de/gesellschaft/zeitgeschehen/2018-08/chemnitz-rechte-demonstration-ausschreitungen-polizei?utm_referrer=https%3A%2F%2Fwww.google.com%2F, last accessed March 2023. Louise Osborne (2918), "In Chemnitz, anti-fascists stand up to the Nazi salutes of Germany's far right," *The Guardian*, September, https://www.theguardian.com/world/2018/sep/01/chemnitz-protests-germany-migration, last accessed March 2023.

they turn to, local people may even find it threatening, because they take it as a sign of resisting integration. This simplified example may sound too rigid and artificial, but as an immigrant who has lived in three different countries, I am sure stories like this one can be found everywhere, sometimes the whole package, sometimes part of it.

At this point, one may point out that those people who turn down immigrants like that are just racists or xenophobic. What they do is wrong, period. That's right, they highly likely are. But the observation should not stop here. Because racist or xenophobic attitude or thinking does not come from nowhere. People who think in that way acquire it from somewhere, they may have been actively trained to see through the wrong lens. What's more, this is not only an agential matter, either. Because if there is such training, there must be corresponding epistemic structures as well, such as norms, concepts and hermeneutical resources. They may be embedded in everyday reasoning, historical narratives or the logic of social orders. That means, not only immigrants but also locals should integrate, since the latter group can also contribute in one way or another both to the integration of immigrants and a better co-existence in an immigration society. This may sound rather counter-intuitive, and someone may point to the etymological baggage of "integration," claiming that "integer" is tied to the assumption that there is a given whole and everything should just become part of it. But etymological origin is not a proper basis for moral judgments. Also, using what has been as the basis for justifying what should be commits a classical induction fallacy. As for what really concerns integration, I shall show later in the discussion that many given epistemic structures contain demeaning and excluding effects. They make immigrants' integration unnecessarily harder by upholding problematic judgments that treat (some) immigrants as undesirable and thereby at odds with social solidarity.

Those problematic epistemic structures cannot be redressed unless locals make an effort to reflect on them and eventually give them up because they are part of those epistemic structures. Immigrants generally do not reject integration, in fact they anticipate it when they decide to move elsewhere, be it willingly or forced. They are ready to make changes, although their changes do not necessarily meet the expectations of the receiving society. However, if they are genuinely treated as equal members of that society, and if their complaints and suggestions are reasonable, then why should that society not consider their voices and make changes accordingly? And when that happens, isn't that also a form of integration? Namely, the receiving society abandons or amends what it took for granted and adapts itself to the new situation based on a reasoning that (partly) originates elsewhere. And these mutual efforts are likely to be asymmetric because people with different social positions and capabilities cannot be expected to make the same amount and the same type of contribution.

Joseph Carens also points out that equal legal rights and the acquisition of citizenship are necessary but not sufficient means for integrating immigrants and their descendants. A functioning formal equality requires the cooperation of officials, ordinary citizens, public cultures and so on. These are the pre-existing contexts with which formal equality *must* interact. Having considered this aspect of integration, Carens remarks that "the value of formal equality is greatly reduced if the representative of the state and the rest of the citizenry *treat you as outsiders who do not really belong and who have somehow acquired a status that is really undeserved*" (Carens 2005, 44, my emphasis). The cooperation of ordinary citizens along with the kind of public culture at hand are factors that determine whether and to what extent formal equality can be real and effective. Formal equality may indeed end up masking substantive inequalities, because by leaving aside relevant pre-existing contexts formal equality generates the misleading impression that rights alone should be enough for social participation. Like this, other crucial participators are exempted from potential responsibilities and immigrants become the only group that is held accountable to a successful integration, whatever that means.

How integration is understood as well as what knowledge supports this kind of understanding are among the pre-existing contexts that I set out to examine in this book. Although I highlight the conceptual and epistemic analysis of integration, I do not mean to say that they are the only two aspects that matter, nor do I mean to deny the significance of the rights discourse. I see my attempt as a complementary approach. Moreover, my discussion will leave out the critical migration and border regime studies, simply because I believe our foci are very different. Unlike those studies, I do not include topics such as irregular migration, reception policies or border control in my discussion. What I am interested in is to challenge the widely shared understanding of integration as a one-way process and point out the epistemic barriers that uphold it. In so doing, I aim to expound that, besides rights, the receiving society can and should also make epistemic efforts for the sake of integration. Due to this focus, I will also omit questions such as states' duties to refugees under international law, the role of global capitalism or the influence of imperialism and neo-colonialism on immigration. Leaving them out does not refute their significance. They are all valuable and crucial topics, but I cannot cover all these within limited space. More importantly, attempting to take them all in will blur the actual purpose of my discussion.

The first chapter includes a discussion about the conceptual obscurity of integration. By engaging with its assimilationist features, I show why an assimilation-like integration is morally problematic and in what sense integration can, in fact, become impossible in practice. Therein, I refer to the notions of generalism and perpetual foreignness in order to illustrate how an assimilation-like integration can end up deepening social divisions rather than healing them. In order to tackle the moral problem as well as to lay the grounds for a mutual integration, I examine the role identity plays. The reason is as follows. Understanding integration as a one-way process conception shows that identity can distribute responsibility differently, be it consciously or not – just like authority and power can be distributed via the social imaginaries of identities. The one-sided understanding of integration exempts certain groups at the outset from any potential onus for integration. This exemption is also a tacit approval that those who are exempted are already an integrated part of society, hence they are allowed to charge those who are yet to become. What's more, another underlying message of a one-sided understanding of integration is that those who do not need to integrate are certainly not to blame if integration goes wrong. Furthermore, although more specific identities like ethnicity, religion or even race directly affect immigrants' life, their legal status and their chance of getting a work permit, they are often not identities that indicate qualifications that are really necessary for social participation and contribution, such as having expertise and professional skills or possessing personal merits like being altruistic and honest. Rather, they are made necessary by the prevalent social orders for other purposes.

In the second chapter, I focus on the role of "immigrant" identity in integration and integration-related issues. Following Bernard Williams' discussion of necessary identity and Armartya Sen's analysis of identity and violence, I argue that social orders often exploit identities for governance purposes and that such exploitation not only gives rise to oppressive practices, both institutional and epistemic, but also gives the wrong impression about what is actually or justifiably necessary. While policies can be abolished overnight, it takes much longer to rectify incorrect knowledge and misleading norms. After distinguishing justifiable necessities from apparent ones, I examine the identity of "immigrant" as well as identities that are related to it. I argue that, for integration, "immigrant" is only an apparent necessity. In the last part of the second chapter, I explain how "identity-based thinking" excludes.

Drawing insights from Sally Haslanger's analysis of assumed objectivity, I analyze the epistemic structure of identity-based thinking. There, I demonstrate how the norm of assumed objectivity sustains unjustified epistemic necessity. Then I concentrate on epistemic irresponsibility and epistemic injustice. Following Lorraine Code's discussion about "epistemic responsibility," I explore what it means for something to be epistemically irresponsible. With the notion of "epistemic irresponsibility," I intend to draw attention to the matter of how ignorance on behalf of knowers and the particularities of knowledge can uphold the illusion of an assumed objectivity. Feminist theorists rightly point out that what we often believe to be neutral or universal facts only mirror the experience of a small, privileged group. Based on Miranda Fricker's "epistemic injustice," I aim to place particular emphasis on the point that identity-based thinking can cause severe, but also hidden, consequences of epistemic structural injustices. Both angles are helpful to make sense of how identity-based thinking works and how it might be possible to tackle it. Regarding integration, identity-based thinking should not simply be considered an agential wrong – it is more structural than expected.

As introduced earlier, identity can distribute responsibility of integration, especially when the concept in question is vague and urgently requires clarification. What's more, identity can also incorporate the needs of social orders in its own principles and discourses. In this way, these two functions of identity form a loop of epistemic necessity, which not only makes salient certain ways of perceiving some people but also hides problems and distorts reality. While individual solutions, such as cultivating virtuous knowers, is undoubtedly useful, structural solutions are also needed for redressing the collective aspect.

Before continuing with discussions of structural matters, I explore an individual remedy for overcoming identity-based thinking in the fourth chapter. In this chapter, then, I develop an account of what exactly it means to know people. Following the discussion in Chapter Three, I emphasize the importance of subjectivity; that is, of how factors such as social positions and personal relations also constitute what who can know. The subjective aspect of knowledge and the process of knowing not only reveal the limits of our knowledge practices, but more importantly they show that our knowledge about other people and ourselves is always, to some extent, particular. This, however, is not necessarily a disadvantage, as it gives us a truer picture about the self and the self-other relationship than claims purport to be universal. In this regard, I argue for the significance of narrative knowledge, i.e. knowing a person in his or her actual contexts. Someone may be an immigrant, but that person is never *just* an immigrant. Their other positions or relations may amplify their disadvantages as an immigrant (or contrarily, compensate for those disadvantages). Without seeing that person in a realistic setting, stereotypes may be reinforced, and inappropriate judgments may thereby be made. The point is this: social orders will always make salient particular perceptions about certain groups of people, but such representations often have their own purposes and do not always reflect what is really going on. At the end of the fourth chapter, I present the ethics of difference – an ethical concept from Chinese philosophy which offers a different moral pattern that treats morality as a matter of know-how and understands the moral conduct as the "self-cultivation" of moral agents and argues that moral recipients are as important to moral relationships as moral agents.

The fifth and the sixth chapters engage with the structural problem and the structural remedy of identity-based thinking. Therein, I narrow my focus to discussing the image of the "stranger." Drawing critically from Miller's *Strangers in Our Midst*, I take seriously the threatening and undesirable representation of immigrants and ask from where it originates. I take such representations seriously because they are persistent and always resurface when domestic problems emerge in order to place the blame on outsiders. Accusing people of being xenophobic or racist, however, is not enough, as there might very well be structures in place within that society that nurture the "us versus them" dynamic in the public imaginary. After analyzing two structures that make "strangers," I argue in favor of dismissing the self-centered model of "strangeness." Instead, I emphasize the emancipatory capacity of "strangeness," since it compels us to notice things that are so solidified in our lives that we would otherwise consider them almost absolute. Behind everything that we view as "strange," there is always an implicit standard about what counts as "normal." I refer to the latter approach as the self-negotiating model of "strangeness."

The sixth chapter is a thorough discussion about structural alienation through a problematic process of normalization as well as how a problematic understanding of belonging and membership is not only a historical consequence of exclusions in the past but also continues to influence how immigrants are viewed and how integration is understood in the present. I theorize in particular the epistemic and the ethical role of history regarding national identity. Based on Iris Young's account of the social connection model of responsibility, I argue that history can function as a model of responsibility and how history can contribute to, what Catherine Lu calls, "structural transformation." In the end, I conclude by summarizing my discussion and unpacking the meaning of the term "mutual" in the concept of "mutual integration."

Before proceeding with the discussion, I still need to point out one thing. I am aware that the classification of "locals" versus "immigrants" may falsely generate the impression that I perpetuate such dualistic thinking. However, since such dualistic thinking indeed constitutes how we think about integration and migration related issues, the decision of using this pair of concepts is mostly methodological because some problems can only be addressed in this way. What's more, readers will realize that in my discussion I also take into consideration the fact that migration issues never affect only those without the citizenship of the society where they live. In fact, I actively problematize the dualistic thinking as an epistemic structure that not only excludes those from outside, but also foments feelings of estrangement and divisions on the inside.

One –
The (Im)Possibility of Integration

Immigrants' integration depends on what the receiving society offers, such as accesses to important goods, the possibility to participate in economic, social and political life, and the protection from discrimination. Without these means, immigrants' integration remains empty talk. That means, while it is reasonable to insist that immigrants should learn about the receiving society, comply with its rules and so on, this should not be taken as the only content of integration. As briefly illustrated in the introduction, integration concerns more than rights. Not only the lack of rights but also problematic norms and understandings of belonging or membership can obstruct immigrants' participation and therefore their integration in the receiving society.

In the first chapter, I shall explain why the widely shared conception of integration – only immigrants need to integrate – is assimilation-like. I will show that this feature not only renders immigrants' social participation practically difficult, but it can even reinforce exclusion and division. The assimilation-like integration makes it impossible to tell whether integration is taking place or not, because integration may be just a different name for assimilation. As the discussion shall demonstrate, this assimilation-like feature is laden with moral problems. For immigration societies, such a feature is especially worrying, because it intensifies the "us versus them" dynamic and often turns out to reproduce stereotypes and misconceptions.

Integration thus becomes impossible because its one-sided focus which ignores that immigrants' integration also involves the group (i.e. locals) that are conventionally not considered part of integration is de facto no different from what assimilation requires: namely, "just adopt our standards, or otherwise you fail." By analyzing the role of locals[1] in the following discussion I will show that they in fact participate actively in immigrants' integration, even if they may not be aware of that. I will primarily pay attention to the epistemic aspects of integration – as explained in the introduction, it is an underexplored and underestimated element in the debates around integration. As an immigrant, my own experience tells me that regardless how equal my status theoretically is, it is useless to my social participation and my sense of belonging if the first thing I need to prove is always that I am not a threat. Integration is mutual and should be recognized as such. This is a realistic, hence appropriate and promising understanding.

The Assimilation-like Integration

The widely shared conception of "integration" seems indistinguishable from that of "assimilation." Like assimilation, integration also insists that only immigrants need to make an effort to adapt, and they alone are responsible for the success of the integration process. As Bhikhu Parekh notes,

"(T)he idea of integration is not as innocent as it seems. It involves a particular way of incorporating outsiders into the prevailing social structure, and is sometimes either indistinguishable or only marginally different from assimilation. […] Like assimilationists, they (integrationists) too see integration as a one-way process: the onus to integrate is placed on the immigrants, and so is the blame for their failure to do so. This is a misleading account of the process of integration." (Parehk 2008, 85)

Understanding integration as a one-way process raises the question of whether integration can really make a difference at all. What is the point of emphasizing "integration" if it is in fact indistinguishable from assimilation? What is integration anyway? Hence, what makes integration impossible is above all its conceptual ambiguity: that is, if "integration" is interchangeable with "assimilation," then "integration" becomes a redundant notion. There is no point in insisting upon a vague concept like integration when there

---

[1] As already clarified in Introduction, I am aware that such a dualist classification of "locals and immigrants" may appear reductionist. However, since this is how the concept of integration as well as its related practices are constructed and conducted, such a classification is necessary because it is the only way to reveal and tackle the unreasonableness of this classification. It would be naïve to think that turning a blind eye to this reality would make these problems go away.

is already a much clearer alternative. Unclear concepts bring about certain practical difficulties as well, as they can make it difficult to know what is actually going on in practice. Some may argue that even if "integration" may be conceptually similar to "assimilation," they are still different, because integration, for instance, does not entail forcing immigrants to adopt certain views or participate in certain ways like assimilation does. But is it really so? Is the one-way conception really capable of avoiding assimilationist consequences?

An assimilation-like integration may not directly enforce practices and behaviors, but it can do so indirectly. The issue here is not primarily whether people are forced to adopt certain things or participate in certain ways; rather, by placing the onus to integrate entirely on immigrants, locals are effectively exempted from any potential responsibility. This understanding of integration basically assumes that locals cannot do anything that is disadvantageous to immigrants' participation in the receiving society, let alone impede their integration. Hence, if integration fails – whatever the standards are – only the immigrants are to be blamed. Likewise, the idea of assimilation also stresses the sole responsibility of immigrants in adapting to the receiving society and presupposes the righteousness and appropriateness of many pre-existing contexts of the receiving society. This ahistorical view does not consider the fact that certain practices and beliefs may turn out to be unjust, exclusionary and morally problematic, given their historical characters. If the only standard for measuring integration concerns the extent to which immigrants have adapted themselves to the given contexts of the receiving society, such an understanding of integration effectively *works* as assimilation.

In the introduction, I referred to Carens' view that formal equality which immigrants enjoy, such as rights, will not function effectively without matching contexts, such as an appropriate public culture and the cooperation of ordinary citizens, officials, etc. Understood as a one-way process, the failure of immigrants' integration in their receiving society can always be taken to mean that "they have not tried enough" or "they should have tried harder." Once the possibility that pre-existing contexts could be frustrating and impeding is precluded, immigrants are basically made into the perfect scapegoat for integration's failure.

Apart from the conceptual obscurity of assimilation-like integration, there are other problems as well. Carens argues that the standard of assimilation is "incompatible with the kind of liberal legal rights" and "with the norm about free choice and privacy that undergird many of those rights" that liberal states promise (Carens 2005). In principle, people should be free to choose how to live, how to exercise their rights like free speech and protest, and so on. But apart from Carens' remark, I believe that there are other reasons why the standard of assimilation is problematic: it is completely unrealistic. If quarrels and conflicts ensue between members of, say, a small family of four people, how can anyone possibly expect a city of two million people or a country of twenty million people to be homogenous and conflict-free? Conflicts are an inevitable part of social life when different people live together. That is to say, conflicts do not necessarily mean that a society will fall apart or that integration is failing.[2] Social problems should not be taken exaggeratedly to be a sign of integration failure, especially when it involves people with a migrant background.[3]

In addition, non-ideal theory's critique of ideal theory reveals a third problem regarding the standard of assimilation. Ideal theory departs from idealized presuppositions, such as a perfectly assimilated society in which everyone shares the same set of values, rather than from conditions that can be observed in the real world. Similar to ideal theory, the standard of assimilation concerns the question of how society should be rather than actual problems in society. It assumes that conflicts result from the lack of homogeneity; and once the society is sufficiently homogenous, solidarity and stability will automatically be enhanced. As Charles W. Mills notes, however, if one wants to change the actual phenomenon P "so it conforms more closely in its behavior to the ideal P, one will need to work and theorize not merely with the ideal [...] but with the nonideal [...] so as to identify and understand the peculiar features that explain P's dynamic and prevent it from attaining ideality" (Mills 2005, 167). That is to say, even if one continues to believe in the homogenous picture of an assimilated society, one nev-

---

2 El-Mafaalani argues exactly the opposite, namely successful integration means conflicts, because protests and dissents demonstrate that immigrants know their rights, local languages and how to use them, see *Das Integrationsparadox*.

3 Parekh notes that religious identities are so salient in Indian society that every conflict between Hindus and Muslims comes to be interpreted in terms of those identities, even though the actual conflict has a completely economic origin. This not only worsens the identity politics that are already present but also makes it useless for solving problems. See chapter one of Parekh's *A New Politics of Identity*. Similar trends can also be observed in immigration societies: the identity of "immigrant" is so salient (more precisely, the "immigrant" identity entailing certain racial, cultural and political components) that many conflicts come to be interpreted in terms of this identity. This will be discussed in Chapter Two.

ertheless has to theorize actual conflicts and problems. This is one of the shortcomings of assimilation.

For non-ideal theorists, ideal theories are too ideological, because they "abstract away from relations of structural domination, exploitation, coercion, and oppression" (ibid.) that shape human agents, social institutions, cognitive spheres and compliance in practice. An ideal theory, like that of a homogenous society resulting from assimilation, presupposes coherence between practices and beliefs which should thereby shape how individuals relate to reality. However, without acknowledging and exploring the gap between the actual and the ideal, ideal theories distort what is actually wrong in reality. Probably conflicts originate from something else rather than lack of homogeneity. One of Judith Shklar's important observations in her *The Faces of Injustice* is that it is a misconception to presume justice to be normal and injustice to be aberrant. According to Shklar, it is vital to know the faces of injustice because rigid definitions of justice cannot account for the historical variability and difference in how victims and spectators perceive the two. The problem with assuming injustice to be the absence of justice is that justice can only be validated when an action does not comply with some known legal or moral rules. If the victims' complaints fail to "match the rule-governed prohibitions," "it is only a matter of the victim's subjective reactions, a misfortune, and not *really* unjust." This procedure ignores a great deal of injustice by mistakenly presuming "a stability of perspectives that is just not there" (Shklar 1980, 7). As José Medina notes, "normalization of a presumed justice and the concomitant abnormalization of injustice [...] contribute to the invisibility of everyday injustices, to the formation of active bodies of ignorance that *perpetuate* the injustices and *desensitize* us to the suffering they cause" (Medina 2012, 13, my emphasis). In short, presuming justice may lead us to ignore real injustices.

For example, regarding integration, the understanding of justice that is restricted to improving the formal equality of immigrants, i.e. distribution of rights, may thereby overlook a great number of real obstacles that are relevant to immigrants' integration in society but remain relatively unaffected by formal equality. Confusing formal equality with justice may lead one to misinterpret the fulfillment of formal equality as an absence of injustice.[4]

---

[4] Felix Bender pointed out to me that the same inference holds vice versa: if we assume the existence of injustice, we also implicitly assume some positive account of justice. I think this is correct, but I would argue that the positive account of justice does not have to come from some abstract theories

Immigrants who enjoy formal equality may nevertheless experience difficulty when participating in social, economic and political life due to prevalent xenophobic attitudes within the public sphere. In that sense, they are not treated as equal members of that society despite their legal status.[5] The only focus on formal equality does not take into consideration how pre-existing contexts may affect its realization; it also generates the wrong impression that immigrants' failure of integration is because they haven't tried hard enough, since they already have the necessary rights they need in order to earn an income and socialize.

As mentioned in both the introduction and the brief discussion above, when talking about integration, the primary focus is on what immigrants should do. Apart from the distribution of rights, the role of pre-existing contexts remains underexplored. Answering the question of "what can locals do?" is, at the same time, an attempt to answer the question of "in what way can integration become mutual in practice?" While there seem to be at least some ideas of what it means for immigrants to integrate, such as whether they learn the local language(s), whether they behave according to the law, whether they sufficiently participate in the receiving society and so on, there does not seem to exist any standard of evaluation on the other side. If locals' behavior affects immigrants' participation, when does it promote integration and when does it obstruct it? In what sense can they integrate? From the above discussion, it should be clear that "assimilation" is not an appropriate guide to integration, but it also begs the question: what is?

One might say that locals should make immigrants feel "welcome," but this prescription is far too ambiguous.[6] Without sufficient elaboration the criterion of "feeling welcome" may turn out to be rather arbitrary. Does the standard of making them feel welcome mean that anything is acceptable? Besides, Carens' suggestion, according to which just integration requires a public culture that recognizes immigrants as legitimate members of society and treats them with respect, appears a bit unclear to me as well (Carens 2005, 29–46).What does it mean for someone to be recognized as a legitimate member of a society? "Feeling welcome" and "recognizing as legitimate

---

like in the case of ideal theory, it could also be acquired from relevant (historical) experiences. This appears to me to be the main difference.

5 Let alone most immigrants don't have the same legal status as citizens. And not being formally equal adds to their lesser social status because a different treatment is legally sanctioned.

6 For example, Bhikhu Parekh (2006), *Rethinking Multiculturalism: Cultural Diversity and Political Theory*. London: Palgrave Macmillan.

members of society" or "treating with respect" all sound good, but they need lots of explanations, interpretations and justifications. Although discussions heading this way acknowledge that immigrants' reasonable voices should be heard and accordingly accommodated, they still implicitly follow the one-way paradigm of integration. What if immigrants' reasoning conflicts with the existing pattern in the receiving society? What if their voices cannot be made sense of according to the prevailing epistemic resources and structures of the receiving society? Without taking this fundamental element into consideration, calls for recognizing immigrants' reasonable voices are prone to superficial and simplified interpretations of integration-related issues. Without first making the stance that integration depends on both immigrants and locals, immigrants' integration remains subordinate to the dominance of pre-existing contexts. What's more, "feeling welcome" may not apply in cases where marginalization results from past injustice. It is not difficult to see this when we take into consideration that many immigration societies used to participate in colonialism. The main source of their immigrants is their former colonies. And since the exclusion these immigrants have been facing is not only unjust in its root but also systematic and enduring, what is at issue here is not "making them feel welcome" but rather "correcting injustice." I will explore this aspect in the last two chapters.

In the following discussion, I shall revisit the Muhammad cartoon controversy from 2005. By focusing on this example, I intend to shed new light upon the issue of integration: 1) since I try to argue that locals can and should contribute to integration, I shall show what may cause integration to resemble assimilation if this group is precluded; 2) when immigrants are blamed for social conflicts and conflicts are primarily assumed to have resulted from their lack or failure of integration, "our" standard and thereby quite possibly "our" own epistemic fallibility are reinforced; and 3) epistemic fallibility can have moral and political consequences, especially regarding the use of "universality" or "tradition"; 4) even if rules have never or rarely been questioned, this mere fact does not automatically provide those rules with natural legitimacy, for this fact may result from other factors. By simply emphasizing that immigrants should conform to a view that is taken to be universal or traditional, the particularities of immigrants are effectively devalued, hence their equal status, and this does not have to involve any violation of rights. Though in the name of integration, this gesture may lead immigrants to feel excluded.

The Muhammad Cartoon Controversy and the Generalized Other

In September 2005, Jyllands Posten published a series of cartoons, which, according to the newspaper's cultural editor, Flemming Rose, was intended to "push back self- imposed limits on expression that seemed to be closing in tighter" (Rose 2006a). By "self-imposed limits," Rose meant "self-censorship" "caused by widening fears and feelings of intimidation in dealing with issues related to Islam." According to him, this self-censorship is "a topic that we Europeans must confront" because it effectively undermines Europe's liberal values. The aim of publishing these cartoons, then, was to "(challenge) moderate Muslims to speak out." In Rose's opinion, these cartoons not only represent satire, which belongs to both the Danish tradition and the idea of free speech. More importantly, he argued, by subjecting Muslims to satire, they (the cartoonists and/or Rose) were treating Islam "the same way they treat Christianity, Buddhism, Hinduism and other religions," which thereby made it a gesture of treating Muslims as equal members of society. Rose says, "(w)e are *integrating* you into the Danish tradition of satire because you are part of our society, not strangers. The cartoons are including, rather than excluding, Muslims" (ibid., my emphasis).

In another article published three months later, Rose further defended his opinion that the publication of these cartoons was meant as an act of inclusion and not exclusion (Rose 2006b). He said that European political correctness – by which he particularly refers to "a politics of victimology" from European's traditional left wing – "perpetuates national and religious differences" and allows Muslims to "resist integration and adaptation." Rose's articles were responses to the reactions that ensued from the publication of these cartoons. Two of the cartoons, which depicted Muhammad the Prophet as a terrorist, were controversial, for they were believed to stigmatize Islam and simply reinforce the existing prejudices that were directed against Muslims. Things escalated rapidly from peaceful protests against the publication of the cartoons to anonymous death threats against the artists and petitions from Danish imams. Eleven ambassadors from Muslim-majority countries even asked to meet with the then Danish Prime Minister, Anders Fogh Rasmussen. Some countries recalled their ambassadors, and in some instances, there were even series of uncalled-for attacks on European embassies throughout the Middle East.

When looking at the disputes, there appear to be at least two opinions at stake here. According to the first, satire should apply equally to every religion without exception; according to the second, however, the cartoons were not a gesture of integration, but inappropriate and humiliating. Rose's defense was to claim that identifying with satire is a matter of "following the customs,"[7] that is, it is simply a part of following Danish tradition and/or the freedom of speech as a tradition of liberal democracy, and following these customs is simply a sign of respect. But I think there are some mistakes here. First, Rose confuses two concepts here: "rule" and "customs." While a "rule" refers to a necessary condition for someone's participation in something, i.e. one cannot play football without following the rules of football, "customs" do not. Without taking one's shoes off, one will not be allowed into a temple, thereby making taking one's shoes off a rule rather than a custom.[8] The comparable situation of a national rule, then, would be something like needing a visa to enter Denmark or of needing registration to reside in a city; identifying with or participating in satire are simply not analogous. Unless the law changes and requires everyone living in Denmark to participate in satire, there is no necessary relation between participation in satire and living in Denmark and/or liberal democracy, no matter how long one has lived there.

What's more, immigrants should not be compelled to think the same. So far, the disagreements concern the matter of the freedom of speech, which entails that people perceive and think about things differently. Freedom of speech does indeed allow Rose and the cartoonists to publish their cartoons, but it also allows people to criticize them when they disagree or feel offended. Enjoying the freedom of speech does not mean being exempted from critique. The problem is that Rose seems to believe that reactions against the cartoons, such as protests and petitions, require (self-)censorship. Of course, death threats and outright attacks are wrong reactions; but that does not mean that the satire is not inappropriate (if I know that some things are someone's or some group's cultural taboo, why provoke? Doesn't it show that

---

7 "But what does respect mean? When I visit a mosque, I show my respect by taking off my shoes. I follow the customs, just as I do in a church, synagogue or other holy place. But if a believer demands that I, as a nonbeliever, observe his taboos in the public domain, he is not asking for my respect, but for my submission. And that is incompatible with a secular democracy." Rose (2006b), "Why I Published Those Cartoons."
8 In a different scenario, "taking one's shoes off" could also simply be an option for one having a more pleasant experience rather than being an actual requirement. For example, the marble of the temple floor is especially cool in the summer and enjoyed by local people. In this instance, "taking one's shoes off" depends on other factors such as peoples' preferences or practicability, such as the matter of whether one's shoes are easy to take off or whether a person's foot or leg is injured, etc.

I lack respect for others?). There is no reason why these two points are incompatible. This is not to say that satire as such is wrong, but rather, that satire can function wrongly, i.e. that there are contexts in which satire may be inappropriate.

Satire is one way to criticize or draw attention to important issues, but not the only way. Sometimes, engaging in satire may not be such a good idea when other factors are taken into consideration. For example, it may be wrong to satirize about B's weight if he is a sensitive person and feels ashamed about it, or to joke about a disease while it is causing social and economic crisis in many places around the world. One can certainly point out the problem and be critical about it, but this does not mean that using irony must be resorted to. One can convince B to lose weight by showing him how his obesity has caused certain health problems, but one does not have to point this out by imitating him having trouble climbing the stairs. Similarly, criticizing failures in institutions and policies that are likely to have prevented officials and professionals from taking timely action is acceptable, but the criticism does not have to be expressed by resorting to associating the disease with other irrelevant but stigmatizing stereotypes, even in a satirical way. Instead of insisting upon how important or essential satire is to the freedom of speech or to democracy, it is important not to forget that there are other ways to exercise one's freedom of speech without the mistake of reproducing wrong or humiliating images. Regarding the Muhammad cartoon controversy, the question should rather be: what was its purpose? Was it making fun of other people and their religion or drawing attention to an issue that is substantially meaningful for improving the scope of democratic values?

Instead of meeting his critics by reassessing the whole situation, however, Rose insisted that those who felt simply offended misunderstood the intention of the publication. For him, publishing the cartoons was a gesture of integration, not humiliation. But in reality, good intentions do not always bring about good results. From the perspective of consequentialism, rightness or wrongness of conduct results not from one's intention, but from the consequences of one's actions. Taken from this point of view, the publication of those two controversial cartoons was wrong no matter what the publishers' original intention was. Good intentions cannot make us immune from liability when bad things happen. Rose drew the conclusion, though, that these reactions stemmed from Muslims' *lack of and resistance against integration* into Danish society. So according to him, those who had (successfully) integrated would have agreed with him and the cartoonists, whereas those who disagreed failed to identify with democratic values and/or the Danish tradition because they had failed to properly integrate. If he and the cartoonists had withdrawn the controversial cartoons and/or apologized, he maintained, they would have been engaging in self-censorship. And according to them, this would be incompatible with both European values and with Danish traditions. Of course, among those who disagreed, there was also a crucial difference between those who simply protested and those who resorted to the use of violence. The use of violence is wrong and should not be permitted. But condemning the latter group does not diminish the reasonableness of the former group's acts, nor does it amount to agreeing with Rose's generalizing claim that all who disagreed were opposed to democratic values or Danish tradition.

There are two claims that need to be addressed here: 1) the claim that, because satire represents freedom of speech, protests against satire cannot be accepted; 2) that since satire is a part of Danish tradition, those who live in Danish society should naturally identify with this tradition, otherwise, they have not successfully integrated. Both are very strong claims, and both are problematic. On the one hand, by associating satire with freedom of speech, Rose attempts to justify the publication of the cartoons by referring to widely recognized human rights. On the other, Rose also associates satire with Danish traditions to culturally justify the publication. So according to him, the publication of the cartoons can be justified both from the perspective of being human as well as of being a member of Danish society. One should see that the cartoons were not (intended to be) offensive; quite to the contrary, they were meant to convey a gesture of integration by treating Islam and Muslims as an equal part of Danish society. And when one fails to identify with satire, one fails to be an integrated member of not only Danish society, but of human society altogether according to the liberal human ideal. So no matter what, not identifying with satire makes one part of an authoritarian society and/or complicit with authoritarianism, Rose drew here from his bad experience of (self-) censorship when he worked as a journalist in the USSR. But this simply does not sound right. By what accounts can Rose suppose that everyone is just like him? Is it because others are also human beings and/or live in Denmark that they should identify with the same set of values, have the same perceptions and interpret things in the same way? And if they don't, does that necessarily mean that they have failed to integrate and/or that they identify with the values of authoritarianism?

Clearly, Rose has his way of moral reasoning. He assumes that all human agents should be the same (or at least not too different), especially those in a similar situation to his, i.e. Danish society and liberal democracy. That is, he assumes that any person in an identical situation with identical access to information should form the same conclusions. Due to the universalizability of the freedom of speech and the Danish culture of satire, when people come to know that the cartoons were not ill-intended, they should come to see his point. In fact, Rose's position falls in line with that of several philosophers. R. M. Hare proposes that role reversal is a necessary step in determining universalizability in moral reasoning; that is, *our* action must be one that *we* are prepared to accept "as exemplifying a principle of action to be prescribed for others in like circumstances."[9] Lawrence Kohlberg's idea of reversibility says that "*we* must be willing to live with *our* judgment or decision when *we* trade places with others in the situation being judged."[10] Both Hare's and Lawrence's positions reflect the so-called golden rule of morality, which states to "do unto other as you would have them do unto you." This is also Rose's point when he insists that what the publishers and cartoonists did was nothing short of common, as they would do the same also to other religions including their own.[11] Since I can imagine certain things done to me, I presuppose that you, whom I treat as an equal human being, should too. This position thus treats supposed reversibility as exemplary of impartiality.

However, what exactly constitute *same* or *similar* circumstances? Does being in an identical circumstance necessarily mean having the same perception? Or does having identical access to perceptual information necessarily mean coming to the same conclusions? In response to Kohlberg's idea of reversibility, Seyla Benhabib points out that moral situations cannot be evaluated independently of one's knowledge about the agents involved in the sit-

---

9 R. M. Hare (1963), *Freedom and Reason*, 88–89. Oxford: Oxford University Press. See also Huang Young (2014), *Why be Moral? Learning From the Neo-Confucian Cheng Brothers*, 133. New York: SUNY Press.

10 Cited from Benhabib (1987), "The Generalized and the Concrete Other," in Seyla Benhabib and Drucilla Cornell (eds.), *Feminism as Critique. Essays On the Politics of Gender in Late-Capitalist Society*, 77–95. Cambridge: Polity Press.

11 One actually does not need to refer to any philosophical discussion to see that this view is very inconsiderate and ego-centric, everyday experience can reveal what is inappropriate here. Suppose making fun of people is your habit or hobby, and you often do it with your friends and family who never complain because this is also their habit or hobby. But is it a justifiable reason for treating your brother-in-law the same way with the emphasis on the gesture of integration? What if this behavior means a completely different thing in his view, such as a lack of respect?

uation (Benhabib 1987). What I think to be harmless may in fact hurt the other's pride; or, while a church for me is simply a (beautiful) building, it is holy for others. How can the meaning of certain circumstances possibly be assessed without knowing *who* is involved? Benhabib notes that "the most difficult aspect" of the "procedure of universalizability" "is to know what constitutes a 'like' situation or what it would *mean* for another to be exactly in a situation like mine" (ibid., 90, my emphasis). Without knowing about the other, moral agents are in no position to assess whether one situation is "like" or "unlike" how it is for their recipient, thus making them unable to determine whether certain actions would be the proper way to achieve whatever they intend to. Benhabib concludes that the problem of assumed reversibility is that of the "generalized other," a term originally introduced by George Herbert Mead. The other is generalized via "right, obligation and entitlement." This standpoint requires one "to view each and every individual as a rational being entitled to the same rights and duties we would want to ascribe to ourselves," and "each is entitled to expect and to assume from us what we can expect and assume from him or her" (ibid.).

The Muhammad cartoon controversy is, in this respect, an illustrative example. In his defense, Rose assumes there to be reversibility between people so long as they live in Denmark and/or a liberal democracy – two things which, for him, constitute similar circumstances. If what I do is common in Denmark or in a secular democracy, i.e. "satire", it follows that you as a part of Danish society or secular democracy *should* also find it acceptable, even if you feel insulted or irritated. How people really think or feel, then, no longer matters because the circumstances, i.e. Denmark and/or secular democracy, determine what people *should* think and feel, which thereby implies the irrationality of how people *actually* think and feel. He alludes to the satire of Christianity to legitimate satire of Islam. Yet, as argued, the premise that "like cases ought to be treated alike" is quite contestable. The fact that both Christianity and Islam are (seen as) religions does not mean that they are sufficiently alike. For example, that A and B are both human and that A eats meat does not necessarily mean that it is appropriate to offer B meat because B may be vegetarian. Syllogisms only guarantee the logical coherence of certain forms of reasoning, but they do not guarantee that conclusions thus derived are true or that the actions derived from such reasoning are justified. By resorting to the notion of a "generalized other" one reasons from a standpoint of moral agency that does not involve any real subject, but only an *assumed* one. To the extent that moral agents act without knowing anything about the other and simply assume what it should be like for them to live in the same place, they are adopting an orientation of assimilation. This is because the moral agent in question is ignoring the difference between themselves and the recipients of their actions.

In opposition to the notion of the "generalized other," Benhabib argues in favor of the standpoint of the "concrete other," which requires everyone to be viewed in their particularities, both rational and emotional. The "concrete other" is meant to be comprehended on the basis of their actual needs, desires, motivations and so on. The expectations of how to relate to a concrete other are not based upon "formal equality and reciprocity," as in the case of the generalized other, but rather upon "equity and complementary reciprocity." That is, the idea that "each is entitled to expect and to assume from the other forms of behavior through which the other feels recognized and confirmed as a concrete, individual being with specific needs, talents and capacities" (Benhabib 1987). In contrast to the "concrete other," the "generalized other" is subject to the obvious danger of self-centrism: that is, by assuming there to be reversibility among human agents on the basis of what "I" can accept or what "I" find rational, one's own standards are taken to be universalizable. This self-centrism could very well perpetuate problems in pre-existing contexts. In contrast, the "concrete other" promotes an attitude of decentralization due to its norm of complementary reciprocity, which will be the topic from Chapter Four onwards. A satire cannot function as intended when all parties involved understand the circumstances differently. Appealing to impartiality or reversibility assumes the view of the generalized other who, however different "they" really are, *should* be just like "us." Once the concrete other is explained away, a similarity between circumstances can thus be forged as if they were truly like cases.

The Problem of Moral Generalism

In the above discussion, I focused on the idea of the generalized other. I argued that generalizations by moral agents, which are assumed to be impartial, wrongly dismiss the particularities of other people. The generalized other can lead to simplistic and misleading conclusions about what a situation is like for another person, based on the assumption that other people are just like "me." Factors such as living in the same society or participating in the same religion may contribute to this seeming legitimacy, for the appearance of the same or similar circumstances can make it appear as if reversibility between moral agents and recipients is indeed justified. Yet quite to the contrary, this can easily lead one to ignore an important fact: that moral recipients and agents are different people. The appearances of sharing the same location or life background can delude one into thinking that moral situations can be evaluated independently of any knowledge about the people who are involved. In this respect, the idea of the generalized other in fact promotes moral generalism.

According to moral generalism, evaluations of moral situations are independent of any knowledge about actual moral agents or recipients, as moral reasons are driven on the basis of principle. In fact, however, moral agents often unconsciously generalize their own standpoints as something universal in the name of principle-driven moral reasons. Moral generalism can thus become a handy tool for moral agents to justify their ignorance of moral recipients. Moral generalism then offers a normative ground for ideas like that of the generalized other. In that sense, I think that it is not unreasonable to explore precisely how moral generalism can perpetuate an assimilationist notion of integration, according to which integration is considered as a one-way process which is solely incumbent upon immigrants.

It should not be assumed that people are the same simply because they live in the same place. The circumstance-argument appears to be too simplified. The cartoons were indeed published in Denmark, which is a secular democracy, but this is far from being the only circumstance that counts. The fact that these cartoons targeted Islam and Muslims, and the fact that Islam has not undergone the same historical process as Christianity produce contexts that are different from a satire on Christianity. This reflects one of the disputes between moral generalism and moral particularism; namely, does a consideration, which is a reason in one case, also count as a reason (with the same valence) in another case? According to generalism it does, while according to particularism it does not. In generalism, moral reasons are principle-driven, meaning that the rightness or wrongness of an action is intrinsic, rather than context-dependent. The claim of moral generalism is so strong as to suggest that actions of a certain type are right (or wrong) overall and that moral law would be right (or wrong) even in a world without agents. In contrast, particularists hold that "there are no defensible moral principles" (Dancy 2017) and that it is always necessary to distinguish and explain why a feature is a moral reason in a specific context. The supposed moral principle does not always constitute a reason when it occurs. The particularist view of moral reasoning is "holistic"; that is, a reason in one case may not count as a reason in another case, or indeed it may count as a reason, but not with the exact same valence. For example, what is funny in one case may very well be offensive in another. In the former case, whether humor is the reason to tell a joke also depends on the background of certain audiences, who find the joke to be funny rather than offensive. In the latter case, however, when the audiences are different, the background may no longer function as an *enabling*, but a *defeating* factor. The audiences may find the joke inappropriate because it is sexist or racist. So, although humor is a reason, there are other factors that may reinforce or weaken that reason.[12]

I believe that similar considerations also apply to the Mohammad cartoon controversy. Free speech and Danish tradition may very well be reasons to act in certain ways, but rejecting those reasons does not at all necessarily mean rejecting free speech and/or Danish tradition as such. To find satire an appropriate form for exercising free speech depends on other factors, such as its content, its timing, the persons who are involved and so on. These factors are not only relevant for satire's intended function, but also important for the consideration of reversibility: that is, is the situation with which one is dealing sufficiently similar to that with which one is already familiar? In order to justify the application of satire, one must either argue that satire is universally applicable or provide a suitable analogy between Christianity and Islam. Before either of these, however, one must first address the question of whether satire is in fact an appropriate way of expressing free speech or Danish tradition. Circumstances need to be investigated first, while also bearing in mind that those who are involved are different people. Rose and the cartoonists may have their reasons for thinking that satire is appropriate, but those who feel offended have their own reasons for thinking the opposite, too. Satire can only function as intended when all parties involved share a common understanding about its justification, its purpose and so on. But as discussed, in the case of the cartoon controversy, there was no common understanding. Was it an exercise of free speech / Danish tradition or of stigmatization / humiliation? As Benhabib observes, "very often we do

---

12 See for reference Jonathan Dancy (2004), Chapter Five of *Ethics Without Principles*. Oxford: Oxford University Press. See also Michael Ridge and Sean McKeever (2016), "Moral Particularism and Moral Generalism," *Stanford Encyclopedia of Philosophy*, November, https://plato.stanford.edu/entries/moral-particularism-generalism/, last accessed March 2023.

not know what *type of practice* is in question, for we do not share a common understanding of the disputed practice itself" (Benhabib 2002, 13). Similar to the veiling controversy,[13] the biggest barrier is all too often that people are not talking about the same practice; they simply assume they are based upon matters of appearance.

Here, "practice" does not refer to a single physical behavior or verbal statement; rather, it has a normative connotation. Benhabib explains, "(w)hat practice we think a specific cultural practice is – religious or aesthetic, moral or legal – will determine which norms we think should apply to it" (Benhabib 2002, 12). Alasdair MacIntyre offers a more thorough notion that I find helpful for capturing the complicated structure of "practice," which he explains as follows:

"By a 'practice' I am going to mean any *coherent and complex form of socially established cooperative human activity* through which goods internal to that form of activity are realized in the course of trying to achieve those standards of excellence which are appropriate to, and partially definitive of, that form of activity, with the result that human powers to achieve excellence, and human conceptions of the ends and goods involved, are *systematically extended*. […] To enter into a practice is to accept the authority of those standards and the inadequacy of my own performance as judged by them. It is to subject my own attitudes, choices, preference and tastes to the standards which currently and partially define the practice." (MacIntyre 2013, 218 and 221, my emphasis)

Practice differs from accidental behavior insofar as it is carried out as part of a social system. It differs from a one-time event insofar as it strives for certain standards of excellence in a continuing process. It also differs from purely individual activities to the extent that it requires human cooperation in order to realize its intended outcomes – intellectual, social or technical – that cannot be achieved in any other way but through this very practice. To have an understanding of a practice necessarily requires understanding how other relevant factors are at work, such as what is fundamental, how meanings are designated, whether there are prohibitions and so on. In

---

13 This refers to the incident which was sparked in France from 1989 to 1990 and which is still ongoing throughout the world. It began with three female students who were suspended for refusing to take off their headscarves at school. Their act was considered to be a violation of the rule of secularity ("laïcité") in public places that discourages or forbids religious influence in governmental affairs or governmental involvement in religious affairs. For the three students, however, wearing headscarves meant religious freedom, which is also one of the fundamental rights of being a French citizen, and by so doing, they had no intention of violating "laïcité." Benhabib has thoroughly discussed this incident in both *The Rights of Others* and *The Claims of Culture*.

granting a certain degree of authority to a practice, neither Benhabib nor MacIntyre means to say that the practice cannot be questioned. MacIntyre points out the problem that some human practices turn out to be highly contestable *when put into a different context*, for example gladiator combat. On the one hand, the epistemic and moral value of a certain practice lies beyond the standards of excellence that the practice can answer, making them another matter altogether; on the other hand, without having any knowledge of a practice, one is in no position to proceed with judgment of any kind, epistemic or moral. That is to say that one is in no position to understand whether it is a legitimate use or abuse of a certain practice.

The artists and Rose upheld their actions as practices of free speech and Danish tradition, whereas the cartoons' target group primarily perceived them as offensive and stigmatizing. While it is true that satire is a socially established practice of free speech and of Danish tradition, it does not follow that such a practice can be taken for granted regardless of its context. Arguments in the name of "Danish tradition" are not always a trump card, even within Denmark, because the practice of tradition requires intellectual cooperation and hence necessarily requires certain identification with that tradition in advance. For this reason, the legitimacy and intelligibility of the tradition in a certain context must always first consider who is involved and who attempts to say what to whom. Not every Dane is equally Danish in the same way; being Danish is not a sufficient reason to make conclusions about how people should identify themselves. Then, being "Danish" is not the only identity possessed by Danes; depending on the context, people may privilege other sets of values to determine the criteria of their judgments. In fact, the artists' and Rose's use of the term "tradition" very much resembles its Burkean formulation, according to which tradition is understood as a static repetition and passive maintenance of what is passed on. This viewpoint has drawn many criticisms, not only due to its ideological use of tradition that abuses cultural practice, but also for its own logical contradiction.[14]

When wearing a veil is considered as a practice of the freedom of religion, it is protected; when seen as a practice of violation of *laïcité*, it is prohibited. Similarly, satire is supported when it is considered a practice of free speech or Danish tradition; but as a practice of stigmatization or humiliation, it is opposed. Apparently, not everything is so clear-cut; like veiling, it is not altogether clear exactly what type of practice satire is. Yet this does not have to be

---

14 See for example MacIntyre, *After Virtue*, Chapter Fifteen.

an either/or issue. Disagreement is an inevitable part of society, regardless of whether freedom of speech exists as a fundamental principle (or whether there is a tradition of free speech). Moreover, disagreement does not necessarily signal integration failure; to the contrary, it may even mean a successful integration, because those who disagree and protest accordingly know the language and their rights.[15] In situations where common understanding is obviously lacking, one party's simply referring to something that should be assumed to be right or true distracts attention away from the actual problem. The crux of the problem here is not that satire is a Danish tradition and that freedom of speech is a universal idea. Rather, it is a question of whether "tradition" and "universality" can justify the satirizing of a group who understands it as humiliating. Neither free speech nor Danish tradition necessarily justifies the use of satire in certain matters, for there are other relevant factors that need to be considered as well. Hence, as moral particularism points out, it is important to consider exactly what other factors are involved.

Rose is clearly a defender of the freedom of speech, both from the point of view of human rights and that of Danish tradition. Generally speaking, when it comes to rights, the freedom of speech should be established and maintained as one of the central values of today's society. However, I am not concerned with rights but with the moral dimension of this matter. At the moral level, Rose's assertion that satire is an (absolute) exercise of the freedom of speech is simply far too strong to be reasonable. According to his interpretation, satire should either be unquestionably legitimate simply due to its connection with the freedom of speech or at least becomes unquestionably legitimate due to its impartiality as supposed by Danish tradition – given that the cartoons are published within Denmark. Yet if I may repeat, doubt about satire is not one and the same as doubt about the freedom of speech or Danish tradition. There may still be other ways to exercise free speech. Moreover, forcing a certain public opinion upon someone in the name of the freedom of speech and accusing those who disagree with that opinion as "failing to integrate," in fact, seems to contradict the idea of free speech and that of treating other people as equal members. Thus, Rose's position is inconsistent in the sense that the type of liberalism he defends is not really liberal to the extent that it attempts to use informal sanctions of public opinion – such as tradition or the majority opinion – to determine how people should identify. In this regard, "integration" turns out to be no different from assimilation, as

---

15 This is El-Mafaalani's point in his *Das Integrationsparadox*.

it describes a practice in which "we" measure the extent to which immigrants have integrated according to how "they" have come to adopt what "we" believe to be right or wrong. Such public opinion is coercive.

From a particularists' point of view, moral reasons are always context-dependent rather than principle-driven. Even when several moral principles are recognized, as some cautious particularists do (Dancy 2017), this still does not mean that the principle-driven reason *always* constitutes a moral reason in certain contexts. In response, Kantian constitutivists offer another argument. They insist that the key point of moral generalism is not about moral principles, but rather about rational agency. From their perspective, moral generalism or a principle-driven moral reason inevitably results from the fact that we are rational agents. Being rational agents commits us to relevant principles, for we would otherwise not be able to understand what is right or wrong, or why we should behave in one way as opposed to another. For example, Christine Korsgaard argues that the principles of practical reasons unify us as agents and allow us to take control over our representations of the world and our actions (Ridge and McKeever 2016). This is the attractive side of Kantian ethics, which requires that "the ground of obligation" be sought "not in the nature of man nor in the circumstances of the world in which he is placed, but solely a priori in the concepts of pure reason." In this way, Kantian ethics seems to help one to avoid "special pleading," which refers to a way of interpreting one's responsibility such that it favors one's own interests. However, Kantian ethics only disguises the problem of "special pleading."

Yong Huang notes that many contemporary philosophers have appealed to Kantian ethics to transform moral generalism from its primitive imperative to a more sophisticated version which is legitimated by the idea of impartiality (Huang 2014, 133–134). Yet this modification runs into the very same Kantian problem, which assumes that "I, as a pure rational agent reasoning for myself, could reach a conclusion that would be acceptable for all at all times and places."[16] From the standpoint of non-ideal theory, the moral agents of Kantian ethics inevitably generalize the experience of a particular group – often privileged ones – while neglecting the actual life experience of those who do not belong to that group. Thus, an implied impartiality is quite misleading, for it replaces the interests of moral recipients with that of

---

16 Benhabib (1987), "The Generalized and the Concrete Other," 91. In the footnote Benhabib notes that this critique comes from Habermas' theory of communicative action.

moral agents. Zygmunt Bauman also emphasized that the idea of reversibility is deceitful, because it falls prey to a tautology: If the judgment of right or wrong comes *not* from the moral recipients but from whether the agents themselves could imagine an action done unto them, this means that "the moral phenomena" that give rise to the corresponding judgment "have been defined and singled out" in advance (Bauman 1993, 47). The Kantian position of pure reason crucially lacks the ability to engage with real people who are rational but not univocally rational. Though I will undoubtedly find certain actions to be morally unquestionable or justified as a rational agent, this in no way means that there is only one form of rationality, or that there should be.

As argued, disagreements should not be taken at face value, i.e. that people who support satire are supporters of free speech and that those who are against it are promoting censorship. Satire could very well be inappropriate depending on its content, its timing, its audience and so on. However, rejecting satire does not in any way impair the freedom of speech – it is not an act of silencing. And from the standpoint of free speech, those who feel that the cartoons are inappropriate should also be able to express their opinions. But then, having the freedom to speak is not the same as having the expertise or experience to speak. In principle, as John Stuart Mill puts it in his defence of freedom of speech, everything can be discussed even if it is immoral. He also adds, however, that the freedom to speak is the freedom to take arguments to their logical conclusions, not to the limits of social embarrassment. And in order to regulate the power of free speech, Mill introduces the harm principle, according to which harm to others should be prevented. Taking this into consideration, whether it makes sense to repeat stereotypes simply because they exist as well as the consequences of repeating stereotypes should be taken into consideration. First, the freedom to say basically anything does not prevent people from saying something stupid. Politicians may have their opinion on disease, but should the public rather listen to their advice or to that of scientists? A person who has had little interaction with people from other countries may be xenophobic, so would this person be a reliable source of meaningful experience with foreigners? The point is that people may have opinions on many things, but freedom of speech does not exempt anyone from critiques and even rejections due to their lack of expertise and/or experience. What's more, other people may as well frown upon opinions if they depart from assuming stereotypes. Second, repetition does not solve stereotypes, but rather reinforces them, no matter how harmless or friendly the original intention was. Claiming that those who identify differently with satire have either failed to integrate or have refused to try at all may thus perpetuate a stereotype with which many immigrants have already been struggling to confront: namely, that immigrants' lack of integration is causing social problems "we" are experiencing now. Immigrants may already face marginalization due to policies, their appearance or cultural background. If, on top of this, they are seen as not having tried (enough) to integrate, this would only reinforce the existing bias against them and confirm the belief that they do not and should not belong in the receiving society. In so doing, not only the needs, feelings and reasons of other people are neglected but the given standard as well as the blind spots are reinforced. Such self-centrism can lead one to remain rather unaware of one's own fallibilities. No wonder that social conflicts are hence often taken to be the immigrants' fault. Here, not only thoughtless conclusions or wrong beliefs but the understanding of membership and who should belong can be exclusionary as well, and this exclusionary understanding may very well influence people's choices about whom to listen to and to trust. Judgments, no matter how universal they seem to be, can be wrong; reflecting upon them can show fallibilities that are otherwise concealed. In general, things that one already knows and believes tend to play a privileged role in judgments. Questioning these assumptions may indeed be extremely difficult and might require adopting wholly new frameworks of thinking. That is the epistemic value of immigrants' perspectives. By providing new resources, they not only challenge established public opinions, but also offer a chance to reveal the coercive and self-regarding ones. I will attend to this in Chapters Five and Six. The less "we" know about others, the easier it is for "us" to take the familiar for granted, and the more foreign other people will appear to be, and the more difficult it will be for them to integrate into the society we take to be our own.

Segregation and Perpetual Foreignness

The second impossibility of integration I would like to identify is the phenomenon of perpetual foreignness. As I have argued so far, an assimilation-like notion of integration not only obscures what is distinctive about "integration," it is also laden with practical problems. The previous impossibility was primarily concerned with unreflective practices or positions that can end up masking one group's ignorance and lead them to make immigrants' participation in society very difficult. Thus, integration may become practically impossible not only because of requirements, i.e. that moral generalism is too demanding, but because immigrants are not treated as legitimate or equal members of society because their actual concerns and needs are unseen. In the first scenario, integration practically became one and the same as assimilation, for in the name of integration locals in fact anticipate that immigrants will think and act just like them. The second impossibility to be discussed in the following is concerned with a by-product of assimilation, that is, segregation.

I understand segregation to be a by-product of assimilation because the preservation and promotion of homogeneity requires identifying what is different and undesirable. So, assimilation can and often will promote segregation. However, this kind of segregation is not necessarily an institutional one, such as apartheid, a practice in which people are physically separated based on their race. Similar to the assimilating orientation analyzed above concerning generalism, segregation can take the form of epistemic exclusion: certain forms of experience, ways of reasoning and so on can be excluded from the conception of membership or belonging in the relevant society. This epistemic exclusion can thereby exacerbate the overall exclusion of those who are already marginalized.

Assimilation goes hand in hand with segregation since the preservation and promotion of homogeneity requires the identification of what is different and what is undesirable. The stronger the demand for homogeneity, the deeper the social division will be – especially when such exclusion is associated with things like (the protection of) sovereignty, universality, tradition, etc. In this way, the desire for an assimilated society will reinforce the legitimacy of excluding some groups of people. Contrarily to what is generally expected, then, the anticipation and promotion of homogeneity will produce a realm of foreignness. In the following part of this chapter as well as in the next chapter, I will provide some examples.

The foreignness I would like to address here does not come from immigrants' inability to communicate or to learn; rather, it results from an exclusionary membership. For example, in *Impossible Subjects*, historian Mae M. Ngai tries to answer the question of how the immigration restrictions from 1924 to 1965 racialized American citizenship. This reshaping process created the category of "illegal aliens," or "persons whose presence is a social reality yet a legal impossibility," and the category of "alien citizens," or people who enjoy the formal status of citizenship but nevertheless *lack the membership of a nation as a matter of identity*.[17] The former category is especially closely associated with Mexicans, whereas the latter is associated with Asians. Both categories emerged due to problematic legal regulations of immigration, i.e. who may enter, who may receive quotas, who may naturalize, etc. This regulation process directly determines what faces and what origins can be legitimately considered "American." Here, the critical issue of racialized citizenship is not the proportion of people of color in American citizens; but rather the fact that restricting this group's access to citizenship implies that people of color are not as entitled to being American as white people do. This issue is even more clearly exposed during the legal process ruling in favor of racialized citizenship.

Sarah Song also recognizes the relationship between legal regulations on immigration and the making of modern American national identity. But her observation is slightly different. Song is concerned with the fact that behind the legal regulations lay the plenary power doctrine of US law, the intent and purpose of which is to protect the country's security, independence and welfare. The reason given in the plenary power doctrine in order to justify the exclusion of the Chinese from American territory was that it is "inherent in sovereignty." According to justices who dealt with cases concerning persons of Chinese origin, the right to exclude or expel aliens is inherent to the state's sovereignty. So, when the government "considers the presence of foreigners of a different race in this country, who will not assimilate with us, to be dangerous to its peace and security, their exclusion is not to be stayed" (Song 2019, 17–29). For states, the right to expel aliens is a matter of self-preservation. But, this reason basically amounts to claiming that certain races form threats to the security, independence and welfare of the US, and that people of such races are undesirable. According to such a reading, Chinese (and Japanese, who were also targets of the notorious Exclusion Act) cannot be "true" Americans, even if they received citizenship.

The stereotype of the "perpetual foreigners" captures this unwanted but unavoidable foreignness, of Asian Americans very well. It is the view that some people are permanent outsiders of a certain society: they might be

---

17 See Mae M. Ngai, *Impossible Subjects: Illegal Aliens and the Making of Modern America* (Princeton: Princeton University Press, 2014).

members of the state but not of the nation. Drawing on his own experience, Frank H. Wu offers his observation on how racial identity marginalizes Asian Americans as people whose "heart(s) must be somewhere else rather than here" (Wu 2003, 80). Their loyalties are questioned and in times of international disputes, they are yelled at by the angry folks to "go back."[18] Studies find that people who are affected by perpetual foreigner stereotypes report greater tension between their ethnic and national belongings, and they also show feelings of discomfort and isolation from their peers.[19] The US is not unique in this matter, associating sovereignty with factors such as religion and ancestry can be found elsewhere as well.[20]

Institutionally speaking, then, some people have already been marginalized due to the contingencies of defining citizenship despite their life-long or even generations-long settlement in a society. Now, this "foreignness" denotes not only marginalized groups but also biased and one-sided bodies of knowledge about who may count as a member and who deserves to belong. For one thing, the development of the concept of the "nation" has always been accompanied by forms of domination and oppression. Hence, the content of national identity may exhibit features that can be interpreted as homogeneity or continuity. For the other, this appearance does not mean that the shared conception of national identity and culture is justified or justifiable. Because this look is achieved only by considering the needs, desires and emotions of a particular group (or groups). Consider the fact that some people have already been marginalized or excluded from the national identity due to contingent factors and that their history and experience of being part of the society are excluded from resources that are used to make sense of that society's history and membership. Also, they rarely get a chance to play important roles such as officials and public figures. Nevertheless, they still exist as part of society. I do not think that the key question here is one about

---

18 See for reference Elisabeth Dennis (2018), "Exploring the Model Minority: Deconstructing Whiteness Through the Asian American Example," in George J. Sefa Dei and Shukri Hilowle (eds.), *Cartographies of Race and Social Difference*, 33–48. New York: Springer.
19 See Q. L. Huynh, T. Devos, and L. Smalarz (2011), "Perpetual Foreigner in One's Own Land: Potential Implications for Identity and Psychological Adjustment," *Journal of Social and Clinical Psychology*, Vol. 30, No. 2, 133–162. See also D. W. Sue, J. Bucceri, A. I. Lin, K. L. Nadal, and G. C. Torino (2007), "Racial Microaggressions and the Asian American Experience," *Cultural Diversity and Ethnic Minority Psychology*, Vol. 13, No. 1, 72–81.
20 See for reference Chapter Four and Five of Benhabib (2004), *The Rights of Others*. Cambridge: Cambridge University Press.

the quantitively-speaking majority/minority division; rather, the problem seems to point to a long-term exclusion of those who have been considered as "not belonging." If, for example, there had not been Exclusion Acts or any racial exclusion at all, Asian Americans may not be struggling with the impression of being perpetual foreigners today, and maybe "Americanness" would have quite different connotations. Though a matter of construction, such a biased body of knowledge reinforces the perception that some people are (and should be) outsiders.

Since identity is constitutive of and constituted by social structures (while racial identities such as Black or Asian are rather manifest in the US case, cultural and/or religious identity more greatly manifest in Europe), it should thus not be grasped simply as a given entity, but a complicated network resulting from varying practices of different kinds. Its functioning requires human cooperation; it is not free floating but closely attached to some real needs. If anything should be learned from the overall exclusion of women in politics, academics and economics, I think it is that an androcentric view only produces knowledge that worsens the exclusion of women. The same point also applies to identities concerning belonging, such as national identity, which is affected by race, ancestry, religion and so on. Once these factors are associated with sovereignty, this connection justifies ignoring people who nevertheless make up the society.

In Elizabeth Anderson's analysis of racial segregation, she argues that despite material inequality, segregation also undermines democracy. She says as follows:

"In societies marked by group segregation, ensuring the competence and accountability of officeholders to serve the interests of the whole public, and not just segregated members of it, requires that offices be occupied by members of the different groups, who must work together to share their symmetrical knowledge, forge mutually respectful norms of intergroup communication and interaction and fill out and implement the ends of office in ways that serve the interests of all." (Anderson 2013, 109)

Based on Anderson's analysis, I think there are two kinds of segregation which remain deeply interrelated and require attention. One type of segregation is what Anderson calls residential segregation, i.e. when communities are divided according to race and when race also becomes one of the criteria which decide where one chooses to live. The other kind is epistemological, i.e. when the making of knowledge only draws resources from, due to one reason or another, privileged group(s) and when such identitarian criteria also become how reasonableness of certain matters is determined.

In this way, a terrible consequence would be what Parekh describes as "cultural limbo," namely where:

> "Immigrants may move out of the communal ghetto and buy a house in a white middle-class suburb. But if the residents of that area move out, these efforts at integration amount to nothing. Or they might adopt the ways of life and thought of the wider society, but if they are dismissed as pushy, presumptuous, not knowing their place, integration not only brings no benefits but also consigns them to a cultural limbo, uprooted from their own community but without acquiring a reasonably secure foothold in the new one." (Parekh 2008, 85)

Carens also points out similar limbo problems, which immigrants face, as "[when] the representative of the state and the rest of the citizenry treat you *as outsiders who do not really belong and who have somehow acquired a status that is really undeserved*" (Carens 2005, 44, my emphasis). Anderson suggests solving segregation through integration. But she does not agree with the idea of solving racial segregation by working out "normative principles that purport to be true in all possible worlds"; in that way, overconfidence could mean the "risk [of] missing out on normatively significant problems and questions of feasibility" (Anderson 2014, 376–382). For her, theorizing integration as a remedy for segregation is not about supposing how a perfect society looks. Rather, it is more akin to the non-ideal treatment of ideals: theorizing ideals by acknowledging precisely what is not ideal. Hence, Anderson's conception of racial integration aims to develop pragmatist methodologies.

With the problem of residential segregation in mind, Anderson posits four stages of integration, which are as follows: formal desegregation, spatial integration, formal social integration and informal integration. In short, to fully integrate a certain population into a society, people within that society more generally should not be divided into separate social units. Moreover, not only should members of different groups be allowed to participate in the same institutions, care should also be focused on how they participate and interact with each other. These points are fair. It is also not difficult to see these four stages of racial integration extended to the integration of immigrants, since race is one of the main factors why immigrants experience discrimination and formal or informal exclusions, explicitly or implicitly.[21]

---

21 See for reference Sarah Fine (2016), "Immigration and Discrimination," in Sarah Fine and Lea Ypi (eds.), *Migration in Political Theory: The Ethics of Movement and Membership*, 125–150. Oxford: Oxford

So solving racial integration will find an answer to the integration of immigrants, at least partly. Besides, given that "race" almost never entails just the color of the skin, a successful racial integration will offer keys to other aspects of integration, such as discrimination and exclusion based on ethnicity, heritage or religion.

Nevertheless, I maintain that the four-stages-model might be too simplistic. Some critics point out that although racial segregation is a social problem, Anderson's expectation of a well-mixed society takes racial diversity at face value and that it is not realistic either.[22] For one thing, some cities or regions are predominantly white due to other historical reasons rather than segregation, but should this racially segregated situation be corrected simply for the sake of racial diversity? Does it mean that racial minorities must be proportionally allocated? Furthermore, critics point out that Anderson underestimates the significance of minority communities for those people. They are the places where they seek what they miss elsewhere due to segregation, such as equality and recognition. In that sense, although a segregated situation, it would be wrong to equate such minority shelters with unjustly segregated neighborhoods. Last but not least, considering that people have different expectations about what racial equality actually looks like, Anderson's concept of "integration" in terms of "racial diversity" depends on a variety of different interpretations. So, questions about problematic or inappropriate identitarian criteria remain. In her case study of racial integration, Anderson also admits that in terms of racial integration she advocates staying away from racial identity politics, which concerns not only how societies are organized, but also how people react to relevant social problems. Hence, when thinking about integration, how to effectively stay away from (racial) identity politics without either ignoring identity completely or falling prey to its rigid ideologies also remains to be answered.

University Press; Michael Dummett (2001), *On Immigration and Refugees*. London: Routledge, especially Chapter Four; Teresa Hayter (2000), *Open Borders: The Case Against Immigration Controls*. London: Pluto Press, especially Chapter Two.

22 See for reference Michael S. Merry (2013), "Book Review: The Imperative of Integration," *Theory and Research in Education*, Vol 11, Issue 1, 101–106. Michael O. Emerson (2011), "Book Review: The Imperative of Integration by Anderson," *American Journal of Sociology*, Vol. 117, No. 1, 317–319. Cara Wong (2014), "Would We Know 'Integration' If We Were to See It? Measurement and The Imperative of Integration," *Political Studies Review*, Vol. 12, Issue 3, 353–360.

When is Integration Possible?

I agree with Anderson whenever she insists on *not* thinking about integration according to ideal models. In Anderson's words, apart from the misleading overconfidence, "the hard work would still remain in figuring out how to apply them [ideal models] in practice" (Anderson 2014). Ideal models offer normative principles, but they are quite ineffective when it comes to modeling the many contingencies and limitations that are nevertheless important parts of reality. Ideals cannot be tested directly, "but their institutional embodiments under particular conditions." Hence, the hard work requires understanding "how institutions work to attribute desired or undesired consequences to the ideal type we are trying to realize, or to contingent features of the practice or its background conditions that we might be able to change" (ibid.). In this sense, the reexamination of pre-existing contexts aims to find out whether anything needs to be changed and whether there are adverse conditions that, for example, produce unjust or unrealistic expectations for immigrants' integration.

Another problem in thinking about integration according to ideal models is the risk of confusing "integration" with "assimilation," as I discussed at the beginning of this chapter. Anderson also warns that integration does not take "a dominant group as fixed and [demand] that other groups join it by abandoning their distinct group identities and conforming to what the dominant group takes to be its defining norms, practices and virtues" (Anderson 2013, 114). In this regard, generalism does not seem to be free from the risk of performing assimilation, for they indeed assume and expect that other groups (should) have certain identifications. I do not mean to deny universalism or certain traditions as such; rather, my point is to deny the kind of exclusionary thinking that has been discussed so far. But arguing that locals can and should also integrate does not mean to say that they alone should adapt themselves to immigrants, as that would be the same one-way process only in reverse. It is important to explore the epistemic dimension of integration because the ways of reasoning and the relevant discursive resources of membership and belonging have not always been subjected to scrutiny. There are many demeaning concepts and norms that not only cause epistemic errors but also moral ones. These can seriously impede and thereby jeopardize attempts for co-existence.

I also agree with the previously mentioned critiques which point out Anderson's concept of integration as a "remedy to racial segregation" to be not very well delimited. First, a minority community could have a positive impact on the marginalized in hard times, although this in fact appears to be a racially segregated situation. The actual meaning of such places will be disregarded if they are treated as "barriers to racial integration." I think Anderson would agree that those minority communities should be respected, and she is rather outspoken about how divisions work(ed) in the interest of the privileged. However, though present racial segregation is often connected with unjust racial segregation in the past and it would be an oversimplification to treat Anderson's proposal as being simply one of allocating people just for the sake of racial diversity, the question of how to understand integration in Anderson's "racial integration" remains unanswered. One may argue that Anderson's proposal should not be taken too literally, and that she intends to argue in favor of structural change that would benefit the participation as well as the representation of people of color. Yet, the question of "how to do it" remains unclarified. How should the proportion of different groups of people look in order to count as well-mixed or "racially integrated"? It is true that racial diversity should not be taken at its face value, but this awareness demands a feasible interpretation of "racial integration," otherwise it is likely to remain empty talk.

Delimiting racial segregation, which at the same time means delimiting integration in Anderson's sense, must therefore take into consideration both the injustices of segregation and the positive significance that minority communities have realized for the underprivileged during hard times. Put in this way, Anderson's notion of integration as a "remedy to racial segregation" appears to be more or less paradoxical, since racially segregated situations cannot be changed when they are seen as constituting injustices on the one hand and having a positive significance on the other. Without first deciding what to change, it is impossible to know how to change.

An anecdote may be helpful for finding some orientations. Michael O. Emerson, who is also a researcher of racial segregation, was once invited to a radio show to talk about racial equality. I quote him at length to capture the interview in his own words,

"The host, it soon became clear, held a staunch Afrocentric viewpoint and did not support in any shape or form racial integration. He continually pushed me to renounce the value of any type of integration ... In the end, as is nearly always the case on talk radio, the host had the last word. He told his audience (I paraphrase), 'This is exactly what I've been warning you about – the dangers of integration, of this ideology that attempts to absorb us, so we lose our institutions and so the white man can have direct control over us. Do not listen!

We must resist such insidious thinking and ideologically motivated and tainted research. Be prepared to defend yourselves."' (Emerson 2011, 317–319)

Being a member of racial minority, the host is likely to be considered a victim of racial segregation – that is, the group that would desire racial equality. Nevertheless, he rejects racial integration since he believes that it is a dangerous ideology. In his thinking, black people should resist integration in order to preserve themselves. In fact, his defense does not sound like anything different from what is normally categorized as "racism talk," if a white person says the same words. The host's opinion that racial integration would "absorb" black people and let whites take control is exactly the same as when a white person claims that racial integration would "contaminate" them. Only here, the race exchanges places. For one thing, I believe that it is reasonable to suppose that the host's belief may be one consequence of long-standing racial segregation; if sticking together with your "own kind" is the only way to survive, it is likely that the underprivileged would internalize this belief as part of their worldview. However, what I want to point out here is that victims of (racial) segregation can also end up embracing (racial) segregation. Anderson's picture of racial segregation meets the criteria of what is normally considered to be "segregation," but her picture might in some ways be romanticized. The belief in racial segregation may not be exclusively white as Anderson supposes.

So, in Anderson's case, if racial segregation is the problem against which integration should be directed, it must be about more than just mixing races. It must also concern how to change the identitarian orientation. Residential segregation is not accidental: people choose to stick with their race and avoid interaction with other races because they think it is the only way to preserve themselves. Measures aiming to improve interracial interactions are one way to combat this misleading orientation. Experience of interracial interactions is helpful, but it fails to explain what is wrong with an identitarian orientation. For positive experiences are perhaps just exceptions. Nevertheless, maintaining that there must be a crisis of segregation when people stay with their "own kind" – however "kind" is defined – is also an inconsiderate judgement. As discussed above, neither racial diversity nor what appears to be a situation of segregation should be taken at face value. People may have practical reasons for interacting with those who speak the same language, believe in the same God and so on. *Overcorrections* should be avoided since "racial diversity" cannot be defined rigidly.

Anderson remarks that her argument does not aim at "proportional representation (of racial groups) in office," nor does it "accord political standing to group based self-definitions and loyalties." The point is rather to "demonstrate the importance for democracy of integration, of cooperation and communication *across group lines*, for the purpose of forging *shared* norms and goals of the democratic polity as a whole, and to that extent forging a shared identity of citizens." Integration, according to Anderson, should change norms when they "incorporate stigmatizing representations of subordinate groups and adaptions to group inequality" (Anderson 2013, 110, my emphasis). So, put otherwise, positive experience is useful insofar as it can help to combat stigmatizing representations and thereby forge shared norms and realize democratic cooperation and communication; this is how to cross group lines. Yet, this proposal can itself be too exceptional, because the chance of having specific experiences, such as experience with foreigners or positive experiences, requires specific conditions that cannot always be equally distributed, such as having sufficient financial support for overseas semesters, having good infrastructures for travel, living in an international city or working in an international company. Positive experience is definitely one way to across group lines, but it is neither a sufficient nor a necessary condition. In spite of increasing the chances of facilitating positive experiences, it is also important to explain why thinking according to or within these lines is wrong. That means we must elaborate what the lines are, what their problems are and how to fix them.

The epistemic dimension of integration, which I have already mentioned several times, makes up the rest of the book. In the next chapter I shall explore the central matter of my discussion: identity-based thinking. Identity-based thinking concerns how memberships are tailored according to some identitarian lines due to the need of social orders and how certain groups' social presence and their legitimacy to belong are thereby re-negotiated. Therefore, identitarian structures constitute one of those pre-existing contexts which formal equality must interact with and can affect immigrants' capacity to integrate.

What's more, although many will agree that differences should be respected, I suppose that few would agree that this also means to tolerate, for instance, sexism. Regarding issues such as women's rights, it is in fact desirable that everyone shares a consensus. However, this should not be achieved by reasonings such as "liberal democracy embodies the true universalism, so conform," or "X tradition is unquestionable, so conform." On the one hand, because liberal democracies are not free from violations of women's rights, their traditions should not enjoy natural legitimacy just because they happen to be (dominant) traditions of such societies.[23] On the other, as I shall thoroughly argue in the next chapter, simply taking given identities – together with their obvious and taken-for-granted connotations – as a ready-made orientation commits the typical mistake of identity-based thinking. The problem is not only a matter of following the wrong standards, as some identities are extremely prone to reductionist negative readings. More importantly, these identities can be the wrong place to begin with because their creations are rooted in the need to sustain certain social orders that gave rise to social divisions. Repeating these identities – especially according to their ready-made logics and vocabularies – only reinforces the existing pattern and makes it look like as if such an identitarian focus is only necessary.

Integration is not possible when the onus of integration is only placed upon immigrants. As discussed so far, such a one-way process will unconsciously adopt assimilating standards and, as a result, worsen different forms of segregation. This is so because exempting locals from any potential responsibility for immigrants' integration assumes that factors which can impede integration only come from outside the context of the receiving society. Based on this consideration I will explore the possibility of mutual integration. By arguing for mutual integration, I want to develop an account that explains why integration is not only the job of immigrants but of locals as well. This is drawn from my experience as an immigrant, but I believe it is more than personal. I cannot truly integrate – such as participate in the receiving society as equal members economically, culturally and politically – if I am only seen as a token of the identities I present and no one is ready to get to know me and accept me as a diverse person beyond those rigid lines. Rights are helpful; yet, if integration simply relies upon rights, this focus may conceal many obstructing factors in the pre-existing contexts. The identity-

---

23 In addition, one key issue here is the to what extent sexism and feminism debates are exclusively "Western": that is, assuming women's experience from the Global North as the standard experience of all women without taking into consideration that "woman" is not a universal group, women are defined not only by gender, but also by race, class and so on. Postcolonial feminism, for example, is one such discussion. Starting from this standpoint, it is debatable whether liberal democracy and certain traditions stemming from such societies are indeed sufficient, or at least genuinely helpful for improving women's status, or whether they can only promote women's status according to the "Western" image.

based thinking that I will explore in the next chapter illustrates one normative foundation there is in meaningfully thinking about mutual integration.

Two –
Identity-based Thinking

Not only immigrants, but also locals should integrate. Put in the terms of integration expectations, one may say: not only immigrants, but also locals should learn or re-learn something. But what should locals learn or re-learn? This question does not seem to make much sense if it is assumed that their given knowledge about the receiving society, about how things are and how things should be, has been subject to scrutiny. As briefly illustrated in the last chapter, it is possible that locals are equipped with ways of thinking that are closed-minded, ill-informed and prejudiced. Given that that they are conventionally exempted from any responsibility concerning integration and that their conceptions about membership and their interpretations of norms and values have a significant impact on, if not determine, whether and to what extent (which group of) immigrants will be accepted as part of society, it is urgent to explore how identitarian frameworks shape the way immigrants' – or some immigrants' – social presence and participation are perceived and explained. There are two identitarian frameworks operating, one is the dichotomous implying that only "outsiders" need to integrate, the other is the one that decides who is to be perceived as "outsider."

In this chapter, I will first explain the concept of "identity" I am concerned with. By identity, I do not refer to group-based identity in general but rather a special kind of identity, namely what Bernard Williams calls "necessary identity," which is necessary for social orders but not for its bearers. I will show how necessary identity, though it often begins with policy, ends up producing a body of knowledge that disguises and underpins related norms and ignorance. I will also show that necessary identity is not restricted to singular identities such as race, religion and gender, but also applies to compound identities which often encompass many singular identities; for example, the identity of "immigrant" in its everyday use, especially when associated with negative meanings, often points at people of a particular race, descent and cultural background. Nevertheless, considering that the term "necessary" or "necessity" carries with it a justifying connotation, treating some identities as "necessary identity" can be problematic, for this approach can easily disguise injustices as being inevitable. Therefore, it is important to distinguish between apparent necessities and justifiable necessities so that moral failures will not be confused with necessary, therefore inevitable consequences. Against this background, I will examine the identity of "immigrant." Then, I will introduce what Amartya Sen's calls "identity-based thinking." I will argue that this reductionist view reduces a many-sided person not only quantitatively but also qualitatively, that is, according to the specific understanding of a certain identity that is predefined by social orders. By borrowing Margaret U. Walker's notion of "epistemic necessity" I will explain how identity-based thinking, which is supported by necessary identity, excludes.

Social Orders and Necessary Identity

In *Identity and Violence*, Sen makes an intriguing observation about classification and identity. Consider a person's shoe size: whatever size one wears is entirely contingent, even though many people share the same shoe size, but this kind of sharing does not have any inherent significance. However, if for some strange reasons, it became prohibited to manufacture or wear size 8 shoes, or indeed if these shoes just became difficult to buy, "then the need for shoes of that size may indeed become a shared predicament and can give reason enough for solidarity and identity" (Sen 2007, 26). As Sen explains, under the new social order, wearing a size 8 shoe would be transformed from a mere classification into an identity that can motivate people to set up organizations to demand change. As "size 8" turns into a source of meaning, it becomes a normative matter and can afford people a reason to act. This transformation imposes a political relationship such that "size 8" now stands for a social role that certain people are made to bear. They must take into consideration how "size 8" transformed their living conditions and reassess their social existence. Not only their social participation and presence will be affected, but they may also be subject to different treatments. Depending on the actual reason why size 8 is banned, those treatments will be legitimized accordingly.

Now, "size 8" might sound like a bizarre example, but what it represents has never ceased to occur across different times and places. There were and there are still numerous identities like "size 8" whose design and implementation result from and serve the needs of social orders. As the discussion of assimilation and segregation in the last chapter shows, Danish, American, Muslim or Asian could all be "size 8"; that is, they all refer to socially designated identities which precede the actual socialization among people just for the sake of a certain social order. Sen, quoting Bourdieu, maintains that such a social arrangement ends up "producing difference where none exists" and "telling people that they're different by designing them" (ibid., 27).

Willliams' concept of "necessary identity" provides a helpful account for further clarifying what exactly the problem is with the externally imposed identity in Sen's observation. According to Williams, "necessary identity" refers to identity that is necessary to certain social orders but not to its bearers. In *Shame and Necessity*, where Williams conducts an enquiry into the ethical ideas of Antiquity, he reveals two incorrect understandings about the Greeks and modern human beings: (1) we believe that we are morally different from the Greeks, because we do not think that (2) the institution of chattel slavery is just and we do not share the view that some people are by nature slaves. Williams argues that these are wrong interpretations of the Greeks' ethical ideas. On the one hand, the Greeks[1] "recognized the simple truth that slavery rested on coercion," not nature. No one is born a slave by nature; it is an externally imposed role. Since "slave" is a necessary role to the then economic system, "someone 'had' to be a slave" (Walker 2007, 163). According to Williams, the Greeks were aware that slaves were made by coercion. They "saw what slavery involved and regarded it as a paradigm of *bad luck* [...] the bad luck of being in a condition imposed and sustained by force" (Williams 1993, 124). On the other hand, the Greeks did not pretend to see the institution of slavery as just. The fact that they recognized this

---

1 For Williams, Aristotle's infamous defense of the institution of slavery is an aberration, in the sense that "various things he says in the course of it are not entirely consistent with each other." Williams argues that "(s)ome of these inconsistencies are clearly ideological products" in which he tried to "square the ethical circle." Aristotle's argument "merely sets the task" but "does not provide the intellectual negotiations and evasions that would be needed in real life to see slavery in that light, and to change it from being what it had always been seen to be, a contingent and uniquely brutal disaster for its victims." See Bernard Williams (1993), *Shame and Necessity*, 110 and 118. Berkeley: University of California Press. What's more, Aristotle cannot speak for the whole Greek world.

coercion shows that they acknowledged slavery to be "a contingent and uniquely brutal disaster" that could even befall free persons. The Greeks' "consideration of justice and injustice was immobilized by the demand of what was seen as social and economic necessity," due to the fact that "slavery" is necessary "to sustaining the kind of political, social, and cultural life that free Greeks enjoyed" (ibid., 124–125). The Greeks saw slavery neither as just nor unjust: they saw it as necessary. Put differently, the Greeks would not have had the life they had if it had not been for slavery. For them, what is socially and economically necessary falls outside the realm of morality.

Williams contends that modern human beings think that they are morally different from the Greeks partly due to their misunderstanding about the Greeks' ethical ideas, and partly because the very idea of slavery is incompatible with the economic system and the widely shared conception of society nowadays (ibid., 128).[2] Yet, this only means that there are different opinions about slaves (and probably also about the economy). It does not, however, mean that modern human beings are morally different from the Greeks. For according to Williams, modern human beings have not eliminated the notion of necessary identity, but simply shifted it to other places. Williams thinks that this misunderstanding about the Greeks is, at the same time, a misunderstanding of us as modern human beings.

In Sen's example, size 8 functions as a necessary identity; that is, size 8 is necessary to some kind of social order, even while it remains relatively insignificant to its bearers. But once an identity becomes necessary to a social order, its meaning and mechanism change as well: it will incorporate new norms or existing norms differently, it will rearrange social structures, redistribute social goods such as status, rights, authority, credibility, and other forms of resource. For my concerns, insofar as necessary identity changes the overall living conditions of its bearers, it changes whether those people are entitled to moral relationships and, specifically, what kind of moral relationships. The term "slave" denotes a certain social status, such as non-citizen and non-human, which permits forms of treatment that are otherwise considered inappropriate or immoral. Those who are slaves are thus excluded from (normal) moral consideration.

There are many other examples of necessary identity as well, such as "black" and "yellow" with respect to racial orders. Yellow or black does not

---

2 However, that slavery is not necessary to the current economic system does not mean that such economic system is a just one, these are two different matters.

refer to a person's actually having the skin color yellow or black, but rather to their non-whiteness – to their lack of certain physical features, ancestry and cultural background that are deemed desirable. Like "slave," racial identities are necessary identities designed to serve the needs of certain social orders. In his study, Michael Keevak describes the prehistory of using yellowness to refer to Asian people, noting that in the early days of travel and in missionary reports, the skin color of people in Asia was rarely mentioned, and if it was mentioned at all, it was described as variously as brown, olive and pale. The use of "yellow" first appeared in medical discourse at the end of 17th century as a way to describe the racial category of the "Mongolianness." However, Keevak suggests that choosing "Mongolian" as the racial category for people in Asia (instead of Chinese or Japanese) was not random but associated with the cultural memory of invasions from that part of the world, such as those by Attila the Hun and Genghis Khan. So from the beginning, identifying Asian people as yellow was linked to danger and threat. Moreover, "yellow" does not refer to the actual color yellow; rather, it is a "developmental color" suggesting illness and not healthy. Chinese and Japanese were not "yellow" when they were considered wealthy, sophisticated and showed willingness to trade with the west.[3] They did not become "yellow" until they were classified as the yellow race which was called "Mongolian" in the 18th century. The yellow race became part of political rhetoric and geo-politics along with the rise of Japan as a military force and the presence of Chinese immigrant workers as cheap laborers. "Yellow Peril" became a politically recognized problem to the sovereignty and well-being of Western civilization.[4]

There is yet another way that identity becomes necessary that does not involve designing new identities to satisfy social orders, but rather through politicizing mere group-based identities – similar to the example of "size 8" – by establishing an "either/or" relationship between that identity and

---

[3] For example, Chinese involvement in American society shifted from being understood simply as common trade to that of stealing jobs and endangering the US economy, see John Kuo Wei Tchen (2001), *New York before Chinatown: Orientalism and the Shaping of American Culture, 1776–1882*. Baltimore: Johns Hopkins University Press.

[4] For a thorough discussion about the development of racial thinking regarding "yellow" and its relation to "Whiteness," see Michael Keevak (2011), *Becoming Yellow: A Short History of Racial Thinking*. Princeton: Princeton University Press. For a discussion about how "White" became a race category against the background of slavery and how it corresponded to the social order which kept black people from voting, see Katharine Gerbner (2018), *Christian Slavery: Conversion and Race in the Protestant Atlantic World*. Philadelphia: University of Pennsylvania Press.

others. Regarding this case, the so-called "divide-and-rule policy" is at its finest. Among authors who discuss the colonial role of the divide-and-rule policy that exploited the opposition between Hindus and Muslims in India, Parekh (2008) points out that the bureaucratic categories of Hindu and Muslim, which were introduced by colonizers who believed that Indians were a deeply religious people, "had serious long-term consequences." Religious identity has become "a primary marker of social identity." This categorization triggered an "exclusivist momentum" such that over time even "public policies came to be tailored to the needs and demands of each religious group." In so doing, their differences were reinforced such that the quarrels between "the Hindu landlords and their Muslim farm workers" were described with "a religious gloss," even if the quarrels had "an entirely economic origin" (Parekh 2008, 17).

In remembering the tragic death of Kader Mia, who was killed during the Hindu-Muslim riots,[5] Sen too condemns the fact that:

"Many-sided persons were seen, through the hazy lenses of sectarian singularity, as having exactly one identity each, linked with religion or, more exactly, religious ethnicity [...] That Kader Mia would be seen as having only one identity – that of being a member of *the 'enemy' community who 'should' be* assaulted and if possible killed – seemed altogether incredible." (Sen 2007, 172–173, my emphasis)

Under the divide-and-rule policy of British India, Hindu-Muslim opposition was encouraged, enmity fostered, and distrust cultivated. To the divide-and-rule policy, both Hindu and Muslim were necessary identities for the conveniences of asserting colonial dominance. Under this kind of social order, it is no wonder that these two identities alone came to be perceived, as these were the only identities that were made perceptible. What's worse, these identities were meant to be perceived in an antagonistic way. Personal and in-group di-

---

5 "My first exposure to murder occurred when I was eleven. This was in 1944, in the communal riots that characterized the last years of the British Raj, which ended in 1947. I saw a profusely bleeding unknown person suddenly stumbling through the gate to our garden, asking for help and a little water. I shouted for my parents, while fetching some water for him. My father rushed him to the hospital, but he died there of his injuries. His name was Kader Mia. ... Kader Mia was a Muslim, and no other identity was relevant for the vicious Hindu thugs who had pounced on him. In that day of rioting, hundreds of Muslims and Hindus were killed by each other...Kader Mia, a Muslim day laborer, was knifed when he was on his way to a neighboring house, for work at a tiny wage. He was knifed on the street *by some people who did not even know him* and most likely had never set eyes on him before. For an eleven-year-old child, the event, aside from being a veritable nightmare, was profoundly perplexing." Sen, *Identity and Violence*, 170–173, my emphasis.

versity is reduced to a friend-and-foe relationship between Hindus and Muslims. One of the consequences of such politicization is the impoverishment of social relationships, namely, the possibilities of how people can relate to each other have been significantly reduced. Social orders ensure that "religious identity" is the only way that one person perceives another.

Another representative example of how a colonial divide-and-rule policy affects, and even forms, present inter-group relations by deploying given identities as necessary conditions for governance is that of Chinese Indonesian. Chinese was made into a necessary identity during Dutch colonization in Indonesia, as Indonesia was divided into three separate groups: Indonesians, Chinese and Dutch. As the rulers, the Dutch considered themselves to be at the top of this hierarchy. Chinese, then, were the "middlemen" between the Dutch and Indonesians, who were involved in the VOC structure ("Vereenigde Oost-Indische Compagnie" meaning "Dutch East India Company") as an important part of VOC's economic activity, particularly in farming, landholding, selling and leasing.[6] This policy tremendously changed the status of Chinese people in Indonesia. For one thing, the involvement of the Chinese in local economic activities was expanded and, due to restrictions on mobility enacted by the *passenstelsel* (pass system) and *wijenstelsel* (quarter system), Chinese economic activities ended up being concentrated in cities. When industrialization began, the Chinese were the best prepared as they were already broadly specialized in matters of business.[7] For the other, however, anti-Chinese sentiment among Indonesians, who were placed at the bottom of the social hierarchy, began to foment at the same time. The perception of the Chinese in Indonesia was transformed from that of "individuals at the mercy of favors or whim of their hosts" (Phoa 1992, 5)[8] to a "threat to the 'natives' well-being" (Urban 2013)[9]. Being singled out in this way, Chinese in Indonesia came to be seen as non-natives, despite the fact that they have been settled in Indonesia since as far back as the 13th century.

---

6 See for reference Liong Gie Phoa (1992), "The Changing Economic Position of the Chinese in Netherlands India," in M. R. Fernando and David Bulbeck (eds.), *Chinese Economic Activity in Netherlands India: Selected Translations from the Dutch*, 5–18. Singapore: Institute of South East Asian Studies.
7 For a reference, see Asvi Warman Adam (2003), "The Chinese in the Collective Memory in the Indonesian Nation," *Kyoto Review of Southeast Asia*, Issue 3: Nations and Other Stories.
8 Phoa, "The Changing Economic Position of the Chinese in Netherlands India," 5–18.
9 Gregory S. Urban (2013), "The Eternal Newcomer: Chinese Indonesian Identity," *LUX: A Journal of Transdisciplinary Writing and Research from Claremont Graduate University*, Vol. 3, Issue 1, Article 19.

This division was reinforced dramatically during Suharto's New Order Regime.[10] During Dutch rule, Chinese Indonesians were no longer considered to be *"pribumi"* (natives); during Suharto's rule, they were considered *"Masalah Cina"* (China Problem), which not only reformulated the distinction between Chinese Indonesians and Indonesians, but went further to emphasize their non-cooperative and threatening existence to the Indonesian nation. It was also during Suharto's regime that both the assimilation of and discrimination against Chinese Indonesians were at their worst. The overall prohibition of the Chinese language, names and cultural practices aimed to altogether eliminate Chinese traits from society through a practice of assimilation while, in effect, maintaining the separation between "Chinese" and "Indonesian."[11] Because if "being Chinese" was a problem for "being Indonesian" and had to be eliminated, in order to do so, the "Chineseness" must first be made visible. So, the policy of solving the "China Problem" was in itself paradoxical because, on the one hand, assimilation policies were supposed to prevent "the amalgamation of the Chinese"; however, on the other hand, such policies ended up reinforcing the exclusion of the Chinese by keeping Chinese features alive (ibid., 472). Such policies end up perpetuating the foreignness of Chinese Indonesians by making their "Chinese" features into a necessity that best serves a corresponding social order, even though they have been part of Indonesian society for centuries.

---

10 I highlight the two periods that, in my opinion, most greatly contributed to the situation of Chinese Indonesians today. This is a very rough account and may be misunderstood to be my suggesting that the treatment of Chinese Indonesians under the Suharto regime was directly inherited from Dutch divide-and-rule. It is worth noting that descendents of Chinese immigrants in Indonesia have kept an active participation in various movements in China, especially those national movements under Sun Yat-Sen's leadership and the confrontation between the Nationalist and the Communist Party. This active contact has, to a great extent if not solely, contributed to the suspicion about their loyalty to Indonesia. This suspicion was specifically reinforced by the fact that Chinese Indonesians owned many assets, and also bought Dutch and Japanese companies after colonization collapsed. For references, see Charles A. Coppel (2002), *Studying Ethnic Chinese in Indonesia, Asian Studies Monograph Series*. Singapore: Singapore Society of Asian Studies. Leo Suryadinata (ed.) (1999), *Political Thinking of the Indonesian Chinese, 1900–1995: A Sourcebook*. Singapore: Singapore University Press.
11 For a reference, see Christian Chua (2004), "Defining Indonesian Chineseness under the New Order," *Journal of Contemporary Asia*, Vol. 34, Issue.4, 465–479.

Apparent Necessity, (Un)Justifiable Necessity, and the Identity of "Immigrant"

Then, what social orders may be associated with the identity of "immigrant" or identities that are relevant to "immigrant"? And are these social orders problematic? If so, how? Examples discussed so far may provide a clue. In general, the history of immigration controls as well as that of citizenship have been guided by various discriminative standards based on race, descent or cultural background.[12] These measures, which are essential to the making of a society, directly determine whose presence in the receiving society is justified and according to what standard; who deserves to belong and why; who "we" are and how "we" relate to "others". As I have indicated so far, these measures are not only part of the past, but their legacy is still felt in the present – they continue to affect how today's policies are rationalized and made.[13] Though hardly any government, organization and individual would explicitly admit that they adore any discriminative principles or criteria, this idea never ceases to play its role in their decisions. What's worse, it seems that although it is widely acknowledged that discrimination based on race, descent or cultural background should not be permitted, discussions concerning these issues only "make a brief appearance," as Sarah Fine puts it, that this kind of simple rejection and condemnation "is the beginning and the end of the discussion of race and ethnicity in the context of migration ethics" (Fine

---

12 See for reference Marilyn Lake and Henry Reynolds (2008), *Drawing the Global Color Line: White Men's Countries and the International Challlenge of Racial Equality*. Cambridge: Cambridge University Press. Teresa Hayter (2000), *Open Borders: The Case Against Immigration Controls*. London: Pluto Press. Christian Joppke (2005), *Selecting by Origin: Ethnic Migration in the Liberal State*. Cambridge MA: Harvard University Press. David Fitzgerald (2017), "The History of Racialized Citizenship," in Ayelet Shachar, Rainer Bauböck, Irene Bloemraad and Maarten Vink (eds.), *The Oxford Handbook of Citizenship*, 129–152. Oxford: Oxford University Press.
13 Such as the Windrush scandal, where Commonwealth citizens, who are also British subjects, were wrongly detained, denied legal rights or threatened with deportation; see Amelia Gentleman (2022), "Windrush scandal caused by '30 years of racist immigration laws' – report," *The Guardian*, May, https://www.theguardian.com/uk-news/2022/may/29/windrush-scandal-caused-by-30-years-of-racist-immigration-laws-report, last accessed March 2023. Or EU visa regulations, which grant "white" list countries (countries with a majority white population) visa-free entry into Europe and require members of "black" list countries (poor countries from Africa and Asia) to apply for visa, see Ojeaku Nwabuzo and Lisa Schaeder (2017), "Racism and discrimination in the context of migration in Europe. ENAR Shadow Report 2015–2016," *European Commission*, March, https://ec.europa.eu/migrant-integration/library-document/racism-and-discrimination-context-migration-europe_en, last accessed March 2023.

2016, 126). As long as immigration controls have been and still are discriminative, distribution of residence permits and citizenship cannot be just or fair. Because the former paves the way to the latter. Moreover, these institutional decisions also have an epistemic impact. For one thing, they will perpetuate racism, xenophobia or ethnocentrism in the pre-existing contexts of the receiving society; for the other, they will lead interpretations of many social problems astray, as if conflicts result from the so-called undesirable features of some groups. Against this backdrop, integration, especially its seeming failure, will be prone to antagonistic identitarian misrepresentations. Similar to the "religious gloss" Parekh uses to capture the misleading framework widely deployed in India to explain social conflicts, it would not be difficult to find variants such as "racial gloss," "cultural gloss" or "ethnic gloss" elsewhere.

At this point, one may disagree and claim that this is rather a problem of unjust distribution of citizenship. As long as the citizenship criteria are improved, immigrants will gain a genuinely equal status. Therefore, this is still an issue of formal equality, i.e. rights, rather than one of knowledge. But as the previous discussion shows, exclusion does not stop after gaining citizenship. Asian Americans, for example, are American citizens, but this does not prevent them from being excluded and treated as not deserving to belong, even though they settled in America generations ago. That second, third or even fourth generation are still being inflicted with marginalization, stigmatization and scapegoating – implying that things would have been better if they were either never here or they had tried harder to integrate – is not an exclusively American phenomenon as similar problems are also to be found in other places with a long immigration history.[14] Among all those with a migration background, not all are inflicted with this sort of exclusion that lasts generations, only those whose race, descent, religion ect. do not fit into the conception – or imagination – of the relevant memberships of the receiving society. This can be explained by Michael Blake's arguments that discriminatory immigration policies will affect existing citizens, in the sense that "[where] there are national or ethnic minorities – which is to say, the vast majority of actual cases – to restrict immigration for national or ethnic reasons is to make some citizens politically inferior to others" (Blake 2005, 232–233).

---

14 See for reference Rogers Brubaker (1998), *Citizenship and Nationhood in France and Germany*. Cambridge MA: Harvard University Press; Paul Gilroy (2002), *There ain't no Black in the Union Jack*. London: Routledge.

In fact, not only citizens but all residents inside the territory with similar features will be made politically inferior to others.[15]

From the standpoint of (some) immigrants, integration is made extremely burdensome because they must fight against prejudices that are attached to the physical and/or cultural features they happen to share. From another angle, this is caused by, or at least conceptually supported by, exclusionary imagination of the receiving society, such as when nationhood is based on racial or xenophobic principles. The hermeneutical aspect of nation-ness, which is famously addressed by Benedict Anderson, captures the discursive and epistemological dimension of "nation." Since it is impossible to know everyone even in the smallest nation, community has to be imagined in one way or another as both inherently limited and sovereign. For that reason, national representations as well as their historical narratives will play an indispensable role. I will discuss this further in Chapters Five and Six. Considering how past injustice, such as colonialism, racism and various forms of discrimination, has shaped immigration controls and thereby framed the conception of who (should) belong, such an imagination can make integration particularly difficult, if not impossible, for some immigrants. It also makes belonging to the receiving society a matter of having certain features rather of than one's merits and efforts, even though those features are not really necessary for a person's social participation. In cases like this, whether immigrants are seen as members of the receiving society who deserve to belong is not primarily judged according to their actual participation and contribution to the receiving society, but on the base of irrelevant elements like race or descent.

Williams' account of necessary identity captures the conceptual relation between some identities and social orders, but it does not offer evaluation of any form. Sometimes this could be confusing, because the term "necessary" usually carries with it a normative tone. As Williams's distinction between "thin" and "thick" concepts shows, some words not only describe but also

---

15 As it appears to me, Blake does not include this group into his argument because his argument rests on the basis that there is a special duty to respect one's fellow citizens as equal members of the political community. However, the deficit of this argument, as Fine points out, is that it assumes, or it must assume, that the existing state is just and unquestionable. But in reality, this is rarely the case since the present demographic situations, such as a homogenous population or certain groups being minorities, are often caused by past injustice. By making the existing states the criteria against which policies are to be measured such past injustice is brushed off, see Fine (2016), "Immigration and Discrimination."

evaluate. The generic use of "necessary" generally implies the objective inevitability of something, meaning that a decision or a choice does not involve subjective preferences but only concerns absolutely objective needs. This framework can be deceiving, for the standard of objectivity can be disguised by power structures. I will turn to this point in the next chapter where I offer a theory of the epistemology of identity-based thinking. The fact that power structures can fake objectivity, thereby necessity, means that it is vital to distinguish justifiable necessities from apparent ones when it comes to human affairs.[16] While explaining that "slave" is a necessary identity to ancient Greek's economic orders, Willliams also points out that the idea of slavery is incompatible with the economic system and the widely shared conception of society nowadays. Since it is the background social orders that decide which identities are necessary and which are not, then as soon as the larger background changes, what counts as "necessary" *should* change as well. However, there are preconditions.

Think about the example of syllogism reasoning. The logical certainty from "(a). all human beings are mortal" and "(b). I am a human being" to "(c). I am mortal" holds independent from whether the first two premises and/or the conclusion are true. That the conclusion in the above example seems rather unproblematic is because, at least according to the current scientific knowledge, the first claims are true. But the same reasoning form can also produce absurd conclusions without ruining the apparent logical certainty. For example, "if a person is White, that person is trustworthy," "Bernie Madoff is White," so "Bernie Madoff is trustworthy" – even though he is the notorious fraudster behind one of the largest Ponzi scheme frauds in history. The point is that the evaluation of the premises, such as whether they are true, whether they are plausible, or whether they are justifiable, is a completely different matter that lies beyond its logical coherence: namely, one that could only be assessed and judged when taking other perspectives into consideration. In Williams' example of "slave" being the necessary identity to the then economic system, though it might be true that "slave" was logically speaking necessary to the background social order at that time, this does not mean that this necessity is justifiable because the premise that

---

16 In purely natural cases, such as regarding the biological features of plants, or in entirely idealized cases, such as in thoughts experiments, it might be safe to say that justifications are not needed. For in those cases, the observed objectivity is highly likely to be the absolute objectivity, therefore the genuine necessity. More on this will be discussed in the next chapter.

grounds the need for such social order could be unjust, therefore morally impermissible. Logical certainty alone is not sufficient for justifiable necessities; contrarily, it could be very misleading if this is the only standard that counts. Reasoning that relies unreflectively on what is given is prone to such apparent necessity, since it assumes pre-existing practices, norms and rules are justified and appropriate. In order to stay sensitive and be capable of spotting problems in the given social orders, different perspectives and resources are needed; only in this way it is possible to see why some necessities are only apparent.

In the above-mentioned cases of divide-and-rule and their aftermath, the necessity of identities such as Chinese, Indonesian, Hindu and Muslim is only apparent because the opposition between groups, the threat one group poses to the receiving society, or the claim that one group is unfit for a certain membership are instituted for the convenience of colonial rule. They are not justifiable, nor do they reflect any so-called nature of the bearers of those identities. Rather, they are signs of domination disguised by power structures. What appears to be necessary is in fact morally questionable preferences or consequences resulting from injustices. The fact that they are still prevailing demonstrates that the legacy of an unjust past continues to play an active role in the present, especially in matters pertaining to immigration and integration. Given that accusations of not trying hard enough or failing to integrate almost always only target immigrants who are also at the same time racial and cultural minorities, it becomes questionable whether the identity of "immigrant" really represents justifiable necessity. It may be intuitive to suppose that "immigrant" is the opposite of "citizen"; hence, as long as "citizen" is justifiably necessary to the modern order of equality, it follows that "immigrant" should be necessary, too. On the surface, this thin definition of "immigrant" may seem correct, but as I have argued with the example of syllogism reasoning, the crux of the problem here is not the logical coherence between premises and conclusions but rather the truth and the plausibility of the premises involved. When the term "immigrant" is used, especially in a negative way such as when combined with "crisis," "threat," "problem," "danger" and so on, "immigrant" never simply denotes the opposite group of "citizen," it is much thicker than that. It entails a great deal of elements, and as the example of perpetual foreigners has shown, whether one possesses the passport is not that significant. This is because such issues rarely concern passports; rather, they concern who deserves to count as one of "us" and who does not.

Regarding integration, the overlaps between "immigrant," the discriminative notions of political membership, and past injustices relating to the receiving society become even more evident. To some extent, the receiving society's resentment against "immigrants" and complaints about their failure to integrate can be seen as old wine in new skins. Because despite the term "immigrant" a closer look shows that this "immigrant" group does not really encompass immigrants – those who do not possess the passport of where they live – but rather immigrants as well as citizens of specific migration backgrounds. And the content of the complaints as well as the reasons for the resentment can be often linked to certain given notions of "who are we." Hence, questions concerning (the success of) integration never only concern aspects such as whether immigrants have acquired the necessary knowledge for participating and living in the receiving society, whether they speak the local language(s), and whether they obey the law; they also concern desires such as immigrants should adopt our values (and in exactly the same way), immigrants should abandon what in "our" eyes are uncivilized practices, and some immigrants should not be let in. Among these implicit but deep-seated integration goals or standards, two, which are also at the same time standard arguments in favor of immigration control, are especially common and seem to enjoy taken-for-granted legitimacy: namely, the preservation of national culture and the protection of self-determination. Neither can fulfill the intended purposes; instead, they only perpetuate existing discriminations.

Chandran Kukathas argues that in order to preserve a culture, one must first clarify what culture and what degree of cultural integrity is desired. If the conception is very thin, then it is hard to see why immigration makes a difference, as the conception of national culture is indeed so broad. But if it is very thick, such as Samuel Huntington's definition of Americanness in *Who Are We?*, i.e. Protestant, then this concept already excludes many people in one's own society, among which there will certainly be important national figures. To do this, Kukathas contends, is to engage in a very deep culture war in one's own society. As for the protection of self-determination, which stresses that "we" want to take control of what happens in "our" society and its future, one must first clarify the question "who are we?" Kukathas notes that policies result from a process of bargaining that changes from generation to generation, from election to election and even from month to month. The results are rather random, and they do not reflect everyone's desires, meaning there will invariably be winners and losers. Nevertheless, this does not mean that the majority's decision necessarily undermines self-determination, nor does it mean that those who lose are no longer part of the "we."[17]

However, one may ask, doesn't the control of immigration lighten the burden of integration, which means that there will be fewer disagreements and less tension? That may be the intuitive impression. What's more, this kind of control still cannot avoid the conceptual implausibility Kukathas points out: a thin notion of national culture or national self-identity will not be able to justify the necessity of control while an overly thick notion will necessarily imply that some members of that society are inferior to others, as the aforementioned argument of Blake's demonstrates. Furthermore, intuition like this still relies on the presumption that conflicts are primarily caused, if not solely, by immigrants' lack of a supposed homogeneity. But whether this homogeneity exists within the pre-existing population, whether this homogeneity is what produces stability, and whether this homogeneity should exist are questions that remain to be answered.

This is not to deny that there are justified criteria for exclusion. For example, in order to be a dentist, one must have certain expertise; in order to secure the functioning of a society, one must obey some rules. But neither hints at the identity of immigrant or the identity of coming from elsewhere. These are what I call justifiable necessities, because the practice is justified, and the qualities needed for that practice are also justifiably necessary. But this is not the case with immigrants. It is not the case that immigrants do not have the willingness or ability to participate, or that they lack the capacity to learn languages and rules; rather, the possibility for them to participate equally and to be seen as members who deserve to belong is greatly limited both institutionally and epistemically from the outset due to their undesirability in one way or another. So, although "immigrant" seems to be necessary for understanding the dynamics of integration, it is often not necessary in a justifiable way, because 1) immigrants who are associated with integration setback or failure are often associated with these negative situations in a discriminative way; 2) in so far as locals also play a part in immigrants' participation in the receiving society as well as to what extent immigrants can

---

17 See for reference Chandran Kukathas (2017), "Controlling Immigrants Means Controlling Citizens," *F. A. Hayek Lecture*, April, https://www.mercatus.org/hayekprogram/economic-insights/features/chandran-kukathas-controlling-immigration-means-controlling, last accessed March 2023. Also see Kukathas (2005), "Immigration," in Hugh LaFollette (ed.), *The Oxford Handbook of Practical Ethics*, 567–590. Oxford: Oxford University Press.

effectively participate as equal members, what locals do and how they think should also be taken into consideration for a more realistic and just integration; 3) violations of rules, especially when people with a specific migration background are involved, are often not judged fairly but with an emphasis on their migration background as if it was the (primary) cause.

But how does an apparently necessary identity fake justifiable necessity? Walker notes that when miserable and demeaning conditions are considered to be culturally or economically given (i.e. necessary), people who are caught in these situations will thereby remain consigned by existent forms of coercion. She draws attention to an epistemic necessity present in some social identities that lies "in the degree of difficulty in making plausible, imaginable, or even coherent claims that it *need not be that way* for those people" (Walker 2007, 178, original italics). That is to say, "the greater the inevitability of this difficulty, the more necessary an identity is" (ibid.). Coercion never works alone. Necessary identity is never secured merely by policies; it is also upheld by allied norms. Together, necessary identity as social order and knowledge "set limits within which there can be interpretation of what undeniably takes place, of whether [...] it is remarkable or typical, in need of explanation or not worth pointing out" (ibid.). Hence, besides the institutional one attributed by social orders, the epistemic necessity "takes the place of certain justifications that might otherwise be required and sought, or experienced as missing" (ibid., 179).

When social environments are rearranged, epistemic circumstances deriving from such environments will nurture specific structures of (mis)perception and (mis)conception. Therefore, the implication of institutional necessity on epistemic capacity must be reckoned with. Institutionally, the necessity of an identity seems to be just for the sake of social order; whereas, in the epistemic respect, the necessity of an identity "refers to just how much certain understandings of some people are needed by some other people to legitimate the latter's treatment of the former" (ibid., 178). This is precisely akin to the effect of assimilation, as illustrated with the example of assimilation policy towards Chinese Indonesians during the Suharto regime: on the one hand, it seems that Chineseness must be singled out in order "solve the China Problem," while on the other hand, singling out this Chineseness turned out to instigate the very understanding of necessary identity that maintains the social order. In this way, epistemic necessity establishes moral legitimacy, which rationalizes the treatment of certain people in such a way as to simply make it look like a *matter of course*. In epistemic terms, just how necessary a specific identity is, is a question of "how firmly" people labeled according to that identity can be "kept in unquestioned, and preferably unquestionable, place" (ibid., 180). The extreme example of such epistemic necessity can be observed in cases where socially attributed identities, such as race and gender, indicate natural properties. The naturalizing pattern appears to show the innateness of certain characteristics of a socially attributed identity, but it in fact simply naturalizes the social order that makes those identities seem to be necessary in the first place. This naturalizing pattern makes it considerably more difficult to change unjust social orders because it distorts the observation in such a way that certain social order is no longer seen as a work of the human world, but of nature.

The recognition of this epistemic dimension should raise certain questions about whether some inappropriate, even wrong, perceptions and conceptions are involved in certain notions of "us" as the taken-for-granted identity of the receiving society. If so, the impact of these perceptions and conceptions should not be underestimated. The examples that I discussed earlier are not just ancient stories, as they continue to be part of the present. Coercion can be institutional as well as epistemic. It is not nature, but our concepts of economy, politics, or society that decide which identities are necessary. Due to the naturalizing pattern, it no longer matters who a person really is, as long as their social existence satisfies the condition of what the social order needs them to be. Their actual identification with certain group is also overwritten by the social order of necessary identity. People are abstracted from their particularities, turned into interchangeable placeholders of generalized claims, such as who are locals and who immigrants, who deserves to belong, who does not, who threatens "our" values and who is one of "us," as if those identities are timeless entities that simply repeat a certain life. In this way, any moral relationship between people becomes "tautologically 'evident'," as Bauman vividly captures, because the truth of moral relationship is guaranteed in advance by the moral phenomena that are pre-defined and pre-selected.[18] Associating "immigrant" with the integrity and security of society can offer such epistemic necessity.[19] As discussed earlier, epistemic necessity functions as a substitute for justifications that would otherwise be

---

18 See for reference Chapter Two of Baumann's *Postmodern Ethics*.
19 Here I do not intend to speculate or prove whether a state or a government intends to do so when they associate immigrants with national integrity and security, I only want to point out that it has this effect.

required, sought or experienced as missing. It refers simply to the kind and amount of understanding about certain people that is necessitated by a social order. Epistemic necessity ensures that immigrants are only conceived and perceived as threatening and undesirable to the receiving society, especially when immigrants are only seen according to their place of origin or cultural background as the prevailing classification does.

Before I proceed to the next part of the discussion, there is one more thing I want to address. While "immigrant" can be taken at face value – that is, used as a thin category simply denoting the institutional and legal difference among a society's population, such as in statistics, this possibility does not weaken the arguments I have put forward so far. There are two reasons. First, claiming that something is possible is not the same as offering a solution to the problem. I do not mean to claim that my discussion can guarantee making "immigrant" free from all the discriminative components – though I hope so; but to see and to understand how certain uses of "immigrant" and certain understandings of "integration" can perpetuate misperceptions and misconceptions inherited from past injustice is at least the first step towards such a solution. Using "immigrant" as a thin concept could be one of the purposes of such critical examination, but in order to get there, it is urgent to clarify what makes "immigrant" almost an equivalent to "undesirable" and "threatening." Second, by pointing out that the mere focus on "immigrant" in integration can be problematic and why it is so, I do not mean to suggest abandoning the concept completely or replacing it with something else. As explained, the purpose is to argue that there are better ways to describe, understand and evaluate integration, therefore the focus should be changed, and integration should be grasped as a mutual process.

So, by analyzing "immigrant" I mean to unveil how the problematic conception of integration relates to the tacit norms and knowledge of political membership and social belonging. Likewise, by distinguishing the justifiable from the apparent necessities, I aim to demonstrate how apparent necessity can make legitimacy seem inevitable and attributes certain apparent properties to those who bear it. Such an appearance, in turn, contributes to how those bearing that identity are perceived. While there are justifiable necessities for social participation, for example, expertise and professional education, there are also a great number of apparent necessities, i.e. those designed to make unnecessary differences seem necessary for other purposes. Of course, Sens' size 8 is an example of how contingent differences can be made into normative categories that determine what kind of treatment and moral relationship people are entitled to. But as discussed, this forged necessity indeed exists in the real world. Necessary identity does more than just fulfill a designated function; it also produces specific epistemic circumstances that shape the experience and the understanding of the world. The latter is likely to endure much more insistently than institutions do, as it is often constitutive of who "we" are. Necessary identity may begin with policy, but it often ends with being part of the epistemic circumstances. While institutional status can be abolished overnight, knowledge persists.

Identity-based Thinking and How It Excludes

Having introduced necessary identity and its association with social orders, in this part I will consider Sen's "identity-based thinking" and explore how epistemic necessity is employed to exclude people. I shall extend Sen's account of identity-based thinking by pointing out that identity-based thinking contains not only a quantitative reduction as Sen notes, but a qualitative reduction of people as well. That is, people classified according to that identity are reduced to a particular version of that identity that serves to morally legitimize a certain social order. Then, I will thoroughly elaborate upon the meaning of this qualitative reduction by revisiting Walker's point mentioned earlier, according to which epistemic necessity is a matter of "how firmly" people classified by that identity can be "kept in unquestioned, and preferably unquestionable, place" (Walker 2007, 180). In the previous discussion, I distinguished justifiable necessities from apparent ones. From now on, I use the term "necessary identity" only to refer to apparent necessities; that is, unless I say otherwise, I mean it to refer to necessities that are associated with unjust social orders and upheld by problematic conceptions.

Sen briefly used the term "identity-based thinking" to refer to the reductionist view according to which people are seen as if they "can be uniquely categorized according to some *singular and overarching* system of partitioning," "which sees human beings as members of exactly one group" (Sen 2007, xii, original italics), as if whatever that person does is primarily, or even solely, caused by that identity. For Sen, identity-based thinking presents a solitarist approach to identity, which he believes is "a good way of misunderstanding nearly everyone in the world" (ibid.). I shall first briefly attend to Sen's account before I move onto mine. Let's recall Kader Mia, whose tragic death was mentioned earlier in the discussion. Sen argues that Mia was not just a Muslim, but also an Indian, an Asian, a father, a son, a husband, a man, a laborer and someone from the underclass who struggled to survive. He had, in fact, many similarities with those who killed him, but in the days of partition nothing else was more visible than what the social order *made* people see. Sen's account stops here without going any deeper. Such a solitarist approach is of course inaccurate and Sen rightly points out how misleading it is. But it is not enough to recognize this approach as wrongful – it needs more analysis. It is important to know whether there are forces or structures that produce and maintain identity-based thinking and what they are.

As a person, Kader Mia was greatly reduced to a single identity. None of his other identities mattered except the religious one. Yet, it is worth noticing that Mia's identity was not only quantitatively reduced as Sen points out, but his identity was qualitatively reduced as well. This often happens in identity-based thinking; namely, that a person not only has fewer identities than he or she really possesses but is also understood according to very narrow conceptions of those identities. Mia's death resulted not primarily because he was reduced to his Muslim identity but because of how that identity was read during the days of partition, i.e. as the enemy of Hindus. For that reason, he was not seen as a person but as the embodiment of danger and as a threat. Identity-based thinking not only excludes but even kills because the prevailing social order generates the impression that an identity can only have a single designated meaning.

Besides examples of individuals like that of Mia, identity-based thinking can also be attributed to collectives. Samuel Huntington's infamous *Clash of Civilizations* divides the world into several civilizations and concludes that these civilizations can be defined in terms of their "civilization identity." According to his picture of the world, China is merely Confucian, India merely Hindu and Europe merely Christian. What's worse is that these civilization identities possess intrinsic features, according to which they are incompatible with each other. They are doomed to clash due to their intrinsic natures and due to the fact that they will inevitably confront each other as the world shrinks via globalization. There are already two reductions at play here: the first is a quantitative reduction, by which countries or regions are associated with a single civilization; the second is a qualitative reduction, by which one interprets civilizations as natural kinds. His so-called description of the world does not reflect how the world really is, but it does serve Huntington's purpose of portraying the world in an antagonistic way rather well, according to which a clash is inevitable.

Sen criticizes this reductionist view by revealing that it rests upon a "foggy perception" of history, which effectively ignores the significant diversities within each civilization and substantially overlooks the interactions between them (Sen 2007, 57–58). Edward Said critiques Huntington's theory by calling it a "Clash of Ignorance," commenting that according to Huntington, *"hugely complicated matters like identity and culture existed in a cartoonlike world where Popeye and Bluto bash each other mercilessly,* with one always more virtuous pugilist getting the upper hand over his adversary" (Said 2001, my emphasis). Said vividly captures the picture conveyed by Huntington's hypothesis: a cartoonlike world, where characters, such as Popeye and Bluto, are purposely constructed in an opposing way in order to best describe the moral battle between "good and evil."

The moral battle between "good and evil" is central to many identity-based social orders. The realm of morality is not always portrayed in terms like "good and evil," as it can also be presented in terms such as "superior and inferior," "civilized and barbarian," "enlightened and backward" and so on. They describe not only the opposition between two sides but also the content of a given morality. For example, by claiming who believes in the true or false God, who is more culturally advanced and who belongs to a better or worse race, all, to some extent, convey not only who is and who is not desirable, but also why. In both Mia's case and the clash of civilizations thesis, complex matters such as person and civilization are reduced to single entities. They are reduced in a particular way that reflects the kind of moral legitimacy which is required by specific social orders. So, Mia is nothing but a religious enemy and the non-Western world is nothing but an ideological enemy. This portrayal immobilizes other possible moral considerations because it establishes a framework in which the latter do not make any sense: when morality is delimited by identifying who is evil, reconsidering the moral status of the evil would altogether debase the notion of being moral.

As I proceed to distinguish justifiable necessities from apparent ones, I do not intend to deny that there are bad or wrong moral views. However, my point is to say that dealing with apparent necessities also encompasses dealing with problematic moral views that are designed to uphold unjust social orders rather than those which have been subjected to careful scrutiny. However, epistemic necessity – as the one that is built into necessary identities – makes it difficult to notice what justifications are in fact missing. It helps to maintain the apparent necessity of certain social arrangements as a matter of course which is simply the way that certain people are meant to be perceived and treated. Such a posture keeps certain people firmly at the limits of morality, as they are considered a threat to cultural integrity or political stability. The more rigid social structures are, the more difficult it is to question the epistemic necessity which supports them, and the more natural certain moral views and behaviors will appear to be. Said's critique of Huntington is sharp and to the point. But dismissing identity-based thinking as exemplified by Huntington's thesis requires more than simply criticizing it as unrealistic and misleading. The same also applies to identity-based thinking writ large. Such thought is reductionist and misperceives almost everyone and everything in the world, but at the same time it shall not be ignored that such identity-based thinking is a pervasive component of everyday political and social life. Thus, while it should be discarded, it is not at all easy to do so because powerful social orders and epistemic norms buttress this identity-based thinking. Before continuing with a discussion about epistemic norms, I shall elaborate upon one last point; that is, how such epistemic necessity excludes.

Epistemic necessity excludes by obstructing the process of knowledge-seeking. Mia's story gives us a vivid example of how a person's image can be radically and tragically distorted by identity-based thinking. From this epistemic necessity, Mia was nothing else but a Muslim; and not just any Muslim, but *the* Muslim that was doomed to play the role of the "enemy of the Hindu." His personality was so dramatically reduced that it put him into a desperate situation. In Mia's case, there was no actual conflict between him and his killers; he was a victim of the Hindu-Muslim riots as were many others. Even if there was an actual problem between a Muslim and a Hindu, like Parekh's example about the economic dispute between the landlord and the farmer, necessary identity makes sure that religious identities are to be perceived as the only or at least the most prominent factor. People identify themselves as distinct even when they share an identity, be it national, religious, gender or cultural. For example, although I can to some extent break down my identity into being Chinese, a woman, an atheist, a traveler, a doctoral student in philosophy, etc., this in no way necessarily implies that by being a woman or Chinese that I am identical with others who are also women and Chinese. On the contrary, it requires further communication and richer knowledge to determine in what respects and to what extent I share commonalities with others who are also women and Chinese. Identity-based thinking distorts the image of a person by leaving out that person's particularity; instead, it treats a person as a mere placeholder of an identity that is imposed externally by some social order.

While Mia's case appears to be one about a singular individual, it should not be dealt with as the consequence of an agential wrongdoing. Mia's death was not merely the result of someone's bad intention to kill him; rather, it exemplifies a case in which social structures partitioned people in such a way that they saw each other primarily according to the necessary identity. Those identities dictated who were to be seen as friends and who were to be seen as enemies. The morality of us-against-them does not afford the possibility of seeing those who do not belong to our social group under any different light. Mia's personal image was distorted because the image of the group to which he belonged was distorted.

Consider *Charlie Hebdo*'s controversial cartoon which was published in 2016 and depicted Alan Kurdi – the little boy who drowned while his family tried to cross Mediterranean Sea – as growing up to be an ass groper in Germany if he had not died (Meade 2016). Under the headline "Migrants," the cartoon shows pig-faced men running after screaming women. At the top of the cartoon, Alan Kurdi was drawn in the exact position in which he died: washed ashore by the drift of the tide. Beside him, the question "Que serait devenu le petit Alan s'il avait grandi?" (What would little Alan have grown up to be?) is written, with the answer "Tripoteur de fessess en Allemagne" (An ass groper in Germany) written at the bottom. As with *Jylland Posten*, *Charlie Hebdo*'s cartoon sparked a debate over racism. The main critique condemns the satirical magazine's exploitation of the boy's tragic death and its stigmatization of refugees by implying that they would grow up to be sexual harassers. This case, too, is representative of topics such as the freedom of speech or political correctness, but I am more interested in how this example shows the way in which identity-based thinking can obstruct our interest in getting to know other people and, as a result, solidify the rigid moral view of "good and evil."

Although it is true that some cultural practices often seem to disregard women's rights or even sexually objectify them, it would be wrong to suppose that these gender oppressive structures are culturally specific, as if they only exist in Asia and Africa but not in Europe and North America.[20] Improv-

---

20 For an interesting discussion about how liberalism produces illiberal social policies, see Desmond King (1999), *In the Name of Liberalism: Illiberal Social Policy in the USA and Britain*. Oxford: Oxford University Press.

ing gender equality requires identifying and redressing unjust structures, but stigmatizing a group of people based on their place of descent, race or cultural background does not solve the problem. For example, immigrants from some places are often considered to be threatening to women's equality due to the practice of "arranged marriage." On the one hand, it is right to condemn arranged marriage when the persons involved reject such an arrangement.[21] On the other hand, the practice of arranged marriage results highly likely from a more complicated network of beliefs, educational and economic situations, gender inequality and so on than just one or two identities. Hence, correcting unjust arranged marriage requires thorough studies. But the simplistic worldview rooted in identity-based thinking assumes that one particular cultural or ethnic identity provides the complete explanation of why people are different.

Furthermore, identity-based thinking importantly overlooks the fact that the conceptions upon which it relies are the products of a social order, i.e. that Muslims are the enemies of Hindus, that Chinese are threatening to the well-being of Indonesian people, etc. They reflect what certain social identities mean in particular epistemic circumstances but not what social identities actually mean or can mean to their bearers. In identity-based thinking, an identity is qualitatively reduced to reflect what the prevailing social order requires. When immigration control is constantly framed in the language of protecting cultural integrity and national identity, this already implies a threatening image of immigrants and points out a direction for interpreting social conflicts involving people with a migration background. There are criminals among immigrants just as there are among locals, but generalizing the threatening image of immigrants does not at all serve the purpose of catching criminals, but of maintaining the moral legitimacy of the "us versus them" dichotomy. Unjust structures can be institutional as well as epistemic. Misleading conception about immigrants' social presence reinforce the apparent necessity that only immigrants need to integrate.

---

21 This may be one of the those cultural differences that some people find it difficult to accept. Marriage, at least in its widely spread idealist version, should be the result of true love. But this is not what everyone believes about marriage nor should it be. If some people due to other reasons view marriage as an alliance for economic reasons and they do not oppose arranged marriage, I do not think they are doing anything wrong by embracing this practice. Because anyway, they should decide how they want to live, not anyone else, no matter how noble their reasons sound.

However, there are people who, nevertheless, would build their whole lives upon a core identity and who would want to be seen exclusively as the bearer of that identity. But this fact does not contradict what I am arguing against. Identity-based thinking is unrealistic and misleading because it does not involve the process of knowing other people, and it results from classifying and conceptualizing those that are identified with an identity according to what certain social orders need. It not only ignores the actual life of that person – for example, how they identify themselves – but also ignores the actual development of a cultural practice or the actual diversity within what seems to be a single entity. Like Sen's critique of Huntington made clear, none of the civilizations which Huntington describes are either as simplistic or isolated as he believes. The problem, however, is that social orders are so powerful as to rearrange social life in a way that only certain regularities can be easily observed. These regularities do not exhibit some supposedly underlying nature but rather the consequence of acts of coercion. But a difficulty remains: to the extent that people are obstructed by epistemic necessities, it is not so easy to go about questioning those regularities. These impoverished hermeneutical resources and oppressive norms may very well justify further acts of coercion as necessary or even simply natural. So, institutional coercions may be interpreted as necessary means to accommodate the alleged nature of social identities, such as exclusion of a group of people is for preserving the national culture or protecting self-determination.

We must be wary of the apparent depth and convenience of identity-based thinking. Drawing on Huntington's thesis, Sen argues that the so-called civilizational approach is appealing because it does indeed *seem* to invoke a "rich" history and a "deep" cultural analysis. Upon a closer look, however, this seemingly considered explanation cannot even account for the basic empirical contradictions of everyday life (Sen 2007, 42–46). The claim about civilizational homogeneity and the singularity of people are based on calculated value judgments, not convincing proofs and reasons. Despite what Huntington claims, his thesis is not at all realistic but based upon carefully disguised selectivity; that is, it requires turning a blind eye to the actual interactions between cultures and regions throughout history. Identity-based thinking is convenient because it seems to capture how the world is. It explains everything on the basis of a presupposed nature while leaving out any analysis of actual structures that give rise to such understandings. In this way, the feud between Hindus and Muslims can *always* be explained in terms of their being "natural enemies," just as the fear of immigrants can *always* be legitimated in terms of a "threat to our well-being" and hostility toward other people can *always* be justified in terms of "protecting our values." Upon closer examination, then, no explanation for feud, fear, and hostility are provided; rather, they are *explained away* by the moral legitimacy that certain social orders require.

Despite their efforts, immigrants may nevertheless fail to participate in the receiving society equally because, in addition to a lack of rights, various forms of necessary identity within the receiving society make such participation extra hard for them. In that case, what seems to be immigrants' failure to integrate lies not in their lack of knowledge about the receiving society or motivation to participate; rather, they are simply unable to participate or discouraged from doing so, as they otherwise would have, due to how they are treated. In this way, being discouraged and rejected may leave immigrants with no choice other than starting their own communities to support themselves. The existence of so-called "parallel societies" will only confirm the wrong belief that immigrants are threatening the solidarity and the culture of the receiving society.

Public culture is affected by both rules and shared conceptions of membership, traditions, values and so on. Those shared conceptions compel people's participation in a society and, specifically, how they do so. The point of raising questions about epistemic structures and how they constitute important shared conceptions of the receiving society draws attention to the fact that what we know and value as a community should not be simply taken for granted. Knowledge and moral views are discursive and result from dynamic processes that are not free from social orders and other contingencies. Unlike institutional rules, knowledge and moral views cannot simply be abolished overnight. They persist in norms and beliefs, which are themselves constitutive of our conceptions of who we are and how we belong.

Once other people come to be seen as nothing other than an enemy, a threat, or a stranger to "us," any moral consideration of those people becomes difficult or even unlikely. In this way, epistemic necessity impoverishes the possibilities for people to form relationships with one another. Once there is only one way of identifying a group of people and only one way of making sense of their presence as a part of the social reality, other choices seem impossible, apart from those afforded by the social order.

Three –
The Epistemology of Identity-based Thinking

Identity-based thinking leads integration into a dead end because it perpetuates unjustified as well as unjustifiable necessary identities. It burdens integration with assimilationist expectations and segregating consequences. Questions regarding integration – its perceived failure, success and problems – should not be restricted to the aspect of rights, but should be extended to relevant epistemic conditions, such as what conceptions and ways of reasoning are involved in making sense of and evaluating integration. Moreover, these questions should not be restricted to immigrants, either; the pre-existing conditions in the receiving society as well as the active role of those who are conventionally seen as its (legitimate) members should also be examined under the light provided by these questions.

In the last chapter, I explained how identitarian frameworks can shape the way some people's – for example, immigrants' – social presence and participation are perceived and interpreted. By referring to Williams' "necessary identity," Sen's "identity-based thinking" and Walker's "epistemic necessity" I demonstrated how solidified epistemic conditions in the pre-existing contexts can obscure political and moral failures and worsen the situation public policies are supposed to address, especially when policies are tailored to the needs of social orders that created such epistemic conditions in the first place.

However, what remains to be answered, before I proceed with discussions of mutual integration at the individual and the collective level, is a clear account of the epistemic structure of identity-based thinking, such as to what norm it ascribes and how it sustains unjustified epistemic necessity. For one thing, knowing these things is helpful to understanding the way cognitive models, social orders and power distribution like epistemic authority work together. For the other, knowing how to strive for mutual integration at both the individual and the collective level depends on a sufficiently clear understanding that shows exactly what should be corrected and improved. As argued in the last chapter, dismissing identity-based thinking requires more than simply criticizing it as unrealistic and wrong because the fact that such thinking is pervasive and longstanding shows that it is not merely accidental but supported by some structures. In that sense, identity-based thinking is not just a reductionist feature, it should also be treated as a substantive epistemic practice. In the following I shall propose an epistemology of identity-based thinking that can account for the fact that identity-based thinking is structural. I will also highlight two of its moral problems, epistemic irresponsibility and epistemic injustice. I shall show how epistemic necessity is engendered and maintained. Both are to be appreciated as individual and collective fallibility. Regarding individual fallibility, they are primarily concerned with the need of virtuous knower and virtuous knowledge-seeking processes; regarding structural fallibility, they are mainly concerned with structural transformation of related epistemic circumstances.

The Model of Assumed Objectivity

In order to outline the possible solutions to identity-based thinking, I shall first analyze how it works, i.e. to which norm it ascribes. In the previous discussion, I discussed that identity-based thinking is related to necessary identities and social orders, and how it reduces a person or a group not only quantitatively but qualitatively as well. For instance, identity-based thinking reduces the existence of actual people to their fulfillment of certain economic, political, and/or cultural functions. I drew particular attention to how epistemic necessity helps to maintain certain structures of coercion. Then, I pointed out that the qualitative reduction of identity-based thinking involves a specific moral view of "good and evil" or "us against them." Epistemic necessity not only keeps some people in unquestioned or unquestionable places, it also immobilizes certain moral considerations by presenting conflicts as unavoidable. By appealing to "necessity," identity-based thinking escapes difficult moral concerns about social orders and acts as if what appears to be happening (all the time) is merely how things are instead of it being the consequence of faulty social structures. Identity-based thinking therefore disguises exclusions and coercions as necessary consequences resulting from the alleged incompatibility between different *kinds* of human groups, though they are in fact epistemic and moral failures. Some people are by nature *our* enemies: there are religious enemies, ideological enemies, ethnic enemies etc., as if no one could have any choice what relationship one develops with other people as opposed to accepting what is given. These claims, which are put in the name of nature, are objectifications.

Feminist theorists have done preliminary work to show how women are objectified as sexual objects. However, objectification exists not only with regard to sexual desires; fear, hatred, or arrogance can also direct one's desires and the need for satisfaction. Like sexual desires that can be cultivated – even twisted – through problematic social structures and thus make certain groups of people particularly vulnerable, fear, hatred, and arrogance are also not always innocent and contingent emotions. In a way, they too are desires that can be cultivated to target certain groups of people and to serve certain purposes. This is not to say that these emotions are intentionally designed to cause harm to other people; rather, when a social order classifies and divides people into groups with designated functions, this order will (indirectly) promote objectifying attitudes towards others as well as towards the self. Put differently, moral failure would not have been so successfully disguised were it not supported by a problematic norm, such as that of objectification.

Sally Haslanger points out that "there is an aspect of illusion in objectification" "on the part of the objectifier" and "that these *post hoc attributions are true by virtue of the object's nature and not by virtue of having been enforced*" (Haslanger 2012, 35–82, my emphasis). Objectifiers share illusions not only about those they objectify, but about themselves as well. Objectifiers objectify other people by viewing and treating them as if characteristics attributed to them were natural properties, but objectifiers also objectify themselves by believing that their artificial superiority is their natural property, thus leading them to view their superior position of power as legitimate. On the surface, this objectification works in favor of the objectifiers. When their man-made superiority is considered nature's work, their exercise of power becomes unquestionable. These post hoc attributions result from social arrangements; they are artificial properties, not natural ones. However, since identity-based thinking tends to conceal problematic structures, it ends up promoting faulty epistemic practices – such as objectification – that reinforce those structures. Haslanger refers to the norm of objectification as *assumed objectivity*.

Haslanger identifies two models of objectivity: "absolute" and "assumed." The model of absolute objectivity is supposed to represent the ideal of objectivity; that is, how things truly are, simply by their nature. Absolute objectivity roughly consists of three norms: epistemic neutrality, practical neutrality and absolute aperspectivity. *Epistemic neutrality* takes "a 'genuine' regularity in the behavior of something to be a consequence of its nature" (ibid., 71). For example, photosynthesis is a natural characteristic of plants, which need sunshine in order to survive. Based on epistemic neutrality, *practical neutrality* thus constrains "your decision making (and so your action) to accommodate things' nature"; that is, knowing that sunshine is indispensable for plants, I should thus place my plant at the window where it will get sufficient sunshine. *Absolute aperspectivity* is a norm of distance that is further divided into three conditions. An observed regularity is only then a "genuine" regularity when it satisfies these conditions, namely that "(1) the observations occur under normal circumstances (for example, by normal observers), (2) the observations are not conditioned by the observer's social position, and (3) the observer has not influenced the behavior of the items under observation" (ibid.). Hence, absolute aperspectivity actually underlies both of the other two norms. In the model of absolute objectivity, absolute aperspectivity is the premise by which an observed regularity is taken to be genuine. "(Only) those observations that satisfy the aperspectivity conditions (1) through (3) are a legitimate basis for drawing conclusions about the nature of things" (ibid.); that is, these are the only observations that exhibit epistemic neutrality. On the basis of epistemic neutrality, one then knows how to behave in order to accommodate the nature of a thing, which thereby expresses its practical neutrality. So, as long as the norm of absolute aperspectivity cannot be convincingly satisfied, the legitimacy of epistemic neutrality and practical neutrality are both in doubt.

The model of assumed objectivity is distinct, however, in the sense that, as the name suggests, objectivity is simply assumed. One assumes by this approach that everything, including people, has a nature; and so long as a certain degree of regularity can be observed, one can also assume the legitimacy for drawing certain conclusions about the nature of the thing in question. According to this assumption, one can ignore the possibility that social orders can produce regularity. This is especially true for human beings, who are not free from social positions and power relations. Social orders can create an environment in which people manifest regular behaviors and beliefs according to gender, descent, appearance and so on. However, the model of assumed objectivity abstracts this aspect away.

In this model of reasoning, *assumed aperspectivity* replaces absolute aperspectivity, as it says that "if a regularity is observed, then assume that (1) the circumstances are normal, (2) the observations are not conditioned by the observers' social position, and (3) the observer has not influenced the behavior of the items under observation." First of all, the causal relation between aperspectivity and observed regularity is changed in this model. Aperspectivity is no longer the premise of observed regularity like in the case of genuine regularity, but the other way around. Now, "observed regularity" determines whether observations are conditioned and whether observers are aperspectival. Second, this change means that epistemic neutrality no longer possesses any limitation, for it is no longer important whether observed regularity *is* genuine; instead, every observed regularity now *is considered* a "genuine" regularity. Therefore, as long as regularity is observable, the condition of epistemic neutrality is satisfied; and as long as this assumed epistemic neutrality is satisfied, assumed aperspectivity is sustained as well. Hence practical neutrality is justified, as one should act according to observed regularity in order to accommodate the nature of a thing. The intersection of these three norms creates a veritable loop: practices based on observed regularities will reproduce conditions that maintain the status quo, thereby inevitably leading to observations of the same regularity.

Haslanger notes that since assumed aperspectivity entitles us to claim that any observed regularity is also a genuine regularity, it disguises the gap between observed regularity and genuine regularity, which should in fact be subjected to closer examination. In so doing, assumed objectivity justifies objectifications and sustains objectifiers' power. At the same time, assumed objectivity also confuses what is really happening with what seems to be happening. In examples provided by feminist theorists, objectifiers claim that being submissive is part of a woman's nature, while women themselves would explain the appearance of being submissive as a result of being deprived of opportunities and the ability to change.

Regarding the examples of necessary identity that were discussed earlier in the last chapter, objectifiers can claim that some people are by nature not part of a certain nation, since their ancestors were from elsewhere, while those who are seen as permanent outsiders would explain their being perceived as foreign as a result of a racist image of the nation itself. Are Chinese people and Indonesians or are Hindus and Muslims naturally enemies?

Objectifiers may say yes and present piles of "evidence" demonstrating that whenever the two groups interact, they conflict with each other, and whenever one side gains, the other side loses. Those who disagree, of course, will point out that this antagonism owes much to policies that were tailor-made to serve the purposes of divide-and-rule throughout the years. Assumed objectivity legitimizes objectification, which is, generally speaking, why following this norm is wrong. More precisely, assumed objectivity normalizes problematic structures, produces fallacious knowledge[1] and disguises moral wrongdoings. From a realist point of view, assumed objectivity not only describes whatever is taking place inaccurately and unilaterally, but it is also politically disabling. By attributing observed regularity to some alleged nature, it deprives people of their agency.

As the mechanism by which a social order preserves itself, necessary identity can cause or constitute assumed objectivity. When people are classified into groups with designated functions, this creates a circumstance that will nurture the practice of objectification. It allows objectifiers to see exactly what they want, thereby reinforcing their beliefs. Once such circumstances are ingrained in principles, conceptions and thinking habits, they will begin to operate as a self-fulfilling prophecy: when social functions are designated according to salient physical, geographical, or ideological features, this may coerce people with similar features into practices that reproduce those post hoc attributions as if they were natural properties. On the one hand, their life opportunities will become so seriously limited that they have no other choices; on the other hand, such repetition is very likely to make objectifying beliefs no longer a matter of what one wants to believe but a "fact" that one must simply accept.

An adequate observation of people's living situations must take into consideration how social conditions shape their lives. A naturalized norm

---

1 My use of the concept of "knowledge" here is very thin, simply meaning "things that are known and can be informative for actions." According to this understanding, knowledge is not necessarily desirable, a closer examination is required to access its actual value. But knowledge can also be used as a thick concept, denoting "things that not only are known but also should be known." This desirable feature ascribed to knowledge in the latter use provides simultaneously an evaluation of knowledge. According to the latter understanding, assumed objectivity should be seen as deliberative efforts to avoid knowledge, like a form of ignorance. For an interesting discussion concerning mechanisms for avoiding knowledge, see Linda Martín Alcoff (2007), "Epistemologies of Ignorance. Three Types," in Shannon Sullivan Nancy Tuana (ed.,), *Race and Epistemologies of Ignorance*, 39–58. New York: State University of New York Press.

is misleading because it precludes the relevance of social structures. It downplays the influence that social structures can have upon a person's capacity to perceive and to know. What's more, it is also important to consider that one's perception and understanding of social phenomena depend on what concepts are available. So-called "women's nature" can be explained in completely different ways from patriarchal and feminist perspectives. Similarly, the Muhammad cartoon controversy in the first chapter can be interpreted in different ways as well. It is not the case that only those who support satire unconditionally are true defenders of free speech or count as successfully integrated into Danish society. People may support free speech but nevertheless reject satire for other reasons.

On the one hand, the interdependence between what one already knows and what one can make sense of demonstrates the hermeneutical character of the knowing process; on the other hand, this interdependence also means that observed regularity can be mistaken for proof about what is believed to be someone's nature. What's worse, the most worrying part is that absolute objectivity can make it only logical to accept the model of assumed objectivity. For under the premise of "by nature," observable regularity becomes a handy tool to complete the hermeneutical loop and portrays the coherent appearance as justified. "Nature" thus becomes a means to justify exclusion and to avoid responsibility; in the name of "nature," people's behaviors are interpreted as pre-determined and inevitable, thereby dismissing the constitutive or even causal role that unjust structures and ignorance may have played. Such misleading interpretations can reinforce existing biases and make it more difficult to examine how existing ideals might be deficient and responsible for wrongs or injustices.

Under the policy of divide-and-rule, colonial governments exploited group differences and social conflicts in order to govern. They politicized accidental features of group belonging by transforming them into determinant factors upon which one's life depends. If you were Indonesian, this meant you should necessarily see the Chinese as enemies because social orders divide these two groups into competing rivals. The Chinese were portrayed as dominating business and seizing wealth; they succeeded by taking what used to belong to Indonesians. Whether the colonial governments genuinely believed Hindus and Muslims or Chinese and Indonesians to be naturally different people does not really matter; what does matter, however, is that they organized their colonies and tailored their policies according to these alleged natures. In this way, they produced self-fulfilling circumstances, in which one side was doomed to see the other as threatening and undesirable.

Similar examples can be found not only in colonialism but also in the building of nation-states. In Chapter One, I discussed the stereotype of the "perpetual foreigner," a concept which captures how some people struggle with being associated with foreignness. For Asian Americans, their Asian heritage renders them less American. However, their "Asianness," of course, is not by nature "un-American." Rather, being Asian came to be treated as "un-American" due to prevailing racism as well as the racialization of state sovereignty. This transformed Asianness from mere physical differences into a factor that, on the one hand, affected or even determined what kind of life one could live on US soil if one was of Asian descent and, on the other hand, defines what "Americanness" contains and what it excludes. Such legislation and discourse change not only the fate of people of Asian origin, but they also change how these people's presence in the receiving society is perceived, what is expected from them, whether they carry an additional burden when participating in the receiving society, and if so, how much of a burden. For them, integration is no longer as simple as learning the local languages and rules because they must first fight against prejudices and discriminations that prevent them from gaining opportunities to begin with. As a Chinese saying goes, "they already lost at the starting line."

The fate suffered by Asian Americans, however, is by no means restricted to Asian Americans. The experience of migration and integration is widespread and resonates with countless immigrants, be they first or later generations. For immigrants, denial of and doubt about the legitimacy of their belonging to a society is not a trivial matter as, without being treated as an equal member of the society, they will be discouraged from participating in the receiving society. In situations like this, attributing regularities to alleged nature – such as claiming that "immigrants *just* have no interest in integration," "immigrants do not respect *our* society," "immigrants *should* learn (our way of life)" – disguises how unjust social structures, exclusionary environment and/or hostile public culture have contributed to what seems to be (some) immigrants' lack of interest or failure to integrate. In this way, necessary identities, along with the unjust structures and misleading knowledge it maintains, will be reinforced unconsciously.

In the following, I shall explore two moral problems of identity-based thinking: epistemic irresponsibility and epistemic injustice. The purpose of this exploration is to offer two possibilities to tackle identity-based thinking.

If it is so far clear and convincing that identity-based thinking is an urgent problem, how to address it? What can be done to weaken, or even break, the disguise of epistemic necessity? As I discussed in the introduction and the first chapter, there is a limit to what immigrants can do in terms of integration. They cannot participate in society equally if they are constantly identified as those whose presence (may) endanger "our" culture, values and stability. They also cannot really become part of the receiving society if the underlying conception of "who we are" is inherently exclusionary and discriminative. Based on this consideration, "responsibility" and "justice" are the two most relevant moral concepts for my discussion about integration because they are the most commonly used in debates of integration, in which integration is often understood as the "responsibility of immigrants" and policies regarding integration are often evaluated in terms of "justice." And I shall explore the epistemic kind of these two moral concepts, since one of my main arguments is that integration concerns not only institutional conditions like rights, but also epistemic circumstances such as discriminatory public culture, narrow-minded thinking and exclusionary understanding of political membership. Moreover, the following moral problems should be appreciated at both the individual and the collective level. At the individual level, they constitute vice, which is to be tackled primarily by cultivating (more) virtuous knowers; while at the collective level, they constitute structural injustice, which is to be tackled by collective efforts such as changing problematic norms and enriching hermeneutical resources. These two aspects complement each other.

Epistemic Irresponsibility

Epistemic irresponsibility, which I derive from Lorrain Code's notion of epistemic responsibility, treats knowledge as an actively sought-after product rather than one that is given. Knowers are irresponsible when they assume that they only absorb whatever is given passively, and that social positions and personal traits play no role in the knowledge-seeking process. By introducing the responsibilist account of epistemology, Code wants to bring to attention that sensory reliability can be delusive. For instance, having functioning eyes is not always sufficient for knowing what is really going on, as the example of observable regularity according to assumed objectivity demonstrates; she also wants to emphasize that out situatedness as knowers makes us all limited and prone to epistemic fallibilities.

According to Code, epistemic responsibility should account for:

" [the fact] (1) that knowledge claims and efforts to know are *events or processes* in human lives; they emerge out of interaction amongst knowledge seekers, their communities, and the world; (2) that there is *no knowledge without knowers, no knowledge without context*; (3) that knowledge cannot be stored equally in a computer or a human mind, because *people have attitudes to knowledge that shape both its structure and its content*. ... A 'responsibilist' approach to epistemology ... maintain[s] that the nature of the knower (who the knower is) and of his/her environment and epistemic community are epistemologically relevant, for they act as enabling and /or constraining factors in the growth of knowledge, both for individuals and for communities." (Code 1987, 26–27, my emphasis)

For Code, responsible knowers not only observe, they also take into consideration how contingent and personal factors may influence their observations and how they make sense of them. Such factors include, but are not limited to, personal aspects of the knowledge source, epistemic circumstances such as the political or economic situation, historical developments, etc. In a similar vein, responsible knowledge practices would be those that acknowledge the limited and perspectival properties of knowledge. Such practices recognize that knowledge is made instead of just being passively absorbed.

Nevertheless, I have several reasons for transforming Code's idea of epistemic virtue into a negative account. First, since I aim to address identity-based thinking as an epistemic fallibility, I am more interested in showing how it actively promotes bad epistemic proceedings; put otherwise, I want to show why identity-based thinking is harmful as opposed to saying that it is simply not good enough. Second, Code's account of epistemic responsibility is not unproblematic. In short, despite her arguments about epistemic responsibility being a fundamental epistemic virtue, some critiques indicate that Code fails to spell out a clear account of what actually counts as being epistemically responsible. In response, Code replies that she does not think that epistemic responsibility can be defined in a rigid way as if there were a single, most responsible way of knowing. She notes that her point has been to urge would-be knowers to be as responsible as possible. Hence, she refuses to develop criteria for epistemic responsibility, as she simply thinks that there are none (Code 2017). However, without a clear account of what counts as epistemic responsibility, it will be difficult to orient oneself within actual knowledge practices because it is not clear what a responsible knower should strive for.

The decision to explore the opposite instead, i.e. epistemic irresponsibility, is my attempt to address the issue through a negative approach. I intend to work out a feasible account of what it means to be epistemically responsible by reflecting upon what counts as epistemically irresponsible. In this way, I believe I should be able to avoid the rigid definition to which Code is opposed while at the same time amending the weaknesses in her position. In the following, I shall first introduce Code's responsibilist epistemology, which was inspired by Ernest Sosa's reliabilism despite there being fundamental differences in their concerns.

Code distinguishes human knowledge from knowledge of things. She points out that Sosa's reliabilism, while it might be appropriate for knowing things, falls short when it comes to questions about the human world. This is because while reliable knowers may be accurate, their passive observations may nevertheless remain unreflective. Like those who believe in a given human nature and adopt the model of assumed objectivity, they might be accurate in reproducing the observable regularity, but they can also be completely wrong. They may produce knowledge that reinforces problematic social structures and existing biases. Their reliability may be too simplistic, since they do not take people's situatedness into consideration. This is where Code's epistemic responsibility comes in as a vital intellectual virtue: being reliable is not enough because as knowers we need more than passive observations of the world around us to understand what is really going on. In order to achieve that, other intellectual traits, such as attentiveness and open-mindedness, are urgently needed in order to make up for our fallibilities as well as amend them.

Following her responsibilism, I aim to emphasize that knowledge should not only be treated as an end-product, but that the knowledge-seeking process deserves at least equal attention. By taking the knowledge-seeking process into consideration, it becomes clear that factors such as dependency, social status, historical situation and so on are also constitutive of knowledge. That means, knowers don't simply know, they acquire knowledge from different epistemic proceedings; thus, knowing is of ethical concern. In that sense, it is important to investigate the ethical aspect of knowledge practices, as some practices may turn out to be better than others. By theorizing about epistemic irresponsibility, I hope to offer a feasible account of virtuous knowing.

First, although Code agrees with Sosa that the discussion of knowledge is always the discussion of *someone's* knowledge, and that knowledge justification involves assessing whom to trust and why, she points out that Sosa's view on knowledge is too general. Knowledge claims such as "the door is open" and "the cup is on the table" are too simplistic, not everything is an all-or-nothing affair which people either know or do not know but cannot know *little* or know *well*. The complex structures of "human knowledge," i.e. *knowledge about the human world that depends on experience*, such as knowledge about history, culture and morality, are greatly undermined and misrepresented. With the notion of "human knowledge," Code makes a distinction between knowledge about people and knowledge about things. Central to knowing people is the recognition that people are active, dynamic and should not be objectified (or be reduced quantitatively or qualitatively according to certain interpretations of an identity). As she states, "there are degrees of knowledge, ways of knowing more or less well," which nevertheless "count as knowledge" (Code 1987, 11). Knowledge of the human world differs from the knowledge of things because the human world cannot be as easily objectified as stones or plants, although it should not be objectified either. As I discussed earlier, objectification means that the social structures which shape people's lives will be left out, leaving questions concerning injustice insufficiently addressed.

Code describes the mode of knowing in Sosa's "reliabilism" as recording. She notes that knowing as "recording" simply captures what seems to be happening from the outside. This mode of knowledge is incapable of saying anything more than repeating observations. Following this mode, one has nowhere to begin inquiries about possible bias or false claims in knowledge structures, since its coherent whole can perfectly justify itself. However, the fact that one knows does not mean that one cannot have wrong or biased knowledge, nor does it mean that there cannot be better "epistemic proceedings [...] more responsible, than others" (ibid., 10). Given that power relations are part of social reality and given the historical character of knowledge, knowers could be wrong, and they could have known better. However, knowers can only realize this when they examine their existing knowledge against a larger, more expansive and more complex background, which is similar to escaping the apparent logical certainty of syllogism reasoning. Code therefore proposes to change the focus on knowledge as an end-product to knowledge as an active process of seeking that involves different epistemic proceedings. This expands the domain of inquiries and allows knowers to attend to invisible structures. By changing the focus, epistemic responsibility aims to reexamine factors that have contributed to knowledge production.

Second, what Code calls "degrees of knowledge" indicates not only the gradual process of knowledge accumulation – such as how I only came to know how hard it is to do a PhD once I started doing it – but also how personal particularities can affect what and how well one knows. For example, I know my mother well but not my neighbors (*personal relations*), or I know what it means to live as an immigrant, but in comparison to those who have little financial support I have poor knowledge about how difficult life can be (*social positions*). One crucial aspect of knowledge about the human world is that such knowledge is not free from experience. One does not know a woman's world if one does not know what a woman's life is like. Experience is vital because it shapes not only individuals, but groups as well. Not knowing such life experience or knowing little does indeed affect whether and how well one can escape and question objectifying and misleading knowledge. Identities such as gender, race and class matter to one's life. Generally speaking, a woman's life is different from a man's, and a person from the global south has a different life than someone living in the global north. But Sosa's reliabilism misses the dynamic aspect of knowing people as well as how situatedness constitute one's knowledge.

Code clarifies that stressing the centrality of cognitive activity means more than assessing the reliability of cognitive faculties. Having functioning eyes or a sober mental state is not always a sufficient condition for knowing what is really going on. Knowledge-seeking processes encompass more than what the notion of "reliability" can capture (ibid., 52). Sosa's emphasis on cognitive practices rests primarily on the functioning of the cognitive senses but is little concerned with the underlying consciousness that affects how one perceives the world and what one can understand. In this manner, claims made on the basis of assumed objectivity may nevertheless be considered reliable because they are accurate.

In this regard, responsibilism brings out an otherwise neglected issue: are our knowledge-seeking methods capable of distinguishing "logical mistakes" from "something false"? The former mistake is easier to detect than the latter because in order to detect the latter knowers must establish contact with bigger and richer reality, they must attend to the experience of different human agents. The key to maintaining the apparent legitimacy of objectification entails establishing norms that only reflect the experience of a particular group (or groups), which thereby excludes those who are undesired.

Code notes, among others, that feminist theories show how serious bias provides the cognitive basis for devastatingly oppressive practices (Code 1988). By shifting the focus to the knowledge-seeking process, responsibilism is concerned not just with the epistemic location, such as someone's knowledge at the time, but also with the basis of epistemic proceedings like premises, norms, and what kind of epistemic circumstance is involved. Person P might be in a position to know, but this does not mean that P cannot be wrong, however accurate P's observation might be. The reason for this is that "something false," as opposed to a "logical mistake," concerns contacts with reality. There is no doubt that "sense" can be made of the world by relying on stereotypes or prejudice. Different examples of objectification show that the world can still be perceived as a coherent whole when based on ignorant or biased basis.

Social conflicts can be interpreted as resulting from immigrants having no interest in integration, from their being different kinds of people or from their not fitting into the receiving society because "they" don't share "our" values. Claims like this might reflect what appears to be observed regularity, but how true are they? Cultural background or descent are often important to one's personality, but they do not always constitute people's motivation or reason for social participation, let alone how they organize their lives. In reality, this can be attributed to an entire host of more realistic factors, such as social positions, financial situations, family relations, career plan and so on. In the case of immigrants' integration, social orders that only focus on or overemphasize the cultural or ideological differences between locals and immigrants are severely misleading because they generate the wrong impression as if immigrants' different cultural background or lifestyles are the only reason why integration fails. Furthermore, such overemphasis implies that these factors are the key to political stability and social prosperity, ignoring completely how the "good life" of some people has always been accompanied by the suffering of those excluded and oppressed. The belief that conflicts, which were absent in a nostalgic version of the past, are brought about by immigrants who are too different and refuse to integrate relies on a very wrong, or even twisted, understanding of the past.

Third, knowers are not, as the paradigm of S-knows-that-P represents, detached and neutral observers. Code notes that the epistemological formula, according to which "S knows that P," is wrong and deeply misleading because it presupposes an interchangeability between human agents. "S" is highly reductive and leaves out many aspects that are essential to our abilities and possibilities to know. As mentioned above, social situatedness shapes how knowers experience and make sense of the world in a particular way, not because such situatedness has a determinant nature, but because it reflects a person's resources and the limits therein. *Who* S is matters. Code remarks that the question of "what *can* I know?" is not complete, for it only concerns the transcendental conditions of knowledge, if there are any; however, another aspect of the question is "what can *I* know?" Apart from the supposed transcendental conditions of human intellects, "who I am" also constitutes and constrains what I can know. However, one would not be able to consider human agents in a non-reductive light if one had merely followed the formula "S knows that P" in the attempt to make sense of knowledge practices.

For every P that S knows, S can only know *that* P due to the very epistemic location which S occupies, including the underlying conceptual framework, the historical limitations, the power relations and so on. Code emphasizes "responsibility," because it highlights the knower's active nature, the degree of choice regarding cognitive structuring and the role as a cognitive agent, which the concept of "reliability" cannot. For this reason, the knowledge-seeking endeavor requires evaluation in terms of responsibility (Code 1984). People *actively* seek out knowledge. They are not always in a simple position to know; rather, they choose, combine and assess. As I understand it, epistemic responsibility draws attention to the indispensable particularity of human agents and the complex structure of knowledge production. This requires that knowers do away with the assumption that knowledge is or can be neutral; contrarily, it requires knowers to recognize their active roles and potential responsibility in the knowledge-seeking process.

I shall now try to transform Code's account of epistemic responsibility into an account of epistemic irresponsibility. I intend to do so in order to provide a more plausible account of epistemic responsibility, as this could clarify exactly what problems it attempts to correct. It could also determine more explicitly the criteria for being as epistemically responsible as possible. Though Code does not believe there actually could be meaningful criteria for epistemic responsibility, she does envisage that knowers and epistemic proceedings can and should be as responsible as possible. I see an opportunity to achieve that through a negative approach; that is, to have an account of what exactly should be avoided or corrected by theorizing about irresponsible knowers. I list four points below to determine when a knower or a proceeding is epistemically irresponsible. These should be taken as illustrative rather than exhaustive:

1. Norm: when an observed regularity is assumed to exhibit an alleged nature, therefore automatically constituting a necessity or justification that must be accommodated
2. Knower: when knowers are not considered as active agents, whose particularities such as interests and experiences matter to the knowledge-seeking process
3. Circumstance: when circumstantial factors such as social positions and power relations are assumed to be irrelevant to what can be known
4. Product: when knowledge is not considered as an actively sought product

According to the above criteria, when an epistemic proceeding involves epistemically irresponsible knowers, this proceeding is likely to be irresponsible as well. Besides, even when no obvious irresponsible knowers are involved, an epistemic proceeding can still be epistemically irresponsible; then it may look like this: (norm) when the proceeding is based on framework that mistakes the descriptive for the prescriptive, such as taking the given make-up of a nation as a normative basis, especially when the existing situation results from past injustice, which applies to most cases; (product) in this case, the knowledge of nation is primarily taken as a given instead of as an actively sought product; (circumstance) such knowledge leaves out how that interpretation of the past derives from exclusion and other injustices; (knower) the successful circulation of such knowledge indicates that there must be epistemic irresponsible knowers who actively maintain unjust structures. This structural account is comparable to Iris Young's analysis of structural injustice, which I will attend to in Chapters Five and Six.

Concerning human knowledge, reliable cognitive faculties such as functioning eyes or mental state are not enough for knowers to be epistemically responsible. Any adequate assessment of epistemic proceedings and knowledge must also include considerations about epistemic circumstances such as power relations, historical contingencies, knowers' particularities and so on. As long as we acknowledge that complex knowledge claims depend upon personal experience and that human agents are always concretely situated, we cannot reasonably expect the same reliability from human agents as we do from machines, if they can be said to be more neutral than human beings. Human agents cannot describe the world independently from how the world is given to them through concepts and values that are available to them. These frameworks shape how people perceive and understand the world around them. To the extent that irresponsible knowers are involved, there are some reasons to assume that an epistemic proceeding might be unjust.

Epistemic irresponsibility is not an insignificant problem. Whether knowers have a rich or poor knowledge about other people makes a big difference, for it could influence one's actions towards and relationships with other people and it will also influence how social problems are interpreted. Immigrants' social presence can be misunderstood, and their participation impeded by irresponsible knowers who rest content with the assimilation-like idea of integration and refuse to reflect that their deeds play a part in immigrants' integration in the receiving society. Moreover, knowers are part of the larger structures that may contain oppressive norms and problematic knowledge. Recognizing and correcting epistemically irresponsible knowledge and practices is a first step to reveal misleading epistemic necessity and overcome identity-based thinking.

Individually speaking, correcting epistemic irresponsibility requires cultivating responsible knowers; that is, knowers should be held responsible for the knowledge they produce and circulate. In the next chapter, where I discuss how to individually strive for mutual integration, I will briefly attend to some examples about to what extent epistemic responsibility can be expected from whom. I will only stay within examples concerning integration, since this is the primary concern of my discussion, though the scope of epistemic (ir)responsibility is clearly larger than that.[2] As far as my discussion of mutual integration is concerned, I don't think there are any justifying conditions when knowers can fail to be epistemically responsible. For one thing, in the highly contextual discussion of integration, my purpose is to argue against the conventional understanding that only immigrants are responsible for integration. In this predefined map of identity roles, my task is to show that such role distribution not only misreads the actual dynamic of the reality of integration, but it could also end up perpetuating existing identitarian oppositions. Hence, by arguing that integration should be mutual I am actually saying that no one can be justifiably exempted from the responsibility to integrate, no matter how insignificant their role seems to be according to the conventional understanding of integration – though the efforts every-

---

2 For example, in *Epistemic Responsibility*, Lorraine Code notes that knowledge about traffic rules can be expected from drivers. When the driver fails to obey the rules and claims that he or she does not know what rules there are, it is justified to conclude that the person is an epistemically irresponsible driver, and the excuses are not legitimate.

one needs to make differ in content and degree: for example, immigrants should be expected to know about the rules and languages of the receiving society, while locals should be expected to know about the immigrants they interact with as concrete and diverse persons.

For the other, justifying conditions for being epistemically irresponsible is confusing because it seems to suggest that knowers can be occasionally allowed not to be responsible for their epistemic participations, which is inconsistent with the notion of epistemic responsibility. The key here, as I see it, is not whether there are justifying conditions, but rather whether epistemic irresponsibility is always an agential wrong. And the answer to that question is "no." Epistemic irresponsibility can be agential as well as non-agential wrongs, but even in the case of non-agential wrongs, I doubt justifying conditions exist. First, it is important to keep in mind here that epistemic responsibility primarily concerns human knowledge, i.e. knowledge about other people, about culture, history, morality and so on. Humans can communicate with each other. A stone cannot actively tell us that it does not want to be thrown, but people can tell us what they think. That means, even in cases where social structures are deeply unjust and individual agents due to their personal limitations cannot keep up with propriate ways to deal with structural wrongs, they still can *at least* listen to those they interact with. That is to say, though individual agents cannot be perfectly responsible, they can try to be as responsible as possible. Hence, individual agents can nevertheless try to live up to their epistemic responsibility, though the extent of fulfillment may be greatly limited in no-agential cases.

Epistemic Injustice

Epistemic injustice, as famously coined by Miranda Fricker, argues that human agents can be hampered in their capacities as knowers precisely because of their social identities. This kind of epistemic marginalization can amount to more than personal harm because people are denied the capacity to impart knowledge based on their group character. The impoverished hermeneutical resources will not only distort the real world but also obstruct the marginalized from making their experience intelligible, which will reinforce the practical disadvantages that the marginalized already suffer. Epistemic necessity can therefore easily substitute justifications that would otherwise be required or experienced as missing and keep some people firmly in unquestioned and unquestionable place. The objectifying element of epistemic injustice lies in the assumed epistemic inferiority of some people qua social identity, which at the same time also assumes an epistemically superior knower qua social identity.

Fricker defines epistemic injustice as that which occurs when someone is wronged in his or her capacity as a knower. Epistemic injustice may take place when someone cannot pass on his or her knowledge due to a deficit in their credibility, which results from identity prejudice, or when someone cannot make sense of a significant area of his or her social experience due to hermeneutical marginalization resulting from structural prejudice, of which identity prejudice is a part. Fricker notes that epistemic injustice has nothing to do with the distributive justice of epistemic goods, such as education. When epistemic injustice takes this form, Fricker explains, there is "nothing very distinctively epistemic about it, for it seems largely incidental that the good in question can be characterized as an epistemic good" (Fricker 2007). Central to Fricker's notion of epistemic injustice is how identity as a form of social power can impair someone's credibility and his or her chances to participate in knowledge practices. Fricker argues that "[t]he capacity to give knowledge to others is one side of that many-sided capacity so significant in human beings: namely, the capacity for reason"; thus, "being insulted, undermined, or otherwise wronged in one's capacity as a giver of knowledge is something that can cut deep ... a direct route to undermining them in their very humanity" (Fricker 2007, 44).

Fricker identifies two types of epistemic injustice: testimonial injustice and hermeneutical injustice. She writes:

"Testimonial injustice occurs when prejudice causes a hearer to give a deflated level of credibility to a speaker's word; hermeneutical injustice occurs at a prior stage, when a gap in collective interpretive resources puts someone at an unfair disadvantage when it comes to making sense of their social experiences. An example of the first might be that police do not believe you because you are black; an example of the second might be that you suffer sexual harassment in a culture that still lacks that critical concept. We might say that testimonial injustice is caused by prejudice in the economy of credibility; and that hermeneutical injustice is caused by structural prejudice in the economy of collective hermeneutical resources." (Fricker 2007, 1)

According to Fricker, epistemic injustice is the product of a particular kind of social power: identity power. Fricker defines identity power as an *imaginative* social co-ordination, which inheres in the "collective social imagination" of identity, and which depends upon the shared conceptions of identities to function. Fricker defines this imagination as "what it is or means to be X." Such imaginative social co-ordination differs from the practical. *Practical* social co-ordination would be, for example, the government making it impossible for people of a certain race to obtain citizenship; a direct exercise of power which controls people's action (Fricker 2007, 11–14). By contrast, *imaginative* social co-ordination would be something like the following: given that the government only makes citizenship accessible to people of a certain race and given that this process of normalization generates a default imagination of what it means to be a citizen of X, people of a different race will automatically be imagined as outsiders.

This imaginative power can be exercised both actively and passively. In Fricker's example, a man can actively use his identity by either pointing out he is a man or that the other is a woman in order to underestimate her opinion. For instance, Fricker mentions an example from the screenplay of *The Talented Mr. Ripley*, where the character Herbert Greenleaf silences Marge Sherwood by saying "Marge, there is female intuition, and then there are facts." The passive exercise of imaginative power also works. In an asymmetrical structure like that of patriarchy, just being a man is enough to exercise authority over women. Now, this pattern of exercising identity power is not restricted to gender identities. It can be applied to other social identities as well, such as race, ethnicity, class and religion. It may be easy to observe identity power in a clear-cut binary system, but in everyday life there are more often overlapping cases, such as national identity.

"National identity" refers to a network of ideology, culture and heritage-based factors rather than whether one possesses a passport or not. When it comes to immigration and integration, what is at issue are far more complex structures than any single identity can encompass, like gender in the above-mentioned case. Fricker's analysis of imaginative identity power still applies here, although it may not seem as direct as it does in simple cases of gender or race. Having a passport or having been living in a place for one's whole lifetime does not suffice to exercise the power of national identity; it may also require other factors concerning culture, ideology and descent. For instance, while debates about immigration and integration are conducted as if they only concern a clear antithesis to national welfare, a closer look shows that not all immigrants are considered undesirable. Those who are unwanted tend to share specific racial and cultural features. It is not a matter of passports but a matter of whether certain features fall within the conventional imagination of being X.

Imaginative power can be exercised actively as well as passively regarding national identity. Song notes that in 1892, the US Congress passed the Geary Act, which extended the 1882 ban on Chinese immigration. The Act also required Chinese laborers who were already residing in the US to register for a certificate of residence. However, in order to obtain that certificate, Chinese laborers needed to have a white witness to testify to their pre-1892 residency. Testimony from people of color did not count, regardless of whether they had been lawful residents, for only white witnesses were considered credible for matters of national security. Justice Field, who handled several deportation cases of Chinese laborers, characterized the Chinese as "an Oriental invasion" and "a menace to our civilization." He expelled them on the grounds of preserving US "independence" "and [to] give security against foreign aggression and encroachment" (Song 2019, 20). Being "white" has been actively used to refer to credibility and authority, whereas being "Asian" and "Chinese" meant one had no credibility and should be excluded in order to preserve the US nation.

The passive use of national identity would be as follows in this case: given that there is a default imagination of national identity that contains race, descent, religion and so on, those who do not fall into this group are automatically perceived as "outsiders" or "foreigners" who do not belong in a society, even if they were born and raised there and even if their group has resided in that society for centuries, like the example of perpetual foreigners demonstrates. In contrast, the residency of immigrants who share features of such imagination of national identity goes unquestioned. This perception exists among citizens as well. So far, I have discussed and illustrated with examples that immigrants' integration involves not only those bereft of citizenship but national minorities as well. Anger and resentment towards immigrants are often directed at national minorities who do not belong to the default imagination of the nation.

Not only racial features can be salient for the imagination of national identity, but ideological features can also play an important role therein. Recall the Muhammad cartoon controversy discussed in the first chapter: in that case, the cartoonists and editors assumed that the targeted group should identify with the freedom of speech as they understood it, namely through the approval of satire regardless of how the group perceived the act. What's more, since satire is considered a Danish tradition, approving it is even taken to be a sign of successful integration whereas failing to do so is considered as not having tried (hard enough), although people may have different reasons to oppose satire depending on the context and such rejection does not necessarily have to mean promoting censorship. Considered as an inherent part of democracy and secularism, identification with freedom of speech qua satire acquires a symbolic meaning of a more civilized life than that under authoritarianism. Therefore, speaking as a supporter of satire gives one the identity power to portray oneself as correct and trustworthy, thereby influencing others' actions.

This kind of power is discursive, hence imaginative (Fricker 2007, 14–17). Identity power prominently relies not on who indeed has practical power to control but on how shared conceptions per se can affect someone's capacity to impart knowledge.[3] And this capacity matters to whether one will be listened to, heard and taken seriously as a knower. Not being listened to and taken seriously as a knower not only excludes a person from knowledge practices but also implies an alleged epistemic inferiority of those who are excluded. Fricker provides two examples of this alleged epistemic inferiority in her account of epistemic injustice: women, who are assumed to be insufficiently rational due to what appears to be their excessively intuitive and emotional femininity, and black people, who are assumed to be not trustworthy due to their assumedly lying nature. Regarding immigrants, assumed epistemic inferiority qua social identity also exists. In the past, it could be observed when the residency of Asian people was not recognized because they could not produce white witnesses, when they were excluded from citizenship as a threat to a nation's sovereignty no matter how hard they tried to prove they were not. Nowadays, similar examples can still be observed when their reason for adopting or not adopting a tradition, their views or values are not taken seriously, but instead treated as an excuse to resist integration.[4]

Identity power is prominent in society. When a society is arranged according to identities, people's lives are predetermined based on which

---

3 A "gentleman" can accuse a "worker" of "imprudence, insolence or cheek"; the "gentleman" may have the same social power as the "worker," but the assumptions underlying the identity of a "gentleman" determines that the "gentleman" will be treated differently as opposed to "worker." This will eventually reinforce some inequality between the "gentleman" and the "worker" in the form of material power. See Fricker (2007), *Epistemic Injustice*, 16.
4 Note here that I am not talking about failing to achieve a certain standard due to a lack of expertise or experience. Rather, I am talking about being excluded because of one's social identities, not sharing a certain worldview or not abiding by a certain way of reasoning.

identities they were born into. Those higher up in the hierarchy will automatically have more authority and options at their disposal than those in the lower strata. This structural privilege or disadvantage will be reflected not only in power distributions but also in knowledge production, namely, which knowledge about the world is available and intelligible. In this way, biased hermeneutical resources and oppressive knowledge practices will be inevitable consequences since only a small, privileged group is seen as capable of knowing and reasoning and their knowledge about the world as trustworthy and intelligent.

Medina notes that both overestimation of the cognitive powers of some people and the underestimation of others will interiorize superiority or inferiority complexes respectively. This will not only result in a lack of self-knowledge and of knowledge about others but will also affect people's "capacity to hear and to be heard correctly." Consequently, epistemic injustice will "affect the production and transmission of knowledge and ignorance" (Medina 2012, 28). Conventionally, the focal point when talking about marginalized voices lies in their inability to speak; nevertheless, epistemic injustice brings to light the way in which our inability to listen can possibly worsen the marginalized status of the disadvantaged. Oppressive knowledge practices disable, on the one hand, those who speak and on the other hand, those who listen.

These communicative inabilities reinforce each other in a structural way and deepen the effect of what appears to be irrational, resulting in a disconnection from reality, especially for the listeners. Consider Fricker's analysis of the concept of "sexual harassment": Fricker uses this concept as an example to illustrate 1) how obscured understanding of social experience prevents women from taking timely actions to protect themselves, because 2) others could not comprehend how their experience could be trying and indicative of wrong behaviors and 3) how obscured understanding worsens existing prejudices against women. In the case of "sexual harassment," the lack referred to more than just the lack of a name; a sense of wrong was lacking as well. What's worse is that this epistemic injustice can very well develop into distributive injustice. For instance, women suffering from sexual harassment can end up with them losing their jobs or their unemployment allowance since they cannot justify their claims due to lacking ways to explain what happened.

Explicitly, identity prejudices leave unexplained why the bearers of certain social identities have the properties they are believed to have; implicitly, identity prejudice normalizes wrongheaded claims by not calling them into question. As an epistemic structure, the assumed objectivity constitutes the underlying structure that keeps testimonial and hermeneutical injustice intact. By taking identities as given, it naturalizes the power relations that brought about identity prejudice in the first place. Those who do not fall within the preferred identity groups are not considered worthy of being listened to for various reasons: they could be too emotional, not civilized or could have simply picked the wrong side. Irresponsible knowers may assume that they are passive recorders, hence leading them to believe that they are innocent in passing on what they believe they know based upon their observations. In this way, they may contribute to perpetuating pre-existing identity prejudices which make epistemic injustice undetectable. The fallibility of prevailing structures indicates that many pictures about the world may be wrong and severely incomplete. And this indicates further that the so-called circumstantial bad luck of the marginalized ought not to be taken as a mere matter of luck.

By "circumstantial epistemic bad luck,"[5] Fricker means that, in some situations, injustice may be accidental and agential if the listener does not mean to undermine the speaker's capacity to provide knowledge when the listener could not know better. I think Fricker is partially right. It is possible that listeners are "epistemically innocent" when, due to personal ignorance and/or historical limitations, they could not know better. However, the epistemic failure herein, then, should not be treated as a mere accident, because the epistemic circumstances result from social structures. In that sense, the epistemic failure can, in some respects, signal ethical and political ones. Here, three things need further differentiation. First, there are different kinds of impossibility to know. For example, in the field of natural science, there is genuine epistemic impossibility, for example, that "until a historical process has run its course there are things which simply cannot be known," such as "information about the DNA molecule" "could not be accommodated within the body of current fifteenth- century biological knowledge."[6] In that case, we may be talking about a genuine "epistemic innocence" because the ignorance comes from *the impossibility to know* but not from *exclusion*.

---

5 It is based on Thomas Nagel's "circumstantial moral bad luck," see Fricker (2007), *Epistemic Injustice*,33.
6 See for reference Code (1982), "The Importance of Historicism for a Theory of Knowledge," *International Philosophical Quarterly*, Vol. 22, Issue 2,157–174.

However, in the case of epistemic injustice, we are dealing with a case of epistemic structures that result from social exclusion.

Second, while there are many identities, not every identity possesses what Fricker defines as "identity power," i.e. an operation of power that depends in some significant degree upon shared imaginative conceptions of social identity. This is because many group identities are not social identities in this strict sense but rather professional identities, which distribute epistemic authority by indicating actual expertise. One of the problematic aspects of social identities is that they are often based on assumed properties rather than real ones. They disregard a person's actual experience and expertise; instead, on the basis of one's externally imposed identity, they assume what qualities that person should have. This brings the discussion back to the distinction between justifiable necessities and apparent ones. The problem is that apparent necessities produce the illusion that some identities are necessary, although in fact they are used to support unjust social orders. It is not always unjust to deny a person's capacities. In professional discussions, such as those concerning disease or climate change, it may even be desirable that people without professional background be excluded. However, that exclusion is not unjust for it is based on actual expertise that reflects a person's real epistemic capacities. Unjust exclusions do not meet this criterion. Why being white would give a person a particular capacity to judge whether another person is trustworthy? Why does having a particular cultural background give a person the particular deservingness to belong to a nation?

Third, there are innocent cases of *prejudice*, but I doubt there are innocent cases that qualify as *injustice*. Regarding injustice, misjudgment does not just result from not knowing about one's conversation partner; rather, it must be supported by the imaginative co-ordination of social identities at the same time. As explained in the first point, the latter suggests exclusion. Let's first consider an example Fricker uses. Fricker gives the example of a philosopher who mistakenly affords her conversation partner a lower degree of credibility in discussions about literature because she assumes him to be a medic (Fricker 2007, 21–22). While that agential case qualifies as prejudice and is innocent, it does not seem to fit with Fricker's definition of identity power and epistemic injustice. The identities of "philosopher" and "medic" distribute epistemic authority on the basis of professional backgrounds which reflect real epistemic capacities, and they are not social identities like "Asian" and "Black," which distribute power on the basis of social imagination and assumed epistemic authority. The philosopher misjudges the medic's knowledge about literature, probably because they've never met, probably she has never met a medic who reads much literature. Even though it seems that in the philosopher's misjudgment there are still traces of imagination involved, this is not the *kind* of social imagination identities like "Asian" or "Black" possess. After all, the assumed lower degree of a medic's capacity for literary knowledge is not alive in any collective social imagination. It may be the philosopher's personal prejudice, but it does not result from any form of exclusion as explained above.

Therefore, in the case of "circumstantial bad luck," as long as social identities are involved, the epistemic failure cannot be ethically or epistemically innocent. For instance, A misjudges B because A assumes that B is not credible or cannot have epistemic expertise due to B's social identities, such as race, gender and class, though they do not necessarily reflect B's epistemic capacity. B's deflated credibility level results from B's one or several social identities, but this externally imposed epistemic inferiority does not appear overnight. Rather, it results from complicated and longstanding processes. What happens to B qua social identity, happens not only to that social group in the same period of time, but also probably to the same social group in different times. What appears to be "epistemic bad luck" often attests to a cumulative result of oppressive knowledge practices that involve certain unjust epistemic circumstances. What's more, knowledge claims resulting from prior exclusions cannot purport to reflect reality. No wonder such epistemic circumstances will end up promoting ignorance and bias. As Code points out, knowers depend upon a variety of factors to know. Knowers don't simply have biases or identity prejudices as individual knowers, but rather *hold them as part of a much bigger epistemic community*.[7] Therefore, epistemic injustice is systematic not only because, as Fricker notes, identity tracks its victim through social domains (Fricker 2007, 27); more importantly, it is systematic because "epistemic bad luck" happens so often and lasts so long even though no individual knower intends to do so.

For people who already suffer from the impact of testimonial injustice, it is very likely that they are or will also be the victim of hermeneutical injustice since their social group is viewed as not worth listening to and marginalized from knowledge production. This hermeneutical injustice will in turn reinforce the testimonial injustice that social group is inflicted with. This

---

7 See for reference Code (1987), *Epistemic Responsibility*, 166–197.

connection between testimonial and hermeneutical injustice demonstrates that they are in fact more closely intertwined with each other than Fricker claims.[8] It also shows why in terms of injustice there are hardly innocent and/or merely agential wrongs. Neglecting the ethical culpability of injustice risks perpetuating existing false knowledge claims as well as the very identity power that preserves its corresponding social orders.

The connection between testimonial and hermeneutical injustice raises another question. Epistemic injustice is clearly structural. Fricker also admits that redressing both types of epistemic injustice requires individual effort as well as efforts at the institutional level although "in terms of our philosophical understanding of epistemic injustice, the ethical is primary," which has been her focus (Fricker 2007, 177). But in my reading, Fricker may have underestimated the political impact of this seemingly individualistic account. I agree with Code's observation that Fricker's "emphasis on the systematic operations of power within and through entrenched social imaginings" in fact already demonstrate its own institutional significance.[9] There, the question transfers from "what virtues do individual knowers need in order to avoid or correct epistemic injustice" to "what hermeneutical resources are epistemically more just." That is to say, the individualistic ethical concern can be extended to collective matters once we take into consideration that, as discussed above, knowers are always part of a bigger epistemic community. To cultivate more virtuous knowers, individual ethics as well as better resources are needed.

So, when Elizabeth Anderson notes that the transactional view of justice as embedded in epistemic injustice is limited, she correctly points out that "the cumulative effects of how our epistemic system elicits, evaluates, and connects countless individual communicative acts can be unjust" without individuals committing any epistemically unjust transaction, and that it is hard for individuals "to keep up the constant vigilance needed for the practice

---

[8] Fricker notes that hermeneutical injustice might often be compounded by testimonial injustice. But in her opinion, the convergence between these two models of injustice is occasional. See Fricker (2007), *Epistemic Injustice*, 158–161. However, Medina argues that these two models are not only intertwined but feed upon each other and deepen the effect of the other. See Medina (2012), *The Epistemology of Resistance*, 96.

[9] See Lorraine Code (2008), "Review: Epistemic Injustice: Power and the Ethics of Knowing," *Notre Dame Philosophical Reviews*, March, https://ndpr.nd.edu/reviews/epistemic-injustice-power-and-the-ethics-of-knowing/, last accessed March 2023.

of virtue to sustain its good effects over time."[10] In cases where hermeneutical injustice is at play, it will be difficult to detect, let alone clarify, testimonial injustice. What's worse, hermeneutical injustice is only identifiable when what remains obscured in experience can be named and how it is unjust can be shown. Before that happens, hermeneutical injustice as well as the very social imagination that co-ordinates unjust epistemic authority will be kept intact.

But there is no reason to be pessimistic. In my opinion, exactly because our epistemic systems have such cumulative effects which can systematically obstruct individual epistemic virtue, it is reasonable to introduce different and diverse hermeneutical resources in the hope that they can provide better resources and ensure, to the greatest extent possible, that epistemic virtue will not operate in the dark. This may be a bit difficult to think in abstract terms. For example, the process of encouraging women to participate in science has been accompanied by an exploration of women's role in science, among other measures. This exploration amounts to more than providing women with role models. Another significant effect is that it breaks the wrong claim that science is a men's job. It shows that the underrepresentation of women in the field of science results not from the fact there have been rarely any women in science. Instead, for example, women were only allowed in science when they collaborated with male scientists, women were not admitted to higher education or scientific institutions, or, given the sexist structure in society and in academia, women as a group were and still are susceptible to the "Mathew Matilda Effect in Science," i.e. a bias against acknowledging the achievements of women scientists.[11] Such hermeneutical exploration brings about more than just an attitude change because enriched hermeneutical resources can point out hidden institutional failures and correct wrong knowledge about historical facts.

---

10 See for reference Elizabeth Anderson (2012), "Epistemic Justice as A Virtue of Social Institution," *Social Epistemology*, Vol. 26, No. 2, 163–173,

11 See for reference, Margaret W. Rossiter, "The Mathew Matilda Effect in Science," *Social Studies of Science*, Vol. 23, No. 2 (May 1993), 325–341. C. G. Jones, A. E. Martin & A. Wolf (eds.), *The Palgrave Handbook of Women in Science since 1660*, (Basingstoke: Palgrave Macmillan, 2022). For an overview, see Claire Jones (2018), "Women have been written out of science history – time to put them back," *The Conversation*, December, https://theconversation.com/women-have-been-written-out-of-science-history-time-to-put-them-back-107752, last accessed March 2023; Louis-Pascal Jacquemond (2020), "Women of science. 19th – 21st centuries," *Digital Encyclopedia of European History*, June, https://ehne.fr/en/encyclopedia/themes/gender-and-europe/educating-europeans/women-science, last accessed March 2023.

Hence, in my opinion, an important element to avoid – or at least to weaken – the abovementioned loop of the two types of epistemic injustice is to introduce diverse hermeneutical resources in the hope that they provide better recourses. Of course, the process of finding or developing those resources itself is also a process in which epistemic injustice is likely to occur. But this does not diminish the importance of this epistemic journey. Regarding integration and immigration, I think the same applies. On the one hand, membership, community and belonging are discursive notions that are susceptible to various social identities and therefore susceptible to epistemic irresponsibility and injustice. Problematic norms and impoverished resources can produce wrong knowledge and perpetuate identity power. On the other hand, this not only excludes immigrants from knowledge practices that are significant to community-building but also ruins their efforts of integration. I shall attend to this in Chapter Five and Six.

In the previous discussion about epistemic irresponsibility, I discussed the indispensable role of situatedness and personal traits in the process of knowledge production. I point out that, from the standpoint of responsibilism, identity-based thinking produces a delusional picture of reality. By leaving out the active role of human agents in knowledge-production, identity-based thinking naturalizes, and thereby disguises, what is in fact the product of unjust social orders and practices. In the discussion about epistemic injustice, I tried to draw attention to the fact that based upon impoverished and biased hermeneutical resources, the picture of the real world is twisted. By excluding some groups of people from various kinds of practices that are at least partially epistemic in nature, such as nation-building, identity-based thinking leaves out a great deal about the real world. Epistemic irresponsibility and injustice should both be attended to and corrected with respect to epistemic circumstances. Apart from cultivating virtuous knowers by orienting people away from these two moral problems, to know the real world in a truer and richer way and to improve the overall epistemic circumstances are also important.

Both epistemic irresponsibility and epistemic injustice are not just epistemic failures but political and moral ones as well. First, they disguise unjust social orders and biased knowledge; in this way, they offer an incorrect picture of the real world. As discussed in the last chapter, identity-based thinking excludes certain groups of people from ethical concern by depicting that picture as inevitable. Women's nature, instead of social structures, determines that they are submissive. Similarly, the intrinsic features of, for example, certain races or cultures determine that some people cannot and should not belong to a nation or a society because they are threatening. So, according to identity-based thinking, the problem is not that "we" fail to listen to and care for "them," but rather that "they" are by nature outside the realm of morality. Second, assumed objectivity conceals past injustices behind power distributions. Here, power does not primarily refer to institutional power but rather to that of epistemic authorities, i.e. those whose knowledge is considered valuable for making sense of a nation or an idea such as universalism. Certainly, no one can avoid following one framework or another, but the problem is when certain frameworks purport to be rationally or morally necessary while in fact they are highly selective. Epistemic injustice and irresponsibility offer another way to think about knowledge and participate in its production. They urge us as knowers to see both the crucial fact that we are active agents in knowledge-seeking processes and that as knowers we are socially positioned. In the next chapter, I shall discuss what mutual integration requires from individuals; in Chapters Five and Six, I shall then explore what it requires at the collective level.

Four –
Knowing People

The onus to integrate should not be placed only upon immigrants because locals also play an important and indispensable role in integration. How they perceive the immigrants' presence in the receiving society as well as how they understand the culture, the value and the community they see as their *own* affect how they interact with immigrants. In turn, their behaviors and attitudes can exert an encouraging or discouraging impact on immigrants. What's more, integration concerns more than the distribution of rights. As argued so far, the epistemic circumstances of the receiving society, especially the prevailing ones, have a significant impact on how immigrants' participations are interpreted, how effective their equal status is (if an equal status exits), how their integration is judged from the outside, how accurate and realistic those judgements are, and so on and so forth. Assuming integration to be a one-way process misses how pre-existing problems that are epistemic in nature can hinder integration itself. This is because in so doing, exclusionary or otherwise inappropriate standards or criteria that can make immigrants' participation in the receiving society difficult are left intact. As the previous discussion shows, these problematic epistemic circumstances can misrepresent what is really going on as well as perpetuate the deeply flawed conceptual frameworks that generate these misrepresentations in the first place. In this regard, xenophobia towards the second or third generation of immigrants due to racial or cultural differences, as well as doubting whether they have successfully integrated into the society where they have lived for generations vividly demonstrate that, in this case, integration is just another name for assimilation.

Therefore, a just integration must take into consideration the fact that immigrants are not alone in their efforts to integrate and that the larger background, such as past injustices, is likely to survive epistemically. Understanding integration as mutual process serves not only the purpose to make "integration a category of its own." More importantly, "mutual" is vital because it makes integration just and realistic: a mutual integration does not see immigrants merely as passive recipients who are supposed to fulfill given orders but recognizes their equal status and active role in the making of a relation that involves them. It also no longer views locals as having the natural authority in deciding what is good or desirable for the society but admits that they can, consciously or not, contribute to unjust practices that are parts of social structures. In this chapter, I shall address mutual integration at the individual level. Based on the previous discussion I shall argue for the practice of knowing people as an individual remedy to identity-based thinking, where I highlight the role of subjectivity in knowledge production and the role of narrative knowledge in a non-reductionist view of other people. I shall explain what knowing people requires and in what sense it constitutes mutual integration at the individual level. I will draw on the ethics of difference from Chinese philosophy as a normative source to demonstrate and defend the position that epistemic capacity is indispensable for morally appropriate relation.

Why Take Subjectivity into Consideration?

Code argues that when it comes to matters of the human world, subjectivity must be taken into account and that doing so does not at all mean denying objective reality. In her defense, such a denial would obliterate the political meaning of many political projects, such as feminism (Code 1991, 45). Code's aim of taking subjectivity into account closely ties in with her model of knowing people, which proposes to stop seeing subjectivity and objectivity as polarized dichotomies. She argues that knowing is not a matter of choosing the subjective over the objective or vice versa; rather, they both constitute a crucial aspect of what one can know. Subjectivity should not be confused with illusion or groundless speculation; it is not the same thing as subjectivism. Subjectivity "involves recognizing the full personhood and epistemological centrality of knowing subjects, of which theory of knowledge need to take account and acquire understanding," whereas subjectivism "is an outright denial of any normative force to realism" (Code 1987, 142). In subjectivism, the concept of reality can mostly be substituted by the contents of one's own interpretation. In this attitude, reality simply does not matter. This is the exact opposite of what it means to acknowledge subjectivity.

Subjectivity *does* care about reality, namely, the reality of knowing subjects. It asks the knower to acknowledge human beings as particular and concrete, i.e. *not* as disinterested, detached or isolated individuals, but as dependent and relational, and as having preferences and limits. She lists some aspects of subjectivity that are constitutive of what a knower *can* know, which includes "(i) historical location; (ii) location within specific social and linguistic contexts, which include racial, ethnic, political, class, age, religious, and other identifications; (iii) creativity in the construction of knowledge, with the freedoms and responsibilities it entails; and (iv) (personal traits such as) affectivity, commitments, enthusiasms, desires, and interests, in which affectivity contrasts with intellect, or reason in the standard sense" (Code 1991, 46). The call to take subjectivity into consideration emphasizes chiefly portraying a truer and richer picture of the world.

As Sen argues, when it comes to knowing people, no one should be seen as having only one identity. We are all multi-faceted persons who are subject to more than one relation or position. When we make choices, we often pass between different domains and compare a variety of different values. It is not as if there is a single, overarching identity that dominates everything we do. Ignoring the diverse constitution of human agents misleads us into seeing the world in a rather rigid und unrealistic way. We may end up fueling existing conflicts rather than mitigating them. I have discussed this matter thoroughly in the previous chapters. Reducing people to a single identity may very well serve some purposes of governing, such as in the case of divide-and-rule; but it also ends up perpetuating the wrong image of a group and the misleading impression that some people are just incompatible with the society, such as in the case of perpetual foreigners. Social orders can make salient certain ways of perceiving some people, such as the incompatibility of Asianness with being American, and the opposition between Chinese and Indonesians that are institutionally produced and sustained.

This applies to immigrants as well. As an externally imposed identity, "immigrant" enables one to identify and perceive certain social problems in particular ways; namely, one can look to immigrants for an explanation for a declining economy or for the increasing crime rates. But this can mislead one in one's efforts to make sense of social reality. The identity of "immigrant" does not really reflect why a person does what he or she does. An immigrant's behavior depends more on other characteristics, such as being career-driven or being financially limited, than it does on being an immigrant. This externally imposed identity is made obvious in comparison to a person's other identities due to how social orders frame the presence of immigrants as part of social reality.

In the previous discussion, I distinguished justifiable necessities from apparent ones. I stressed that apparent necessities, such as place of origin and race, do not reflect real needs or actual abilities that are required in social participation, such as expertise; rather, they are made necessary by social orders, and they disguise forms of epistemic coercion by obstructing epistemic inquiries of justification through epistemic necessity. Regarding the integration of immigrants, which is often framed in the language of cultural preservation or protecting self-determination, the extent to which such factors are made necessary begs the question as to what degree of supposed cultural integrity or what kind of self-identity is actually desired, as Kukathas argues. While a thin notion of national culture makes it rather difficult to see why immigrants would make any real difference, a thick notion would mean having to deny the national membership of many existing citizens. What's more, turning those unnecessary factors into necessary ones also means, as I shall argue in Chapter Six, perpetrating structural alienation and disregarding how past injustice has contributed to some particular conceptions of a nation. The identity of "immigrant" thus poses an obstacle for knowing people to the extent that it generates and emphasizes a particular way of making sense of immigration, especially by means of the cultural- and self-preservation frame. It reduces immigrants to nothing but cultural, economic or ideological units. In this way, it prevents observers from seeing their actual in-group diversity as well as from understanding how their actual situatedness within the society motivates them to act.

Knowing people means more than knowing about their age, height or marital status; it requires undertaking non-reductive perceptions and engaging in on-going interactions. People are socially positioned. Changes in their social status, relations and so on will affect how a person behaves, hence dictating what can be observed about them. In a similar vein, changes in one's relations with or knowledge about another person can also change what one observes. Consider the following example: John's neighbors claim that John is a Christian because they see John every Sunday in church, but in fact, John only goes to church every Sunday to please his grandmother who is religious and, more important to John, she is the only family he has. Due to their insufficient knowledge about John, John's neighbors see John as a religious person rather than as a caring grandson. The neighbors' perception, then, would change after they get to know John and his particularities better. After getting to know John, they would also notice that their earlier judgment was poorly informed and that they might have taken certain things for granted; they would have simply gone on assuming that his going to Church necessarily meant that he was religious. Individual examples such as that of John may be a familiar part of everyday life; it is a truism that without knowing someone personally one is often not in a position to make appropriate judgments. In the following, let's consider a collective example.

Zhouxiang Lu and Weiyi Wu notice that studying the in-group diversity of Chinese immigrants in Ireland – such as their generation, profession and education – can better account for their different levels of social participation and help to understand how they identify with Irish society than the old paradigm of immigration studies, which relies on nationality, ethnicity and so on.[1] The old paradigm of the "citizen-immigrants dynamic" only takes into consideration the immigrants' descent, thereby missing the immigrants' other social positions that are in fact far more relevant to their lives in the receiving society. The problem is not that observers mistake the ethnic identities of immigrants; rather, they assume that being "Chinese" is the only identity that counts. Among their interviewees, some people – especially those who are first generation immigrants – have a lower level of social participation due to a lack of fluency in the national language. Many among the second generation experienced a shift in their identification from "being Irish" to being "both Chinese and Irish" due to their experience of being rejected as Irish. Some students are discouraged from participating in social life because they are not familiar with pub culture while others endure a substantial amount of stress in order to finish their coursework within a certain period of time. Blue-collar workers tend to struggle to earn more money at the cost of their social lives, and immigrants from Fujian province have often been drawn to Ireland by their overseas communities.

When observing from the outside, the immigrants' Chinese identity may appear to be the most salient. When immigration is primarily understood in terms of descent or cultural background, it is almost impossible not to see someone according to his or her cultural, racial or ethnic identity. But according to the interview results, nobody bases their choice of social inter-

---

[1] See for reference Zhouxiang Lu and Weiyi Wu (2017), "Rethinking Integration and Identity: Chinese Migrants in the Republic of Ireland," *International Review of Sociology*, Vol. 27, Issue 3, 475–490.

action on their "Chinese" identity, however they identify. In the eyes of an outside observer, Chinese immigrants as a group may exhibit signs of being unable to integrate, since they may not have enough Irish friends, they may not go to the pubs often enough, they may seem to hang out only with other Chinese people, etc. However, all these appearances are closely related to the social positions of immigrants and their experience. Yet, the old paradigm of immigration studies does not reflect such in-group diversity because it focuses *too much* on descent or cultural identities that are neither primarily relevant nor really necessary for a person's choice of social participation. What's more, Lu and Wu also note that a comprehensive understanding of the in-group diversity among immigrants will improve the feasibility of government policies and strategies regarding immigration because knowledge about immigrants' in-group diversity can provide a more realistic picture of immigrants' actual situations and needs.

Knowledge about in-group diversity among Chinese immigrants in Ireland changes how their apparent lack of social lives and how their relation to the receiving society are viewed. However, in comparison to individual examples such as that of John, judgments concerning groups seem to be more prone to generalizations, although collective examples such as that of Chinese immigrants in Ireland are not altogether unfamiliar. On the one hand, one may insist that foreigners or immigrants (of a certain background) all share some properties by which they are incompatible with the receiving society.[2] For example, Rose in the Muhammad cartoon controversy stresses how identifying with satire is a feature of successful integration. On the other hand, one believes that "our" friend or colleague, who happens to be a member of the immigrant group, is an exception. Somehow, coincidently, "we" just happen to know the one or two exceptions instead of the "regular" members. But we do not just happen to know the exceptional individuals from an otherwise homogenous group; rather, since we know our friends or colleagues better (which also explains why they are our friends), they become more than just Chinese or Christian to us. Their images become richer and truer than we would otherwise assume. We begin to see them as persons with more than one identity and more than one way of identification – we

---

[2] For example, Asians and Mexicans were considered "non-assimilable" to the American identity. See Mae Ngai (2014), *Impossible Subjects: Illegal Aliens and the Making of Modern America*. Princeton: Princeton University Press.

see them as concrete persons who are subject to multiple social structures and entangled within various relations.

Similar to personal diversity, supposedly homogeneous groups are also characterized by in-group diversity. An investigation of in-group diversity is conducive to an appropriate understanding of observations by breaking the illusion of assumed objectivity because such investigation requires would-be knowers to pay attention to the overall circumstance – that is, it requires would-be knowers at least to try to act responsibly and just in epistemic practices. In such investigations, knowers become aware of factors that are contingent and particular, but which are nevertheless relevant to people's behaviors. This is also an opportunity to rectify identity-based thinking. Like the Chinese immigrants who act due to their financial situation, familial relations, career plans or existing immigration policies, their actual situations will be disregarded when they are only seen according to their descent or cultural background. Thinking according to identity not only objectifies other people as if the identity-related properties define who they are; that identity also turns out to be the wrong focus as it fosters a failure to understand why people do what they do. In this way, their images can be distorted, their behaviors and social existence misperceived, and our relations with them misconducted.

In the first chapter, I followed Benhabib and argued that assuming the interchangeability between agents may underestimate the actual complexity of the situation being dealt with. By mistakenly assuming that moral agents and moral recipients are or should be the same people, particularities which are relevant to moral conduct will be wrongly disregarded. Sharing the same identity or the same physical location does not necessarily mean sharing the same situation; what is morally relevant can nevertheless be different, since moral situations cannot be appropriately assessed independently of knowledge about those who are involved therein. The assumption of interchangeability between moral agents and recipients makes "truth" appear more obvious than it actually is, as if a person is just too stupid if he or she does not understand it. By assuming that others are just like "us," we do not acquire knowledge about others, but rather, we reduce them to what is obvious to us and judge them accordingly.

Consider the expectation behind "assuming another's position" by "putting oneself in another person's shoes." "Assuming another's position" is a common technique in social life, but it does not happen as easily as one might expect. It is not quite so easy to assume others' position without knowing about them in a more or less personal way or sharing any comparable experience. The imperative to "assume another's position" is not a magic spell that happens easily. There are preconditions for it to function. Moreover, failing to make sense of others' opinions or behaviors does not necessarily mean that they are just insane, for it is also possible that an answer is mistakenly supposed to be obvious. In his early work *Madness and Civilization*, Michel Foucault explores the relation between madness and civilization. He argues that madness is a cultural rather than a natural phenomenon. For one thing, it has been associated with different groups of people in different times, such as patients with leprosy and women; for the other, the meaning of the term "madness" has always been associated with the juridical system, which is supposed to be responsible for maintaining social order by correcting the undesirable behaviors of that group of people. It is easy to characterize other people as having no interest in integrating, as threatening because they do not support liberal values, or as insane or brainwashed. It is also easy to attribute those "characteristics" to an alleged group nature. But despite all these apparent answers, our knowledge about those people who are supposedly mad is not enriched; instead, we only reinforce what we already take for granted.

Necessary identity not only organizes social life and preserves social orders, but also makes salient certain ways of perceiving particular people. Examples of such perceptions would be how women are associated with submissiveness and hysteria, how immigrants are associated with threats to social welfare, how certain races are associated with danger to the national sovereignty and integrity, etc. This broader background explains how one does not just happen to bear prejudice against some people, but that such prejudice is related to particular epistemic circumstances and that it may even be reproduced and maintained by such epistemic circumstances. Individual solutions can be conducive to redressing identity-based thinking and to improving pre-existing contexts to some extent, although they are not sufficient. In the next two chapters, I shall attend to the structural aspect of this problem.

Anderson praises racial diversity and holds it to be an essential element for promoting integration, especially in a racially segregated country such as the one in her example, the US. But like moral generalists, she may have idealized racial diversity too much. She ignores the fact that, on the one hand, victims of racial segregation can also become advocates of segregation and, on the other hand, the positive significance minority communities, which are racially segregated places, have had for their members in difficult times. In Chapter One, I argued that racial diversity should not be taken at face value and that achieving integration means more than just realizing racial diversity. It remains contestable whether replacing the ideal of homogeneity with the ideal of racial diversity suggests that people who choose to live or associate with those who speak the same language or have the same place of origin as themselves are doing something wrong. From this perspective, the ideal of diversity (in no matter what sense we mean) does not seem to differ much from the ideal of homogeneity in any substantial way. The crux of the problem is not with whom immigrants or locals associate or what language they prefer to speak, but the reasons behind it.

What is actually worrisome in the cases of both assimilation and segregation is that one's ignorance about others seems to be justified by a noble cause, be it universalism or self-preservation. Either case entirely dismisses the question of how this ideal is constituted by particular social orders and epistemic circumstances. Code introduces the notion of "knowing people" as a model that does not assume the incompatibility between objectivity and subjectivity. She emphasizes that subjectivity also constitutes an essential moment of our knowledge. Not only do the subjectivities of others contribute to what they know, but our own subjectivities contribute to what we know as well. However, we may delude ourselves into thinking that subjectivities do not contribute to our knowledge when we simply follow what is given. Apart from the way in which social orders and power relations keep certain epistemic practices in place, thereby ensuring the predominance of one form of knowledge over another, there is also a logical dimension to how what we take for granted comes to appear as obvious. As I will explain now, the logical aspect is that sometimes things we suppose to be indisputable are in fact *nondisputable*.

Jiwei Ci notes that premises will not appear to be indisputable to those whose premises they are.[3] There are two ways in which a premise can lack disputability. "Indisputability" refers to the situation when "premises have been subjected to scrutiny," while "nondisputability" refers to situations when disputability dose not arise at all. He notes,

---

3 See for reference Jiwei Ci (2014), *Moral China in the Age of Reform*. Cambridge: Cambridge University Press, 63–87.

"the concept of indisputability misses what is going on, and nondisputability seems more appropriate: Something is nondisputable either in the sense that it is simply not called into dispute or in the sense that it is considered sufficiently plausible not to make (further) dispute imperative or necessary." (Ci 2014, 69)

Based on Thomas Metzger's discussion of modern Chinese political thought and modern Western political thought, Ci points out that Metzger's description of Western political thought as having a thin parameter of freedom and Chinese political thought as having a thick parameter of freedom is too simplistic. Metzger describes Western discourse as "thin" due to its preference for individual agency while he describes Chinese discourse as "thick" because it is conducive to conformity. Ci notes that in fact, both discourses involve individual agency as well as conformity. When carried too far, this oversimplification becomes an illusion, as if the thin parameter does not involve the production of conformity and the thick parameter does not allow room for individual initiative and subjectivity.

In modern Western discourse, the disputability of individual agency does not arise easily whereas conformity does not seem to be disputable in the Chinese case. However, this does not mean that individual agency or conformity alone is sufficient to constitute a political order. Ci notes that in a way, Chinese discourse may be said to represent the limit case of Western discourse. Similarly, Western discourse can be seen as representing the precondition for Chinese discourse. It is not, as Metzger describes, as if one discourse completely lacks what the other emphasizes; rather, the two discourses amount to two different paradigms for satisfying the twin needs of individual agency and conformity. So, just because the disputability of an idea does not seem to arise for the we-group in question does not necessarily mean that the idea is indisputable to them; it may very well mean that the question of disputability simply does not arise, given the way in which the discourse is constructed.

The distinction between indisputability and nondisputability also applies to the discussion of knowing people. For example, when talking about religions, believers' thoughts and actions can be regarded as products of the religion's worldview and consequences of its historical development. As demonstrated by the Muhammad cartoon controversy that was discussed in the first chapter, satire *seems* to be indisputable for some because it *is* nondisputable for the same group of people, whereas for others, satire does not seem so because it is in fact held to be disputable. On the one hand, when something is considered sufficiently plausible not to necessitate further disputes, something else that is coherently related with the former can be thereafter smoothly applied because the success of the former guarantees that the latter will not be called into question. On the other hand, this relation can be constructed in an opposite direction as well: for the same pair of concepts, which can be used smoothly one after another in certain circumstances, if the former is considered highly disputable, then it follows that the latter will inevitably be called into question as well.

The practice of secular politics means that satire is logically coherent with freedom of speech; its nondisputability is thus *discursively* guaranteed beforehand. Christianity also underwent times when, for example, material representations of God and saints were prohibited. In that case, mocking God or saints did not seem to be indisputable. Nevertheless, Christianity underwent a different course of development due to any number of historical contingencies. How society develops in other aspects will affect a religion's role as well as how "the secular" is constituted and understood in different ways.[4] My point is that in order to explain why and how Christianity is a different religious practice from Islam, one must look beyond the religion itself. By exploring other social aspects, one can better answer the question than if one were to just focus on the religion itself. That Christianity may to some extent better fit into the discourse of secular politics has something to do with the very status of Christian discourse *now*, which is not free from the historical course of many historically Christian societies. For instance, many churches have abandoned the old homophobic beliefs that they used to profess. This opens up space for thinking about co-existence with homosexual people in society more generally, which had previously been impossible. In this way, the current discourse of Christianity has a different epistemic capacity of what is indisputable or nondisputable.

Once it is clear how nondisputability can be confused with indisputability and thereby contributes to the apparent plausibility of one thing over another, I suppose that it is not hard to imagine how this appearance can reinforce the universal impression of a certain prevailing discourse and its epistemic necessity. If the above discussion primarily deals with the theoretical aspect of what different discourses make salient and what epistemic output they can have, now the effect of a specific output needs to be considered.

---

4 For a general but also interdisciplinary discussion about the relationship between religion and the secularism in public sphere, see Craig Calhoun, Mark Juergensmeyer and Jonathan VanAntwerper (eds.) (2011), *Rethinking Secularism*. Oxford: Oxford University Press.

When discussing epistemic injustice, Fricker uses the example of dental care to illustrate the point of how general equality can result in practical inequality. Imagine a society with no free dental care: this does indeed appear to be equal for everyone, but effectively, the lack of free dental care only impairs the dental health of the poor, as the rich can all afford to see a dentist. So, despite what one wants to believe at face value about no-free-dental-care-for-all, this apparent equality in the end only promotes what seems to be equality from the perspective of the rich (Fricker 2007, 161). Thus, emphasizing the capacity to pay implicitly selects a discourse that does not put the capacity to pay in question; that is, it takes the perspective of the group with sufficient financial resources. In that sense, the discussion is caught up in a tautology, since the indisputability of a concept depends upon a discourse in which it is taken to be nondisputable, i.e. in which the question of its disputability does not arise.[5] Now, consider that everyday life is just full of such unequal discourses, that people are more questionably accustomed to one discourse rather than another. In the words of Fricker's epistemic injustice, the hermeneutical resources of one discourse are richer than those of others.

Fricker's theory points out that epistemic poverty can disable would-be knowers from understanding those whose rationality they don't share. A lack of concepts is more than just a lack of words; it might as well indicate the inaccessibility of an entire discourse. The more the concepts reflecting the collective perspective of one group are used, the easier it is for people to understand them. For instance, in a world where "woman" is constructed as the opposite to "man," the more familiar we are with the androcentric human ideal, the easier it is for us to render women's experience and thoughts unintelligible. This is not to say that there is any such thing as a natural woman's or man's thought. Rather, when society is oriented according to identities like gender or race, people will be classified into different groups and observed and judged accordingly. A black person is more likely than a white person to experience the world as ripe with distrust, just as an immigrant experiences the receiving society as having more barriers than a citizen, and so on. Group experiences thus give rise to distinct discourses with different epistemic ca-

---

[5] That is not to say that a medical system cannot be questioned. Questioning a medical system that emphasizes the capacity to pay requires at least taking into consideration people with various financial situations or treating (basic) medical products as public goods. If medical service and products are only considered part of the market controlled by an invisible hand, then this kind of medical system basically excludes the medical needs of the poor.

pacities for nondisputability and indisputability. This is not to say that life worlds are solely made up by discourses. However, discourses are noteworthy because they demonstrate the different epistemic capacities that follow from and reshape social interactions. They can also show how invisible structures, i.e. those of an epistemic nature, can reinforce visible difficulties, inequalities and forms of marginalization. Regarding identity-based thinking, social order can not only reinforce perceptions about the presence of certain people, it can also objectify this impression by appealing to the apparent objectivity of such an appearance.

The distinction between indisputability and nondisputability shows that, when the given framework is changed, what appears to be indisputable may become irrational or impossible to understand. It seems that the inaccessibility of discourses has not been taken seriously enough, particularly with respect to the question of how such inaccessibility can affect the way we see other people and even ourselves. Instead, we seem to be more comfortable with the idea that both rationality and irrationality (or truth and falsehood) are simply apparent. We seem to assume an understanding of what is rational and what is not that is all too easy and which may very well work in favor of identity-based thinking. For one thing, identity-based thinking persists because social orders shape how certain groups of people are perceived, from which it follows that different perceptions of those people may be helpful to rectify identity-based thinking. But people should be seen in their actual life situations, with a particular emphasis on those aspects of their lives which highlight what is actually relevant and necessary for their social participation rather than those which simply portray them as too different to be desirable or compatible. However, impoverished epistemic circumstances yield knowledge that keeps certain people firmly in place and makes it difficult or even impossible to perceive them in any different way. That is to say that we may very well be held captive by our own discourses, such that we fail to recognize that it is not others' irrationality but rather our own particularities and inabilities that render them irrational to us.

Narrative Knowledge and the Concrete Other

As I understand it, nondisputability shows that knowledge cannot be treated simply as agentless information. As far as the human world is concerned, much of what one knows is primarily knowledge of concrete agents; that is, knowledge from knowers who are *not* free from social positions and personal traits. The notion of "conflicts between discourses" captures how epistemic factors contribute to conflicts without presupposing any essentialist views or reducing people to one overarching identity. An examination of discourse reveals that claims are always based upon some premises, as premises establish the criteria for what may or may not be disputable. This is true for things like social positions: being a woman, an Asian, or a Chinese person (depending on where I live) means that some things may be inevitable for me. Those inevitabilities may indeed happen so often that they come to form what I believe to be true about my world, even though it does not have to be true for others. However, my knowledge is always knowledge based upon certain premises. Without being a woman, an Asian, a Chinese person or having specific families and friends, I would not come to know things the way I do. There is always a context to what I know, and that context constitutes the intelligibility of my claims. The context may not exhibit features like prompt verifiability and self-evident comprehensibility, but it constitutes its own values.

Walter Benjamin refers to information and experience as two distinct forms of knowledge. In his *Der Erzähler* (The Storyteller), he presents this distinction as follows. News communicates information while stories communicate experience. Information is indeed advantageous to storytelling in some aspects, namely, through its prompt verifiability (*prompte Nachprüfbarkeit*) and self-evident comprehensibility (*an und für sich verständlich*). By drawing attention to this new form of communication, i.e. information, Benjamin intends to give an account of the background of the decline of storytelling in his time and the value of experience. A story, however bizarre, does not manifest its value in how factually true it is, which is the case for information, but establishes its value in its capacity to provide something *useful*:

"All this points to the nature of every *real* story. It contains, openly or covertly, something useful. The *usefulness* may, in one case, consist in a moral; in another, in some practical advice; in a third, in a proverb or maxim. In every case the storyteller is a man who has counsel for his readers." (Benjamin 2006, 364, my emphasis)

For Benjamin, the quality of a story lies in its "orientation toward practical interest," which differs significantly from how the notion of what is "real" is understood in the case of news. The latter is exhibited in its being propositionally true and observable, even though this apparent truth might not reflect what is actually going on or be of much use in practice. In contrast, the validity of narratives from afar – both spatial and temporal – lies in their capacity to give something useful that enables people to engage with the world.

According to Benjamin, experience surpasses information in having something useful to say. These messages might be something like "don't judge people according to their appearance," or "we only realize the value of things when we lose them." Such messages might also take the form of questions to reflect upon, such as "Is it better to live a miserable life or to die in happiness?" or "Does 'sacrifice for the greater good' necessarily mean giving up on individuality?" On the surface, the usefulness of these messages seems to be in their having lessons to teach. At a deeper level, they can teach lessons about the way in which people engage with concrete particularities because they give an image of human beings with actual life concerns. Stories – including fictional ones – reveal people's particularities. In comparison, information falls short as it sacrifices subjectivity in order to resolve uncertainty, and it strives after an almost meaningless objectivity in order to achieve its self-evident comprehensibility, whereas in practice, this objectivity becomes hollow and can be interpreted arbitrarily. Furthermore, the apparent objectivity of information may also turn out to be of misleading value when it ends up disguising oppressive structures. A lack of concern for subjectivity not only leads to misunderstandings but also makes it convenient for subjectivists to twist reality for their own cognitive purposes.

It is important to take subjectivity into consideration, especially when it comes to knowing (other) people. Treating information and experience as two distinct forms of knowledge implies that some knowledge can be only acquired by means of subjectivity, since what is apparent also very much depends upon what concepts are available or which discourse is at disposal. From a different angle, taking subjectivity into consideration is indispensable for knowing people because subjectivity also matters for a person's capacity to communicate: a person cannot communicate his or her world intelligibly if other people do not share or cannot comprehend his or her particularity. Thus, making sense of others can be obstructed not only by a lack of information but also by the inability to appreciate the intelligibility of certain ways of reasoning.

Experience does not sacrifice intelligibility for the sake of self-evident comprehensibility, since its intelligibility does not lie in prompt verifiability or comprehensibility. When it comes to getting to know people, it is not so much a matter of information but of experience. Since it is not easy to assume the universality of certain concepts, the challenge posed by nondisputability herein must be taken seriously. That is, the question of disputability might as well not arise because the ideas in question are characteristic of "our way of reasoning." Some hidden premises, which facilitate seeing some of our claims as nothing less than apparent, may in fact reflect "our" particularity rather than some alleged impartiality. Factors like social positions and historical contingencies can function in a similar way as premises, meaning that we should not so readily conclude that our way of thinking and of living is the only intelligible and moral one.

Experience provides us with access to an enriched picture of a person and at least some access to their particularity. Reflection upon others' experience, then, is vital for knowing people. By means of engaging with one's experience, we can come to know a person in a non-reductionist way, or at least better approach this aim. What's more is that experience also provides an effective method for combating the epistemic irresponsibility that I discussed in the last chapter. Knowers are epistemically irresponsible when their process of seeking knowledge ignores people's particularities and their epistemic circumstances. Knowers can also be said to be irresponsible when they assume that knowledge is simply given instead of actively sought out. Observable regularity can be deceptive, meaning that the active role of human agents in the production of knowledge should not be dismissed, nor should knowers neglect how their own particularities and epistemic circumstances affect what they know.

Benjamin laments the decline of storytelling and the decreasing value of experience. In this way, the advantage of information is also its disadvantage, for its self-evident comprehensibility can mislead readers into assuming that understanding is easy, whereas information becomes a handy tool for supporting subjectivism. In comparison, although experience does not offer quick answers, it gives both speaker and listener a chance to reflect upon their particularities. Such is the process of exchanging experience: we talk about personal situations, what factors may have made things easy or hard for us and may or may not have contributed to our success or failure. Whether and to what extent this experience also suits other people is up to them to decide. But through this process, knowers get a picture that is much richer than the one they initially had. This rich picture can more or less correct identity-based thinking, especially when the person is a member of the group that is closely associated with certain perceptions that fall under specific social orders.

In Chapter One, I discussed how assimilation and segregation can turn out to make integration in practice impossible. In both cases, the concrete agent vanishes. Both assimilation and segregation describe situations where people are thrown into epistemic or moral vacuums where only a series of isolated actions can be seen. Bauman describes this disappearance as real people dissolving "in the all-embracing 'we' – the moral 'I' being just a singular form of the ethical 'us' within which "'I' is exchangeable with 's/he'." Bauman refers to this process as "depersonalization," meaning that "whatever is moral when stated in the first person remains moral when stated in the second or third" (Bauman 1993, 47). Depersonalization takes place when the process of knowing people is reduced to thinking according to identities. Neither assimilation nor segregation engages with people's particularity: in the case of assimilation, particularities are obstacles to universalism and in the case of segregation, they exhibit a nature which no one can change. In contrast, narrative "rescues" the agent from an epistemic-moral vacuum and turns seemingly isolated actions into part of the life that someone lives by filling in the contexts. Using this approach, knowers can, at least to some extent, better assume another person's position than they would otherwise do without any knowledge of that person. Hence, narrative is a better epistemic proceeding for knowing people, i.e. one that is epistemically more responsible than randomly combined information. In addition to knowing what someone thinks, one further ought to know why this person thinks that or, in addition to knowing how someone identifies, one ought to know more about why they identify themselves that way. The latter forms of knowledge approach the person concretely, thereby they can help us correct simplistic and generalized knowledge that may be readily available.

For Benjamin, narrative knowledge is the form of storytelling. I think, however, that narrative also resembles how we know people in real life circumstances. We know friends, family members, colleagues and neighbors when we spend time with them and experience things together. We not only see how they react but also know their motivations and constraints. There is always a context, which can be taken as a reference point for appropriately assessing a person's decisions. Such personal knowledge about them gives rise to the relation we build with them. It also generates a solid basis for being able to judge whether, for instance, someone lies, cheats or is trustworthy in certain matters. To that extent, our judgments of other people no longer rest upon their social identities, such as man and woman, black, yellow, and white, or rich and poor. We no longer need those rigid identities to tell us what to do with someone or what to expect from them, for we have truer and richer knowledge about who that person is than what social identities can communicate. For one thing, narrative knowledge prevents knowers from mistakenly generalizing contingent features into properties of a certain group; for the other, narrative knowledge can help knowers to develop a more robust understanding than assumed objectivity. No one simply remains an agent in a vacuum. Narrative knowledge reveals what social positions and power relations are involved in producing certain world views, meaning that one can develop more realistic strategies or policies rather than believing that there isn't much one can do with other people because of something intrinsic to their nature.

There are different ways to generate contexts, such as personal relationships and long-term engagements with a topic. Without background knowledge, one is not in a position to make appropriate judgments or claims. In my discussion of identity-based thinking, I argued that reality can be distorted if one only relies on what is given or made salient by social orders. Behind the appearance of what one believes to be a lack of integration, many more complicated factors may be at play, as the example of the in-group diversity of Chinese immigrants in Ireland shows. It may also be the case that misguided by the homogenous picture of society offered by assimilation, the meaning of what immigrants do and the expectations of what they should do can be misinterpreted. Some of those who are "one of us" may also prefer being alone over social life, but they are not seen as failing to integrate. While certain behaviors per se may be nothing surprising – in the sense that they happen no matter what – the reactions these behaviors trigger differ significantly when they are conducted by immigrants or locals (especially when the locals involved do not belong to a minority). One of the reasons for overinterpreting the role someone's "immigrant" identity could have played is that the dichotomous pattern of "locals vs immigrants" as deployed by the conventional conception of "integration" overemphasizes – often in a prejudiced and self-centric way – the threat "outsiders" could bring. Observers thus lose sight of how diverse certain groups of people in fact are. No one is just an immigrant. Positive experience, such as getting to know an immigrant in person, can be of great significance for thinking across lines of division, be they racial or cultural. However, as I argued in Chapter One, positive experience is also very contingent. No one always has positive experiences with other people. Nevertheless, even if an experience does not turn out to be pleasant, one may at least get to see how personal particularities could have contributed to a person's behaviors that they do not appreciate. In this way, it is at least possible to prevent people from developing simplistic generalizations about some alleged properties of a group.

Overall, narrative knowledge does precisely what Code emphasizes in her responsibilist epistemology: namely, it shifts attention away from knowledge as an end-state product to knowledge as a seeking process. The mistake of taking knowledge as given is that knowers dismiss how contingencies and particularities contribute to the very production of knowledge claims themselves. As I shall discuss later in Chapter Six, human knowledge is also not free from its historical character. In this regard, feminism and post-colonial studies have done immense work in showing that things which are assumed to be universal often turn out to be particular.[6] In this respect, narrative knowledge highlights the processes of *embeddedness* and *disembeddedness*: on the one hand, as listeners, we must embed ourselves in the speaker's epistemic circumstances to make sense of their behaviors, while on the other hand, this embeddedness is simultaneously a disembeddedness from the epistemic circumstances with which we are so familiar and almost accept as a matter of course. Knowing people requires knowers to be more attentive to and mindful of the lives of others. However, this mindfulness ought not develop into blind following. Knowing people as they are does not serve as an excuse to unconditionally pardon their wrongdoings, such as the "culture excuse."[7] Taking into consideration people's subjectivity simply helps knowers to understand what leads them to do what they do and to think what they think. This further knowledge allows knowers to see factors that would oth-

---

6 For feminism-related literature see for reference Louise Antony and Charlotte Witt (eds.) (1993), *A Mind of One's Own: Feminist Essay on Reason and Objectivity*. Boulder, CO: Westview Press; Sandra Harding (1991), *Whose Science? Whose Knowledge? Thinking from Women's Lives*, Ithaca: Cornell University Press. For a general view of postcolonial literature see for reference Leela Ghandi (2019), *Postcolonial Theory. A Critical Introduction*. New York: Columbia University Press; Nikita Dhawan (2013), "Coercive Cosmopolitanism and Impossible Solidarities," *Qui Parle*, Vol. 22, No. 1, *Special Issue: Human Rights between Past and Future*,139–166; and Dhawan (2021), "Die Aufklärung vor den Europäer*innen retten," in Rainer Forst and Klaus Günther (eds.), *Normative Ordnungen*, 191–208. Frankfurt am Main: Suhrkamp. Also Dahwan (forthcoming), *Rescuing the Enlightenment from the Europeans: Critical Theories of Decolonization*.
7 Here, I mean to refer to excuses such as "my culture made me do it" or "that is their culture," both of which imply judgment is inapplicable. For a reference, see Benhabib (2002), *The Claims of Culture*.

erwise remain hidden in the background. This applies not only to those who we intend to know, but to ourselves as well. Regarding knowing people, the subjectivity at issue is two-fold: the subjectivity of the listeners and that of the speakers, or put differently, that of the moral agents and that of the moral recipients.

Based on the generally outlined methodology of narrative knowledge, an additional matter should be considered: the fact that one may nevertheless have reasons to reject others' claims or behaviors, partially or even completely. The possibility that one's initial judgment may be right cannot be ruled out completely. However, what is important to recognize here is that people should not be rejected on the mere basis of their identity, nor should they be affirmed only on the basis of their identity. Instead, narrative knowledge serves as a way to avoid oversimplification and generalization. Through the lens of subjectivity, it is important to see that people are motivated by more than what a social order makes salient about them. One should appeal to concrete reasons rather than mere identities to affirm or reject someone; furthermore, as Code puts it, knowers should be aware that not everything is an all-or-nothing affair which people either know or do not know but cannot know little or know well. The latter set of criteria indicates that knowing as well as understanding is a dynamic and ever-changing process. Knowledge claims should not be simply assumed based on the social status of different identities or due to an overly symbolic meaning attached to some identities, such as members of liberal or authoritarian regimes.

This is what "the concrete other" requires. Other people are to be comprehended by virtue of their real needs, desires, motivations and so on. No one is a depersonalized member of an all-embracing We, but rather, a concrete agent with specific capacities and constraints. From the perspective of "depersonalization," which Bauman criticizes, other people are not seen in terms of who they are but what they are. They are perceived according to what social orders reduce them to and confined to the framework of identity-based thinking, be it in terms of economic, cultural or political purposes. So far, I have analyzed numerous examples. Once reduced, those people become undesirable objects, and it may also become difficult for them to make plausible or imaginable claims that their lives need not be the way they are. It becomes simply a matter of course that we perceive them as economic units, cultural threats or political enemies. They do not enjoy the "multi-faceted" quality that we grant to people who are considered as "one of us." In this way, they fall out of the realm of morality. For one thing, they will no longer be treated equally, regardless of whether they enjoy formal equality or not. Moreover, once reduced to roles designated by social orders, the possibilities of relationship with them are simultaneously impoverished. Indeed, our relations with them are pre-determined. Before we know any one of them, we are given a set of concepts to make sense of their social existence and what we can expect from them.

Yet, the tricky part is that on the one hand, as knowers, we acknowledge what is misleading in identity-based thinking; namely, it is reductionist. It gives us a misleading picture of other people as well as of ourselves. So, it is plausible to suggest not making judgments simply according to identities, especially when the prevailing social orders give some identities particularly narrow meanings. However, on the other hand, one may argue that this is not yet the whole picture because completely excluding social identities from the discussion is not realistic either. Society is more or less organized according to identities; this is not something that one can just walk away from as one wishes. Similar to the relation between subjectivity and objectivity that recognizing the role of subjectivity in the making of knowledge does not deny objectivity, arguing not to think according to identities should not simply be equated to denying identities. This conclusion is too hasty. Identity-blindness won't redress the wrongs identity-based thinking has done. The point here is to say that identities should not be viewed in an absolute way, as if it either plays a role or it does not.[8] An identity, such as "immigrant," can affect one's life to a greater or lesser extent depending on both one's living circumstances and what other identities one has.

Generally speaking, an immigrant's life is different from that of a citizen. But, if this person happens to share the prevailing physical appearance in the receiving society and the receiving society happens to have a xenophobic public culture, then his or her immigrant identity will not affect him or her as much as it does those who do not share the same physical appearance. Similarly, other identities such as being rich or being an academic will all affect, at least to some extent, the practical significance of "being an immigrant" in different ways. A rich person can afford to buy privileges, which makes up for the disadvantages he or she has as an immigrant, whereas a scholar with

---

8 Even problematic identities, such as race and gender, constitute, in one way or another, how people experience the world. But no matter how salient they are in the way resources are distributed or social life is organized, there are at the same time other identities that can weaken or reinforce the impact of those identities.

a migration background works in an environment where most people possess a rich knowledge of immigration issues. Such knowledge makes it less likely that the scholar will be discriminated against. In both cases, it is not that "being an immigrant" does not affect the person's life, because it does. As an immigrant, one does not enjoy an unconditional residence permit, work permit or voting rights; one has to take into consideration many restrictions that locals do not have to deal with, such as institutional and personal disadvantages in renting apartments and finding jobs, extra bureaucracy and costs for civil affairs like registration and getting married, let alone the additional problems diplomatic relations and geopolitical matters can cause. But there are also other identities at play, such as being rich, white or an academic. They can make up for (or worsen) the disadvantages being an immigrant brings. Suppose that an immigrant is not rich but poor and works with people who are xenophobic; these additional factors only aggravate the disadvantages that come with being an immigrant. He or she may need to work extremely hard just to make ends meet while also being discriminated against constantly by his or her co-workers. What's worse, this experience may also discourage him or her from having a social life. All this may motivate him or her to self-isolate, reinforcing the co-workers' belief that immigrants, which group that person represents, have no interest in integration. In short, identity does affect how one lives and what one knows. That is why identity should not be unseen as if it does not matter.

Now, here are two points that need to be taken into consideration. One is that in order to rectify identity-based thinking, judgments should not be based solely upon identities, as this simply reinforces problematic social orders. The other is that how identity contributes to one's knowledge should, nevertheless, be taken into account. So, while this may sound paradoxical, identity should be left out as well as included. Let me explain. How identity should be both left out and included in knowing people concerns what function identity should play in our getting to know and evaluating other people. Sandra Harding argues that group identity is epistemologically relevant *not* because identity alone can offer justifications, but because groups operate "with different starting belief sets based on their social location and their group-related experiences, and these starting sets will inform their epistemic operations such as judging coherence and plausibility."[9] Identity

---

9 Cited from Linda Martín Alcoff (2007), "Epistemologies of Ignorance: Three Types," in Shannon Sullivan and Nancy Tuana (eds.), *Race and Epistemology of Ignorance*, 39–58. New York: State Univer-

does not determine how one thinks, but since it constitutes or influences how one experiences the world, it is epistemologically relevant. This epistemic relevance is best manifested in the fact that people draw different conclusions even if they have identical access to identical information. But however epistemologically relevant a given identity is, many other identities may be just as relevant. Who a person is always implies a complex network of various identities. Identity does not determine how one thinks because there is never just one identity at work in an individual. Human agents reason and choose among the positions and relations they have. Hence, identity plays a constitutive, rather than a determining, role.

In this part, I have discussed narrative knowledge, how it helps to rectify identity-based thinking by means of shifting the focus to knowledge-seeking as a process and makes visible epistemically relevant background factors that were previously invisible. I argued that narrative knowledge provides a richer picture of a person by portraying them as a concrete other. Immigrants are people with particularities rather than a homogenous group; they cannot be reduced to figures and stereotypes. While the identity of "immigrant" may be more visible than other identities, a closer look shows that it does not really reflect the person's actual living situation. The process of knowing people will also enable us to know more about ourselves than what we already know. This process prevents us from generalizing personal traits into group properties. In the next part, I shall introduce the ethics of difference. I shall argue that for the practice of knowing people, ethics of difference are more appropriate and morally defensible than conventional ethic theories that are moral agent centric because it correctly points out that 1) moral recipients are as important to the moral relationship as moral agents, 2) when different parties are involved, knowing-how is more significant than mere knowing-that, and 3) epistemic failures of moral agents can be morally and politically disabling.

---

sity of New York Press. See also Sandra Harding (1991), *Whose Science? Whose Knowledge? Thinking from Women's Lives*.

Ethics of Difference and the Moral Significance of Self-Cultivation

So far, I have argued in favor of the practice of knowing people. I emphasized that knowledge of subjectivity is indispensable for knowing people because it provides a truer and richer picture of people than rigid identities do. Regarding integration, how well immigrants can participate in the receiving society and how motivated they can be when it comes to interacting with local people as well as adopting local values or traditions are closely related to not only how "being an immigrant" shapes their lives but also their other identities. As argued above, these other identities can function as an enabling or defeating factor depending on the epistemic circumstances of the receiving society. In this regard, what effect the identity of "immigrant" along with other identities can trigger and how such an effect depends on the pre-existing epistemic circumstances of the receiving society are worth examination and reflection. As far as the pre-existing epistemic circumstances of the receiving society are concerned, it is the locals, rather than the immigrants, that should be expected to subject their ways of reasoning to closer scrutiny, though they are conventionally exempted from any responsibility of integration. They should scrutinize how their given understanding of the place or the community where they live, of things they take to be universal, and of other people who they deem to be different from them affect or even impede their ability to listen, understand as well as self-questioning. Again, this is not to encourage a blind acceptance in an opposite direction, just like questioning that satire can be inappropriate is not the same as denying satire per se. I pose these questions from the standpoint of an immigrant because I know clearly from my own experience the following fact: that is, I would not be able to integrate successfully – if I can describe my life situation like this, though I can only speak for myself – had I not met the people who were able to see me beyond my most obvious identities, such as immigrant, Asian, woman and Chinese. At the level of individual relations, they were open to reconsider what they knew about the groups I present; moreover, they were also willing to know me as a person who is not limited by these identities. In this sense, they integrated because they renegotiated the distribution of epistemic authority by – consciously or not – decentralizing the role they play in my integration in the receiving society. They grant me the same significance in the making of the relationship we share together.

Theoretically speaking, I take interest in a particular moral view here. In the previous discussion, I criticized the simplistic moral view identity-based thinking manifests. I noted that the reductionist view of identity-based thinking delimits the realm of morality by defining precisely who is undesirable, such as in terms of "threatening" or "illiberal." Moreover, the definition of "undesirableness" used in such a morality is often based on the standard of the self. Like moral generalism, such a moral view is based upon a presumed principle of what is good or right and leaves those who do not fit into this conception outside of the realm of moral concern. Like the generalized other, this conception takes the self as the standard of (all) human agents and assumes that other people would want the same things that "we" would want to ascribe to "ourselves." As far as I am concerned, such a moral view is problematic because the so-called commonality it presupposes often turns out to have resulted from unjust and irresponsible epistemic practices. The moral view I shall introduce in the following is called ethics of difference. On the one hand, it offers an alternative moral view that is not based upon a self-centered pattern; on the other hand, ethics of difference provide the normative argument why epistemic capacity is indispensable for morally appropriate relation.

In *Why Be Moral?*, Huang provides an account of the ethics of difference[10] based on the Chengs' (Cheng Yi and Cheng Hao)[11] virtue ethics theory. Its point of departure is that moral agents and moral recipients are *not* the same

---

10 See for reference Yong Huang (2014), *Why Be Moral?*, 131–160. In a footnote, Huang adds that his account of the ethics of difference also owes much to the Daoist text *Zhuangzi*. For the latter discussion, see Huang (2010), "The Ethics of Difference in the Zhuangzi," *Journal of American Academy of Religion*, Vol. 78, Issue 1, 65–99.

11 Cheng Yi (程颐) and Cheng Hao (程颢) are philosophers of Neo-Confucianism, a leading school of philosophy in the Song and Ming dynasties of China. I do not share the translation "neo-Confucianism" because what is denoted as neo-Confucianism is a school of thought influenced by Confucianism as well as Daoism and Buddhism. In Chinese, this school is called "Song-Ming-Rationalism" (*Song Ming Li Xue*宋明理学). A different translation is "Song-Ming Confucianism." However, the English translation only preserves the Confucianist influence. For a brief introduction, see Justin Tiwald (2020), "Song-Ming Confucianism," *Stanford Encyclopedia of Philosophy*, March, https://plato.stanford.edu/entries/song-ming-confucianism/#HistContBuddDaoiNeoConf, last accessed March 2023; Wai-ying Wong (n.d.), "Cheng Yi," *Internet Encyclopedia of Philosophy*, https://iep.utm.edu/chengyi/, last accessed March 2023; Yong Huang (n.d.), "Cheng Hao," *Internet Encylopedia of Philosophy*, https://iep.utm.edu/cjemg-omgdap-cheng-hao-neo-confucian/, last accessed March 2023. Also see Chan Wing-tsit (1963), *A Source Book in Chinese Philosophy*, 518–571. Princeton: Princeton University Press; Peter K. Bol (2008), *Neo-Confucianism in History*. Cambridge MA: Harvard University Asian Center.

people. It "underlines the importance for moral agents to learn about their patients' (particularities) before they can determine the appropriate ways to love them" (Huang 2014, 160). Here, "love" does not necessarily mean having a strong and positive emotion of regard or affection towards something or someone but rather refers to "having a moral relation with or a moral consideration for someone." In Confucianism and its related schools, "love" is considered as a form of humanity (*ren* 仁). From this point of view, "hate" can also be understood as a kind of love in the general sense and does not have to refer to ill will.[12] So, because moral agents and recipients are different people, "we cannot just go ahead and love them [other people] but must first learn about their unique ideas, ideals, customs, and ways of behaving" (Huang 2014, 160). Otherwise, one may inappropriately generalize one's own standard, disregard others' particularities and misidentify what is morally relevant in a certain situation.

One thing deserves particular attention here. According to Huang, the Chengs maintain that true love cannot be transcendent love; rather, love is always concrete, such as one's love for their parents, friends and even for people that one does not know. This idea reflects the Confucian idea of "love with distinction" (*ai you cha deng* 爱有差等). For Confucianism, true love is not about a universal or abstract law but a matter of how to love. That is, one does not know love when one does not know how to love, and one only knows how to love when one can love with distinction. I explained above that for Confucianism, "hate" can also be viewed as a kind of love in the general sense that it describes a kind of moral relation. So, to hate someone can also be said to "love with distinction." In the eyes of the Chengs as well as of the Confucians, a person is humane – or, put otherwise, moral – only when he or she knows how to love (and how to hate) in ways appropriate to the objects of love (and hate).

For the Chengs, being moral is primarily a matter of *ability* rather than a matter of looking for some supposed moral truth. This contrasts starkly with

---

12 See for reference Chan Wing-tsits (1963), "The Humanism of Confucius," in *A Source Book in Chinese Philosophy*, 14–48. The discussion of "love" (and "hate") has always primarily been a discussion of "know-how" in Confucianism and its related schools. Concern about love has always been a concern about "how to love," not what love is. This is due to the Confucian standpoint of seeing morality as moral cultivation of oneself. A related passage in the *Zhongyong* (中庸) says that "superior persons may not neglect self-cultivation; to cultivate themselves, they may not neglect to serve their parents; to serve their parents, they may not neglect to know them; and to know them, they may not neglect to know heaven (*tian*)."

conventional moral views, which typically place their primary concern on moral truth. Huang argues that the ethics of difference is particularly significant in the contemporary world because, with the emergence of a global village, "(w)hat used to be members of remote clans have now become our immediate neighbors, in both actual and virtual reality." Consequently, "(a)n appropriate global ethics should thus *enable* us to deal with such entirely new interpersonal relationships in an appropriate way" (ibid., my emphasis). Conventional moral systems, such as moral generalism, often turn out to be based upon ignorant and/or oppressive structures with severely deficient epistemic capacity. On the one hand, as Huang notes, the moral view, which supposes a moral truth, may no longer be suitable for dealing with many contemporary issues; on the other hand, there is something more to be said about epistemic deficiency.

Regarding know-how as a matter of knowing things, Jason Stanley offers an argument explaining why knowing propositional facts does not amount to the whole picture of knowing things. In *Know How*, Stanley argues that when we learn to swim, we don't just learn abstract theories about swimming. Rather, we learn how to swim by really swimming in water and the same is true for many things, such as riding a bicycle, playing the piano or learning languages. In learning how to do something, we learn "some facts" about that thing or activity. Stanley calls these facts "a special *kind* of fact about swimming" "that answers the question, 'how could you swim?'" (Stanley 2013, vii, original italics), which unlike abstract theories leaves us with *skills to engage with the world*. This kind of fact is certainly not propositional, since the knowledge embodied by this kind of fact does not take the form of statements but *abilities* or, in his words, "skilled action." Factual knowledge is not isolated knowledge for it also plays a role in guiding action. Hence, Stanley contends that separating know-that from know-how is a "false assumption" about what it means to know a fact.

According to Stanley's account of knowing, know-how is no less important than know-that, especially when the primary purpose of knowing is *to act*, as evidenced by swimming and languages. For these activities, skilled action is epistemically valuable. For moral conduct, skilled action is important as well. However, moral views that rely on a supposed moral truth often lack the conception of know-how. While much attention has been placed upon debating moral principles or impartial truth, little attention has been given to moral recipients who are equal participants in a moral relation as moral agents. Stanley's argument on the importance of know-how brings to light this epistemic shortcoming of those moral theories that only focus on abstract principles; that is, if knowledge about morality does not leave one with the ability to engage with other people in morally appropriate ways, then one still does not really know what it is to be moral. In this regard, emphasizing the ability to act no longer looks like a matter of mere preference; rather, know-how is an indispensable part of knowing things. So, the Chengs' virtue ethics may not be just an alternative moral view; it also compensates for a disadvantage of moral views which we will only come to learn about later.

The lack of know-how also reflects an inability to deal with certain issues concerning integration. Consider the Muhammad cartoon controversy discussed in Chapter One. While satire is a common tool of critique and a traditional part of the practice of free speech in Denmark or liberal democracy, how well it works greatly depends on the actual context, i.e. what topic is being discussed, which group is being addressed and so on. For some matters, satire may not be an appropriate approach although this is not the same thing as rejecting free speech. Critics can still express their opinions, but in this case, they need to pay attention to how they do it. That is, they need skills to engage with people whose religious doctrine is different from that of Christianity. They should learn about the group if they want to conduct their critiques in a morally appropriate way: if they really treat the other group as equal members of society, they should take into account the fact that the other group, though likely to be different from them, is an equal participant, whose concerns and needs should be given due consideration.

Another example worth noting is the debate about whether multiculturalism is bad for women.[13] Gender oppression exists in many places.[14] One of the challenges many immigrant societies believe they are confronted with is how to deal with the oppression of women while maintaining a multicultural society. When male perpetrators claim that what they do is just part of their culture, they use their minority status to try to get away with their behavior. Nevertheless, it would be naïve to treat a whole culture or an entire group of people who are associated with that culture as threatening to women's rights. Because this would effectively adopt an androcentric view of the culture or group-identity in question, ignoring that within that group or culture there

---

13 See for reference Susan Moller Okin (1999) (ed.), *Is Multiculturalism Bad for Women?* Princeton: Princeton University Press; Benhabib (2002), *The Claims of Culture*.
14 Western political philosophy is also not free from gender oppression, see for reference Susan Moller Okin (1979), *Women in Western Political Thought*. Princeton: Princeton University Press.

might still be (gender) hierarchies – this manifests the in-group diversity, but in a bad way.[15] What is required here is to know how oppressive gender structures are incorporated into and disguised by certain cultural practices, and how to redress those structures without denying a whole culture. As I argued in the previous chapters, it is wrong to suppose that oppressive gender structures do not exist in liberal democracies.[16] Besides, multiculturalism or recognizing different cultural practices should not be carelessly equated with the androcentric view of that culture or that group. As feminist theorists from postcolonial tradition pointed out, elite monopolization exists elsewhere, too.[17] A better understanding about what is going on and whom one is dealing with necessarily requires moral agents to know in a more responsible and more just way rather than assuming who "they" are and that "they" should adopt one's own moral standard.

Defending a morality that is primarily concerned with know-how, knowing people becomes indispensable for the Chengs' ethics of difference. Without knowing people, one would not know how to love with distinction: that is, it would be impossible to know how to engage with other people in appropriate ways. One may cause harm to others or humiliate oneself.[18] Therefore, one must learn about the uniqueness of one's objects of love, which is precisely why the Chengs emphasize the importance of "knowing people (*zhi ren* 知人)" (ibid.). An ethics of difference hence urges moral agents and their conducts to take moral recipients into consideration and to see them as equal participants, whose needs, desires and ideals matter to the moral relationship as much as the moral agents. In this sense, Huang describes his view in

---

15 The image of a cultural or ethnic group should not be reduced to its male version. "Arranged marriage" may be prevailing in certain areas or cultures, but treating this practice as the essence or character of a group is to adopt an androcentric view of the group in question because it actively ignores the in-group diversity.

16 If the oppression of women is a non-Western thing or something that will not happen in liberal democracy, then how to explain social movements like "Me Too," or phenomena like the gender pay gap that disadvantages women or the historical fact that many liberal democracies only granted women voting rights long after universal suffrage became constitutionally established?

17 See Dhawan (2013), "Coercive Cosmopolitanism and Impossible Solidarities," *Qui Parle*, Vol. 22, No. 1, *Special Issue: Human Rights between Past and Future*, 139–166.

18 "(W)ithout knowing people, one may be affectionate to their parents not as they are ... As a result, the person may humiliate himself or herself and cause harm to their parents." See Huang (2014), *Why Be Moral?*, 141.

the name of an ethics of difference as a patient relativism.[19] As the name suggests, it means granting moral patients or moral recipients a central position in moral considerations and conducts.

The practice of knowing people aims at correcting inappropriate generalizations, such as those associated with identity-based thinking, and enabling the moral agents to build morally appropriate relationships with the recipients. It does not urge moral agents to accept the standard of moral recipients unconditionally but to indicate that the epistemic capacity of the agents can be faulty or incomplete. Regarding moral relationships, the purpose of correcting or avoiding identity-based thinking is not necessarily about developing positive personal relations. One may still end up disliking or rejecting a person, but this should be grounded in the knowledge about that person's actual personality or behavior rather than supposed qualities attributed to them by social identities.

Another source of the Chengs' virtue ethics, Daoism, also grants an essential role to the practice of knowing people in moral conduct. For Daoism, the biggest obstacle to our moral conduct is our opinionated mind (*cheng xin* 成心), i.e. pre-conceived and biased opinions. The opinionated mind "is nothing but one's tendency to regard one's own standard of right and wrong as the universal standard" (Huang 2010), which can be also said as the biggest obstacle in the moral agents' attempt to consider moral recipients as equal participants. The preference of both Confucianism and Daoism for the practice of knowing people reflect their shared view on the role of the self in moral conduct. For Confucianism, the practical significance of morality lies in self-cultivation: namely, to engage in moral conduct, moral agents ought to cultivate themselves. For Daoism, the practical significance of morality means to lose oneself. A common misunderstanding is to equate "losing the self" with denying moral autonomy, as if Daoism urges people to give up their individuality. This is too literal an interpretation. The self that Daoism thinks one should lose is the self that attempts to legislate for all others, such as the self as understood in moral generalism. In losing or reconstructing this self-centered self, one acquires a new self that moves between different social domains; put otherwise, one renews one's capacity and learns to access discourses that were previously inaccessible. So, by means of losing the (old) self, one in fact reconstructs the (new) self.

---

19 See Huang (2010), "The Ethics of Difference in the Zhuangzi," 65–99; also Huang (2018), "Patient Moral Relativism in the Zhuangzi," *Philosophia*, Vol. 46 No. 4, 877–894.

This view on the role of self also contrasts starkly with the paradigm of morality that is common in the continental and Anglo-American philosophy traditions. This paradigm is used to center on moral agents in the sense that moral agents determine moral relations. Even in the case of what seems to be simply appraising moral behaviors, it is assumed that the moral agent can function as an impartial observer who is capable of discerning the universal truth.[20] Little attention has been paid to the other end of moral relations, i.e. moral recipients. Yet, how can I be moral if *all* I think about is what *I* want, how much *I* want it and why *I* want it? People at the receiving end must be taken into consideration as well; otherwise, in what sense is a practically arbitrary relation moral? So, the paradigm changes. Since the moral recipient is also seen as a crucial part, the moral agent must consider precisely *who* the recipient is. Moral agents are thus required to learn about the recipients so that the agents know what the adequate (or a more adequate) way to participate in that relation is. That means, for a relation to be morally appropriate or justifiable, all participants must engage in the practice of knowing people. Knowers are only epistemically responsible and just when they consider both themselves and others as particular agents who seek knowledge actively and do not pre-determine epistemic authority based on given identities. Nevertheless, this does not amount to the requirement of knowing everything about the participants, which is not only demanding but also not required by the ethics of difference. From the perspective of ethics of difference, moral agents should be expected to know about their recipients because moral recipients are as important to the appropriateness or justifiability of the relevant moral conducts as the agents are. Given the context-dependent feature, moral agents' knowledge about their recipient should be directed at facilitating the kind of relation that is required by the context in question. Here, "require" does not mean asserting some external perspective such as that of assumed objectivity; rather, it underlines the mutual attribute of such interactive relationship.

The ethics of difference concerns primarily knowing-how, which is more significant than knowing-that when what is in question involves different parties and is chiefly a matter of interaction, or so I think. By highlighting the importance of knowing-how, the ethics of difference questions whether

---

20 Kantians hold that moral principles derive from pure reason, so a moral principle inevitably results from the fact that we are rational agents. However, I think this still does not explain what makes the "I" generalizable.

knowers' epistemic deficiency – especially that of the moral agents – could bring about knowers' moral failures. And the answer is "yes." Both epistemic responsibility and epistemic justice can benefit from the ethics of difference because, by urging knowers to avoid identity prejudice (epistemic injustice) and to be aware that knowing is not always a matter of knowing-all-or-nothing but also a matter of (striving to) knowing better and more (epistemic responsibility), they also advocate that knowers' epistemic failure is morally and politically disabling. And the remedies they point at are also in the direction of correcting and/or improving the pre-existing epistemic capacity of the knowers, who in fact are the moral agents according to the ethics of difference.

In this chapter I proposed the practice of "knowing people" as a solution for how to make integration mutual at the individual level. I stressed that getting to know other people in their actual living situation is the beginning of a practically meaningful moral relation that overcomes identity-based thinking. In this regard, the pattern of self-cultivation acknowledges the equal significance of moral recipients and that moral agents' epistemic deficiency can hinder them from engaging with others appropriately – or put differently, their ability to deal with diversity will thus be obstructed. In this sense, the self-cultivation paradigm of moral conduct is conducive to mutual integration because it is decentralizing. As argued in the first chapter, there is a hidden loop in the agent-centered paradigm of morality: namely, if the judgment of right or wrong comes not from the recipient but from whether the agent him-/herself could imagine an action done unto him/her, this means that the moral phenomena that give rise to the corresponding judgment have been defined and singled out in advance. Moral recipients should enjoy an equal entitlement as well, their needs and concerns should not only constitute the content of moral principles but also inform the moral conduct. In contrast to the agent-centered paradigm, the ethics of difference offers a different approach to thinking about the goal of morality, the dynamics between moral agent and recipient, the moral (and political) significance of knowers' epistemic capacity as well as the importance of improving it.

Before concluding this chapter, I want to draw attention to another common misunderstanding I have discussed in the previous chapters: namely, one should not romanticize "integration" as if successful integrations are capable of producing a conflict-free or complete harmonious society. On the one hand, it is highly unlikely that such situations are possible; on the other hand, it is also highly questionable whether they are (or should be) desirable.

When immigrants are expected to learn the languages and rules of the receiving society, which is a very loose meaning of "integration," it should also be expected at the same time that, once they master the languages and know the rules, they are likely to complain, to question, to disagree, to protest, to strike, to express their opinions on why something should change[21] – they are likely to do many things a local person without a migration background would also do. But the fiction of integration – once "they" are integrated, conflicts will automatically vanish – refuses to accept the realistic side of integration. Through its rose-tinted spectacles, integration should only bring submissive results. For knowing people as the practice of mutual integration at the individual level, there are similar pitfalls. The purpose of knowing a person more and better is to generate more comprehensive knowledge about that person than what social orders makes salient through necessary identities. Not only can such knowledge help knowers avoid identity-based thinking, it can also enable knowers to deal with that person in a morally justifiable or appropriate way, which does not exclude the possibility of negative relationships. But the presence of negative relationships does not mean integration fails, they are simply what happens when different people live together.

Nevertheless, epistemic failures are not only individual and interactive, they can result from structural problems as well. In the latter case, morally inappropriate conducts chiefly result not from moral agents' epistemic deficiency but from structural epistemic fallibilities prior to those conducts. In cases like this, it is possible that individual knowers are unable to keep up with the structural wrongs, hence it is difficult for them to always stay alert. More importantly, redressing structural wrongs requires primarily structural changes. Regarding epistemic fallibilities, this could mean transforming logics, norms, hermeneutical resources and so on. An analysis of this aspect is the concern of the next two chapters.

---

21 This is what El-Mafaalani argues in *Das Integrationsparadox*. He contends that conflicts are in fact indications of successful integration.

Five –
Making Sense of "Strangers"

In Chapter Two and Three, when I explained identity-based thinking and its exclusionary nature, I suggested that in order to rectify it, both individual as well as structural remedies are needed. Regarding integration, immigrants' efforts alone are not enough as, without the right public environment and the cooperation of ordinary citizens, not only may immigrants' formal equality remain ineffectual, but their efforts to integrate may also be in vain. In Chapter Four, I mainly focused on the individual remedy, to which I referred as the practice of knowing people. I stressed the importance of personal knowledge, which, on the one hand, reflects the in-group diversity of a supposedly homogenous group and on the other hand, opens the possibility of a non-reductionist way of knowing the person in question.

The acknowledgement of one's particularity means that one cannot so easily generalize one's standard as universal. It also means that self-knowledge may contain many different misconceptions about what it actually means to be one of "them" or "us." Conventionally, moral agents have almost always been granted the central position in moral conduct, be it an actual agent or an allegedly impartial observer. In the case of an allegedly impartial observer, the observer also often turns out to be the actual agent who imagines him- or herself as impartial. At the end of Chapter Four, I proposed an ethics of difference, which emphasizes the importance of knowing people. Such an ethics questions the self-proclaimed impartiality of moral agents and draws attention to moral recipients, who are just as important to moral conduct as moral agents but neglected by most traditional moral theories.

In this chapter and the next, I will concentrate on the structural aspect of identity-based thinking and mutual integration. Here, questions about what is justifiably necessary and what is only apparently so also matter. Apparent necessities can derive from deficient epistemic capacity, which is itself caused or constituted by problematic epistemic circumstances. Conceptions about who (should) belong are also closely related to various kinds of normalization. As Carens notes, one important issue concerning the integration of immigrants is that despite their efforts and even after perhaps a long period of settlement, some people continue to be treated as outsiders who do not belong and who do not deserve what they have. This notion of belonging is not unrelated to the shared conception of political membership, such as national identity. In the following, I shall begin with David Miller's account of the "stranger." As I understand it, Miller's way of identifying immigrants as strangers illustrates a typical way of understanding the presence of immigrants as part of social reality.

Who are "Strangers" in Our Midst?

According to Miller, "calling immigrants strangers" is not an arbitrary decision, but simply empirically undeniable. He writes:

"Why call immigrants 'strangers', and why assume a homogenous 'we' in whose midst they are being set down? I believe, though, that it captures how immigration is often experienced, at least on first encounter, in settled societies most of whose members have a sense that they and their ancestors are deeply rooted in a place." (Miller 2016, 18)

Miller calls immigrant "strangers" because they are not deeply rooted in a place in the way that locals are. However, how long is long enough in order for a group to be considered "deeply rooted"? A century or two? Or is it the fact that a person was born and raised in that place? What exactly is "deep rootedness" supposed to mean? And why should this matter to the legitimacy of a person's or group's presence? Besides, is it really the case, as Miller claims, that immigrants are not deeply rooted?

In everyday language, the word "immigrant" covers a wide variety of people. It refers not only to people who move to a country that is not their place of origin, but also to people with a migrant background; for example, people who are born and raised here, but whose family originate from elsewhere. When the population of a particular society is diverse, it is impossible to tell whether a person is an immigrant just by their appearance. If a person was born and raised in that society, it would hardly be justifiable to say that that person is not deeply rooted there. Indeed, why wouldn't a person's lifetime count as long enough? In fact, many minority groups are not newcomers. Their histories date back many centuries, as is the case of those of Bangladeshi, Pakistani and Indian heritage in the UK and those of Chinese heritage in the US. However, the deep rootedness of these groups does not really help them to belong in the eyes of some. Many of them continue to be seen as strangers, just as Miller describes.

One important, but rarely mentioned, phenomenon is that not all immigrants are considered "strangers," but only some immigrants, for example, those from the global south or the so-called third world. Immigrants from wealthy countries and places with similar cultural, social and political backgrounds are not considered threatening and undesirable. Contrarily, they may very well be welcomed, as they are not too different. Since they share enough similarities, they are not strangers but one of "us." This is true for Miller's use of the term "strangers." Here, it is important to note that Miller's notion of the "stranger" is highly abstract and arbitrary. It does not simply refer to "people one does not know." According to Miller, compatriots, for example, cannot be strangers, regardless of whether one really knows that person. "Strangers" are those who are *too different* to belong.[1] Miller stresses a particular notion of national identity, which includes national history, symbols and other cultural elements. He believes that "with national identity comes a kind of solidarity that is lacking if one looks just at economic and political relationships" (Miller 2016, 27). But regarding this claim, critics point out that there is no empirical evidence supporting this claim and that liberal nationalists simply take for granted the emotional tie national identity is supposed to provide.[2] Miller emphasizes particular racial differences or differences of descent when analyzing social conflicts, as if these were the only or primary reasons why some people are treated as strangers. But this leaves out the question of how more realistic factors, such as income gaps and infrastructural inequality affect political stability and social solidarity.[3]

---

1 In John Plamenatz's 1965 article, "Strangers in Our Midst," whose title Miller adopts for his book, strangers are not only those who are culturally too different, but also racially. See John Plamenatz (1965), "Strangers in Our Midst," *Race*, Vol. 7, Issue 1, 1–16. See also Miller (2016), *Strangers in Our Midst*, 178n37.
2 See for reference Sarah Fine and Andrea Sangiovanni (2019), "Immigration," in Darrel Moellendorf and Heather Widdows (eds.), *The Routledge Handbook of Global Ethics*, 193–210. London: Routledge.
3 See Chapter Eight of Miller's *Stranger in Our Midst*. I argue elsewhere that Miller overemphasizes differences in cultural backgrounds and descent, thereby ignoring how material and institutional

"Too different" may seem to be a valid criterion to include in discussions of these matters, but just what does it mean? What counts as sufficiently similar or too different? Being born in the same place, believing in the same God or speaking the same language does not guarantee that two persons will develop any intimate relations. And why couldn't two different people become friends or lovers, independent of their being a little, if not very, different? Even if the vague standard is put in seemingly concrete terms like "deep rootedness," as I pointed out above, this still does not provide a convincing reason for associating immigrants with strangers. Not only is the notion of the "stranger" rather abstract and arbitrary, so is the notion of "homogeneity" which it implies. Generally speaking, "homogeneity" is a considerably vague notion, as this concept describes any number of things from physical appearance to political ideals. In this respect, Wittgenstein's "family resemblance" offers a helpful account for understanding how the norm of "homogeneity" conditions the way one sees the world. Wittgenstein argues that, while things are often thought to be connected by an essential core, they may in fact be connected by "a complicated network of similarities overlapping and crisscrossing." These similarities are much like family members resembling each other; there is no one feature which is common to all of them, but they are nevertheless connected by various resemblances.[4]

Today's British soil has been receiving people from outside of this area from as early as the eleventh century if one counts the Norman Invasion. That is to say that this soil has witnessed a number of different versions of imag-

---

conditions can intensify social conflicts. As a result, he not only misrepresents conflicts but also reinforces the stranger-impression that is associated with some immigrants. See Wang (2021), "Imagine 'Strangers' in Our Midst," in Wolfram Cremer and Corinna Mieth (eds.), *Migration, Stability and Solidarity*. Baden-Baden: Nomos. For more reflections on Miller's self-proclaimed realistic approach to the political philosophy of immigration see Robin Celikates (2017), "Weder gerecht noch realistisch – David Millers Plädoyer für das Staatliche Recht auf Ausschluss," *theorieblog.de*, https://www.theorieblog.de/index.php/2017/12/lesenotiz-weder-gerecht-noch-realistisch-david-millers-plaedoyer-fuer-das-staatliche-recht-auf-ausschluss/, last accessed March 2023. Alex Sager (2016), "Book Review: Strangers in Our Midst: The Political Philosophy of Immigration by David Miller," *LSE Review of Books*, https://blogs.lse.ac.uk/lsereviewofbooks/2016/09/06/book-review-strangers-in-our-midst-the-political-philosophy-of-immigration-by-david-miller/, last accessed March 2023. Paulina Ochoa Espejo (2017), "Strangers in Our Midst: The Political Philosophy of Immigration. By David Miller," *Migration Studies*, Volume 5, Issue 3, 465–469.

4 See for reference Ludwig Wittgenstein (1958), *Philosophical Investigations*. Translated by G. E. M. Anscombe, § 66 and § 67. New York: Macmillan.

ining the strangers. Even in light of the usage of the concept of migration in contemporary political and academic discourse, i.e. referring to the arrival of populations after the construction of nation states of the nineteenth and twentieth centuries, it is still possible to see how the Irish were imagined as religious strangers, how Germans were imagined as strangers due to the World Wars, how Italians' loyalty was questioned during the second World War and so on.[5] Different groups of people have been imagined as strangers all throughout Britain's modern history. But now, people of Irish, German or Italian ancestry have ceased to be considered strangers because they share far more similarities with the British than people from Asia and Africa. One way to relieve the concern about immigration is, as the UK government did, to change the criteria of counting immigrants. They would then see an immediate drop in immigration numbers.[6] But this is even more proof about how arbitrary such standards are.

Nevertheless, dismissing such standards as arbitrary cannot answer an important question: why will people of certain backgrounds be considered "local" after one or two generations, while other groups will remain "strangers" after generations of having been settled? It seems that "stranger" and "being strange" are not random constructions after all, but part of some enduring structures. One may refer to notions such as deep rootedness and a particular version of national identity, as Miller does. Yet, apart from the unconvincing arguments that these notions offer and the lack of empirical

---

[5] See for reference Panikos Panayi (2014), *An Immigration History of Britain: Multicultural Racism since 1800*. London: Routledge.

[6] Chandra Kukathas mentions that the UK government stopped counting students as immigrants in 2017, which "dramatically reduced the immigration numbers that the government has been trying to bring down unsuccessfully for years." This change in the criteria of counting immigrants, Kukathas maintains, shows that defining immigration is not only a legal matter, it is a matter of political preference as well. See Kukathas, "Controlling Immigration Means Controlling Citizens." I cannot find news fitting precisely into the timeline. But later recurrences of similar affairs show that "who counts as an immigrant" is rather a matter of political operation seeking to balance economic goals, a country's international image and competence as well as public opinions that view immigration in a predominantly negative way. See for reference Sean Coughlan (2018), "Overseas students should 'stay in migration target,'" *BBC*, https://www.bbc.com/news/education-45483366, last accessed February 2023. Sophie Hogan (2022), "Remove international student numbers from migration figures, says MPs," *The Pie News*, https://thepienews.com/news/intl-student-numbers-removal-net-migration/, last accessed February 2023. Bridget Anderson and Scott Blinder (2019), "Who Counts as a Migrant? Definitions and their Consequences" (continuous updates), *The Migration Observatory*, https://migrationobservatory.ox.ac.uk/resources/briefings/who-counts-as-a-migrant-definitions-and-their-consequences/, last accessed February 2023.

data supporting the claim that national identity is the primary source of how people identify themselves with each other, there is an additional problem with adopting such criteria. The stranger-immigrant association exhibits a similar circularity to that of anti-Chinese resentment in Indonesia. That is, in order to identify "'strangers' in our midst" and to prevent them from transforming the nation, one needs to be on the lookout for certain qualities, such as physical appearance or cultural characteristics signaling that some people are not as deeply rooted as the locals are. To some extent, the very process of identifying strangers presupposes that some people cannot be viewed as equal members of society. When "deeply rooted" – however that may be defined – is seen as part of being "one of us," those who do not share this quality bear it much like an "original sin." According to this way of thinking, applying a reactionary and exclusionary concept of national identity becomes the only possible way to "protect" the nation.

Apart from "deep rootedness," Miller also particularly stresses factors like the place of origin or the cultural background of people involved in riots or unpleasant behaviors, as if belonging to a different community is the only or the overarching reason why some people are not law-abiding. His continuous references to riots and crimes in places with large immigrant populations, such as Paris, Stockholm and so on, reinforce the alleged causal link between immigrants and social problems.[7] Of course, this impression may very well seem true for some people, but certainly more proof than what Miller provides would be needed to determine whether immigrants are in fact more likely to commit illegal acts and cause social problems, and if so, what kind of illegal acts or problems and what are the motivations and reasons.[8]

Even when assuming the claims that immigrants or some groups of immigrants are more likely than others to commit illegal acts and therefore threatening to society were true, several points would have to be considered

---

7 See Miller (2016), *Strangers in Our Midst*, 68, 117, 152 and Chapter Eight.

8 For example, according to recent research about immigration in the United States, when undocumented immigrants are arrested for criminal offenses, it tends to be for misdemeanours rather than violent and property crimes, although being foreign has been consistently associated with overall crime. Data gathered by the study also suggest that undocumented immigrants are less likely to engage in serious crime because they seek to earn money and do not want to draw attention to themselves. The research also suggests that immigrants who have access to social services are less like to engage in crime than those who do not. See for reference Frances Bernat (2019), "Immigration and Crime," *Oxford Research Encyclopedias*, https://oxfordre.com/criminology/display/10.1093/acrefore/9780190264079. 001.0001/acrefore-9780190264079-e-93, last accessed March 2023.

in order to make adequate sense of the claims. First, most people would agree that behaviors such as stealing, smuggling and fraud are wrong. But these behaviors are wrong regardless of who commits them. Being British or Christian does not make one's bad behaviors any less wrong, just as being Asian or Black doesn't make one's bad behaviors more wrong. Stealing, gun violence and sexual assault are not new phenomena that were brought upon society by immigrants; they existed long before the so-called "migration crisis." Second, one may argue that certain problems have increased since the recent arrival of immigrants, but there are many other practical reasons for this, such as how growth is defined or how one defines having an immigrant or migrant background. Having an influx of greater numbers of people into a society is simply more likely to generate greater numbers of crime in general but not necessarily a greater crime rate. References to wrong behaviors, migrant background or perception are not convincing due to their double-standard application: 1) If the criterion is wrong behavior, then why does the category of stranger only apply to immigrants and not locals? 2) If the criterion is one's immigrant background, then why do the wrong behaviors of particular individuals count as *the* representation of a vast and diverse group of people? 3) If the criterion is locals' perception of immigrants, why do only negative perceptions count? Locals do not perceive immigrants in a homogenous way, so why leave out positive perceptions?

Besides, theoretical developments in humanities and social sciences can contribute to fluctuations in crime statistics because they can sharpen our sense and help us distinguish wrongs that have been inaccessible. For example, the emergence of the concept of "sexual harassment" is likely to increase the number of reported sexual crimes, since the improved sense of injustice can enable people to now recognize that many behaviors are "violations." Of course, this is not to say that the growth of certain problems is only conceptual but simply that concepts play a constitutive role in one's understanding of what is going on around them. What's more, it is important to note that although these claims are based on observations, they do not necessarily indicate what is really happening, as not everything is observable. As discussed in Chapter Three, observations are often consequences of deeper structures that should not be treated simply as innocent natural phenomena.

For one thing, certain social structures turn some groups of people into "strangers," though Miller omits any discussion of this; for the other, why does the experience of the "strange" only lead to the one-sided blame of immigrants? In the following, I shall first examine two structures that are responsible for making strangers and then proceed to clarify in what sense they are examples of what Iris Young calls structural injustice. I will then proceed to analyze the self-centered model of "strangeness" in epistemic practice and explain in what way this model is problematic. After that, I will introduce Georg Simmel's sociological account of the "stranger," which emphasizes the emancipatory capacity of the "stranger." I shall argue that this capacity is not only conducive to reflecting upon incorrect knowledge or oppressive epistemic structures, but also to rectifying identity-based thinking. More importantly, it is more realistic than the self-centered model because it carries less preconditions and assumptions.

Structural Injustice and Two Structures That Make "Strangers"

"Structural injustices," as Young argues, "are harms that come to people as a result of structural processes in which many people participate" (Young 2003, 7). They are hard to detect because these harms do not occur in direct and/or individual form, such as A robs B of money, or a truck driver runs over a boy. Rather, structural injustices result from "the relation of social positions that condition the opportunities and life prospects of the persons located in those positions" (ibid., 6). In the case of structural injustices, mutual reinforcement is at play which makes change rather difficult. For one thing, the positioning "occurs because of the way that actions and interactions reinforce the rules and resources available for other actions and interactions involving people in other structural positions" (ibid.); for the other, the "unintended consequences of the confluence of many actions often produce and reinforce opportunities and constraints" which "make their mark on the physical conditions of future actions" "as well as on the habits and expectations of actors" (ibid.). As far as I am concerned, two structures are worth noting here, one institutional, the other epistemic. Institutional structures concern regulations, such as the ways institutions operate, while epistemic structures concern the process of normalization. In the following discussion, I shall first revisit Young's examples of structural injustices and then proceed with my analysis of structures that are responsible for making "strangers."

In Young's example, Sandy, a poor single mother of two children struggling to find an apartment that is affordable, near her work and safe for her children eventually faces homelessness since her social position of being poor, losing her apartment to a real estate developer, having children to raise, working as a salesclerk etc. determines that she does not have much of an option. Sandy possesses few resources and what is worse is that, in a real estate market like that of the US, there are very few regulations in place that could help her. Her only chance is to find a decent apartment which, via a housing subsidy program, requires a two-year waiting period. So however helpful this subsidy program sounds, it does not really work in practice as it fails to help people like Sandy who really need shelter. Sandy is suffering from structural injustices and these injustices are exacerbated with time, as her chances of finding a suitable place to stay may become less because she now has to move further away and spend more time and money on commuting. All this only makes it more difficult for her to find a place near work and convenient to take care of her children.

Multiple structural injustices intersect to result in Sandy's difficulty in finding an apartment. An economic structure that leads to the decision to turn Sandy's apartment building into condominiums, unequal pay and a public transportation system that is unfriendly to the low-income population are further possible factors that contribute to Sandy's financial problems. The absence of state-run childcare associations and the inefficiency of the housing subsidy program only add to her hopelessness of managing work and family. In the end, her circumstances may just *look like* the typical tragic life of a single mother when in fact multiple levels of injustice accumulate and combine into a mutually reinforcing mechanism of obstacles against her well-being. These injustices become so invisible that the failure of the housing subsidy program in Sandy's case seems to be simply a matter of bad luck. But as readers, we may very well ask ourselves when we see a single mother like Sandy, are we really in a position to *observe* everything and to judge her fairly? Are we really able to claim that "she hasn't tried hard enough" or that "she's unlucky"? In order to make a minimally fair judgment, one at least needs to get to know Sandy in order to have some sense of her struggles. Young points out that structural injustices are hard to detect because they result from the normal operations of certain institutions in which many people participate, and do not follow from any direct or individual harm. In Sandy's example, this would refer to something like the normal operations of markets, land use regulations, lack of public transportation choices etc. Structural injustices arise even when everyone is just following the rules, though the result is nevertheless individual, such as exploitation of the workers and people in need facing homelessness.

In a similar vein, immigrants are also subject to institutional structures. Their social participation – both the degree to which they participate and the way they participate – depends upon regulations. These structures include, but are not limited to, regulations that determine who can work, what kind of work people can do, how many hours they may work per week or year; when a person is employed, whether employers are required to justify their choice of a foreigner over a citizen; how complicated it is for landlords to rent apartments out to non-citizens, such as are they required to check the tenants' visa, and are they liable for a civil penalty when the tenants overstay their visa; how easy it is for immigrants to send their children to public schools etc. These structures are actual obstacles that limit immigrants' options with respect to work and residency. Not only do immigrants have fewer choices, but they also have fewer potential opportunities since many employers and landlords do not want to bother dealing with complicated regulations. And yet, these real obstacles are only ever visible to immigrants since these regulations are part of their lives.

Immigrants' social participation can be structurally impaired through the normal operations of institutions. In fact, there are several examples, both past and present, which show that local authorities are behind the apparent disintegration of immigrant communities. Chinatowns are now places of interest in many cities across the world. However, the formation of some early Chinatowns directly resulted from structural injustices. For example, the Chinese Exclusion Act transformed the early Chinatown in San Francisco from a place of leisure and trade into a place of refuge.[9] When Chinese Americans couldn't find any place to stay or work, they had to start their own communities to support themselves. Of course, structural injustices were not the only causes responsible for the formation of Chinatowns as other contingencies were at play, but social structures nevertheless formed an important part of their origin.[10]

---

9 See for reference Charles J. McClain (1994), *In Search of Equality: The Chinese Struggle Against Discrimination in the Nineteenth-Century America*. Berkeley: University of California Press. Philip P. Choy (2012), *San Francisco Chinatown: A Guide to its History and Architecture*. San Francisco: City Lights. Shih-Shan Henry Tsai (1986), *The Chinese Experience in America*. Bloomington: Indiana University Press.

10 For example, the formation of Liverpool's Chinatown was due to the trade link between Liverpool and Shanghai. That the Chinese mainly stayed in the dock area resulted from, on the one hand, the fact that they were mainly seamen working on ships, and, on the other hand, their actual difficulties with communication. The dock area was the only place where they could communicate and

I emphasize the role of social structures in a person's life and social participation because these conditions are constitutive of people's choices and actions. Judgments of other people without considering their actual social position are misleading and unreliable. Having no knowledge about immigrants' institutional restrictions and the formation of ethnic suburbs, one may easily perceive immigrants' behavior as a sign that they are not interested in integration and simply prefer to remain among their own people.[11] Consider the example of Chinese immigrants in Ireland in the last chapter: having no knowledge about the in-group diversity of Chinese immigrants, it was convenient for outside observers to follow the rigid citizen-immigrant dynamic and thereby adhere to an us-versus-them opposition, and a closer look demonstrates how severely misleading it is. People participate in a society in different ways and to different extents due to their financial situations and career plans rather than due to their descent or cultural background. However accurate or reliable one's observations may be, one can only observe sensory occurrences, not causes. Thus, interpretations of observations always depend on one's pre-existing concepts and hermeneutical resources. Before jumping to the conclusion that immigrants are strangers who have little interest in integration, it is important to examine concepts and theories that are responsible for those conclusions in order to see whether they are controversial, biased or counterproductive.

Not only institutional structures but also the general public environment can impair immigrants' chances for social participation and make

---

make themselves understood. For reference, see Ian G. Cook and Phil G. Cubbin (2011), "Changing Symbolism and Identity in Liverpool and Manchester Chinatowns," in Mike Benbough-Jackson and Sam Davies (eds.), *Merseyside: Culture and Place*, 37–60. Newcastle: Cambridge Scholars Publishing. Keith Daniel Roberts (2017), *Liverpool Sectarianism: The Rise and Demise*. Liverpool: Liverpool University Press.

11 In some metropolitan cities such as Hong Kong and Singapore, rental racism is a common obstacle for certain groups of immigrants and hence responsible for their geographical concentration; take, for instance, the African population in the Yuen Long district of Hong Kong. As another example, the constitution of Singapore prohibits any discrimination based on race, religion, descent and place of birth, but it only protects citizens against forms of discrimination, which leaves non-citizens vulnerable to discrimination in renting markets. For a reference, see Xiaochen Su (2018), "Racism and Apartment Hunting in East Asia," *The Diplomat*, August, https://thediplomat.com/2018/08/racism-and-apartment-hunting-in-east-asia/, last accessed March 2023. See also Paul O'Connor (2019), "Ethnic Minorities and Ethnicity in Hong Kong," in Tai-lok Lui, Stephen W. K. Chiu and Ray Yep (eds.), *Routledge Handbook of Contemporary Hong Kong*, 259–274. London: Routledge.

immigrants' contributions to the receiving society invisible. For example, the Chinese workers who built the transcontinental railroads in the US during the nineteenth century have not been recognized as part of US society until only very recently.[12] In photographs of ceremonies that marked the completion of the railroad, no Chinese workers who took part in the actual building of the railway appear in the crowd. Though more than 10,000 Chinese worked on the Central Pacific Line, the Central Pacific did not keep any record of those who died on the railroad. On 28 April 1869, ten miles of track was laid in one day, which later came to be considered one of the hardest parts of the railroad's construction, but not a single Chinese worker's name was recorded in official documents.[13] The fact that these Chinese workers went unseen and forgotten is not unrelated to the then-prevailing racism and the racialized understanding of national identity thus formed, which set the tone for the idea that some people are less important or valued than others due to their descent or race.

It is not that immigrants have not participated at all in their receiving societies; it may also be the case that their efforts to participate are neglected or forgotten for other reasons. As a part of social reality, identity is very often not only the cause of unequal treatment but also the result of it. For example, the failure to recognize women scientists in the field leads to women's further marginalization in science. This marginalization concerns not only the actual difficulties women can have when pursuing a scientific career, it also concerns how the concepts of "science" and "scientist" become so deeply associated with men. This androcentric understanding of science then only further contributes to the supposed rational inferiority of women. Likewise, national identity can also take up various forms of homogeneity, whether it is according to race, descent, culture, etc. Such homogenous concepts can write the presence of (some) immigrants entirely out of history, as the example of the Chinese railroad workers demonstrate. Here, it is no longer the institutional structures alone that make "strangers" but another kind of structure, the epistemic structure.

---

12 For a reference, see U.S.Congress.House (2019), "Recognizing Chinese railroad workers who worked on the Transcontinental Railroad from 1865 to 1869, and their important contribution to the growth of the United States," *Congress.Gov*, February, https://www.congress.gov/bill/116th-congress/house-resolution/165/text, last assessed March 2023.

13 For a reference, see Stanford University's research project from 2012 to 2020, "Chinese Railroad Workers in North America Project," https://web.stanford.edu/group/chineserailroad/cgi-bin/website/, last assessed March 2023.

Evidence of immigrants' contributions, especially those from the past, raises an important question: namely, why are some perceived as strangers, regardless of how long they have settled and participated in a society? Why does this stranger-perception only happen to people of a particular race, descent or cultural background? In Young's discussion about basic social structures, she draws attention to the structure of normativity. Young explains,

"Some people claim that they suffer injustice because others identify them as belonging to groups which dominant ideologies construct as abnormal, problematically different, or despicable. Especially when dominant norms and expectations either encourage discrimination, avoidance, segregation, harassment, or violence, or fail to discourage these harms, those who suffer them are not only victims of individual morally blameworthy actions, but also suffer systematic injustice. Issues of justice such as these concern the way institutions, discourses, and practices distinguish the normal and the deviant, and the privilege they accord to persons or attributes understood as normal. While processes of normalization have important and sometimes far reaching distributive implications, they are not themselves distributions." (Young 2006, 95)

There are two things to note here. First is how the process of normalization can be unjust. Second is in what sense the process of normalization can be structurally unjust. I will address these two points separately.

Young argues that the distributive paradigm mistakenly reduces social injustice to matters of distribution. The distributive paradigm represents social goods "as though they were static things" and "evaluates justice according to the end-state pattern of persons and goods that appear on the social field" (Young 2011, 16–18). This paradigm disregards the fact that social relations and the functioning of social processes also concern justice. The model of distribution assumes "a social atomism, inasmuch as there is no internal relation among persons in society relevant to consideration of justice" (Ibis., 18). Correcting the unequal distribution of material goods does not correct the unjust process which determines how goods are distributed. That is, correcting the end-state distribution cannot prevent unequal distribution from happening. What also matters is how conditions of production are distributed, as Marx emphasizes. Young explains how the distributive paradigm is unable to capture the injustices of oppression and domination. For example, the working class suffers not only from the injustice of unequal pay; being deprived of the means of production, they are also systematically disadvantaged by lacking the power to change what determines the distribution of material goods.

"Conditions of production" concern not only material production but also knowledge production. Whose experiences are accounted for, whose vocabularies are adopted, whose worldviews are recognized and so on all affect the way of reasoning, the wrongs that can be understood, the context in which institutions operate and the kinds of justice that can be brought about. For instance, the kinds of injustice that women and homosexuals have experienced are rooted in more than just individual wrongdoings. The gender role ascribed to women and the stigmatization associated with homosexuals result, on the one hand, from structural processes in which many people participate, such as how girls are raised and how homosexuals are represented in media. On the other hand, these beliefs are also closely related to some concepts of what is normal, such as what is normal for women and what is generally normal for human beings. Concepts such as "normal" and "deviant" are more than descriptive; they are evaluative and prescriptive as well. By describing something as normal, one also implies what is right and desirable. The social structure of normativity concerns what knowledge is produced, what practices are promoted, what values are reinforced and so on.

Young cites the situation of handicapped people in order to illustrate how the lives of certain people can be practically *disabled* when the life experience of those with functioning legs becomes normalized. Handicapped people are *disabled* to the extent that a city is only equipped with infrastructures for people with functioning legs. What's worse, they become further disabled when the concept of "disability" depends *not* on "that person's attributes and capacities" but "on the extent to which the (given) infrastructure, rules, and interactive expectation of the society make it difficult for some people to develop and exercise capacities" (Young 2006, 95). For example, a person is defined as "handicapped" not because he has no capabilities but because having little use of his legs he cannot live *normally* in a society "whose basic structures include frequent stairs, curbs, narrow doorways, or machines operated with feet" (ibid.). Unfortunately, being viewed as a handicapped person, his life options will be significantly restricted, which indeed disables him.

Norms have cognitive consequences, as they condition how people see the world, themselves and others. In the case of handicapped people, when "normal" is defined as having functioning legs, it ensures that other peoples' actual capabilities will be ignored; the focus narrows solely to what is "different" or "abnormal" about those people according to a given sense of normativity. The distributive paradigm simply cannot adequately capture injustice related to normativity. As explained earlier, the injustice at issue here refers to the conditions and processes of knowledge production more than to a distributive end state. The domination of certain concepts of capability, femininity and human nature oppresses those who do not fit. Such oppression does not necessarily have to take on the form of physical violence. It can also simply make life difficult for people to participate in a society by establishing concepts and discourses that do not really allow them to render their social presence valuable, meaningful and normal.

Is there, then, a problematic epistemic structure at the heart of belonging instigating structural injustices that are responsible for constituting "strangers"? I believe that there indeed is such an epistemic structure of injustice. As I explained earlier in this chapter, Miller's "stranger" does not refer to people who one does not know but to people who somehow are not considered as deeply rooted in a society or do not belong to some kind of national culture. While in the first case, i.e. that of a stranger as someone whom one does not know, "stranger" is merely descriptive and does not in any way involve a normative standard of exclusion, in the second case, i.e. that of a stranger as someone who does not belong due to a lack of a certain feature, "stranger" results from exclusion. What's worse is that the type of exclusion in question here is neither justified not justifiable. Why should descent or cultural background be considered necessary for legitimizing someone's presence or participation in a society?

When "strangers" are identified by relying upon a presupposed concept of national identity, "strangers" are in fact made by an imagined conception of a nation. I have shown that national identity can be racialized and excluding, thereby associating it with a particular descent, cultural background or even ideology. These imaginations are forms of knowledge production that result from specific modes of processing the past and past-present relation. Which past to recount and how to recount it are matters of selection, which are themselves active choices that are often intertwined with many other factors. Things like race, descent or ideology are often pre-existing factors that are related to economic status, geopolitical context and domestic social movements other than the idea of the nation. However, these circumstantial factors can play important roles in how a nation is imagined, thereby reinforcing specific epistemic structures. As the example of the Chinese railroad workers shows, the lack of government recognition can also contribute to the making of "strangers." Thus, rectifying the domination of an oppressive and excluding understanding of national identity requires some kind of epistemic change. This means not only developing awareness of what is unjust and unjustified in the shared conception of national identity, but also how to think about belonging and co-existence in an epistemically more just way. I shall continue this discussion in Chapter Six.

Institutional as well as epistemic structures can impair immigrants' participation in the receiving society. In the contemporary world, institutional structures concern, for example, residence permits and regulations, work permits, the liabilities of employers and landlords regarding their non-citizen employees and tenants. These factors can determine how much and how difficult it is for immigrants to participate in society. Institutional structures can also make immigrants' social participation and contribution invisible or unseen. Such was the case of the Chinese railroad workers who built the transcontinental railway in the 19th century, who only recently came to be recognized. It is not that, as may be widely believed, some immigrants are not deeply rooted or made little contribution to their receiving society; rather, there are other reasons why they are neglected and forgotten. Here, I draw upon Young's account of normativity, as normativity is one of the basic social structures which can explain how injustice is not only distributive but a matter of domination and oppression as well. The latter paradigm captures how injustice inheres in the condition of production and in social relations and processes. Those who are forgotten are often people who, according to certain concepts of national identity, should not belong. They may be undesirable for various reasons, but they are all "strangers" who are not part of the nation. Their participation and contribution are unseen because they are not expected to stay or join the receiving society from the beginning. They are seen as economic units, as in the case of migrant workers, who are supposed to finish their job and leave. In that sense, they are not considered a normal part of the nation. In the next part, I shall explain how strangeness can be self-centralizing and why this use of the notion of strangeness is misleading and morally problematic. My self-centered model of strangeness is based on Linda Martín Alcoff's notion of the "not-self."

"Not-Self": The Self-Centered Model of Strangeness

Being "strange" is not an intrinsic property of someone's or some group's character. In order to identify something as "strange," one must first presuppose what is normal. That is, just because people may experience something as "strange" does not necessarily mean that there *is* something wrong in the subject matter of experience; it could also simply imply a particular tension between two sets of epistemic structures about what is normal. The self-centered model of strangeness defines the other according to the self and thus generalizes the other by replacing their particularities with what they are not according to the self. This effectively *reduces people's social existence to their relationship to a pre-existing system of norms*, without taking into consideration the possible tension between two epistemic structures.

Linda Martín Alcoff's analysis of the image of the "not-self" captures precisely this self-centered model of strangeness. She writes:

> "The people of Africa came to be viewed as [...] the disobedient son in the Bible who [...] deserved his fate of being made a servant to his brothers. [...] For the Greeks the term *barbaros* was used to designate non-Hellenophones, though in the Christian era the contrast class came to be predictably defined as one who is heathen, meaning non-Christian. [...] Thomas Aquinas defined the barbarian as one whose manner of life defies common sense...and as such, their lives do not accord with human nature. But this again works via negation, denying the Other a substantive difference. One needs to know nothing about them, their beliefs or practices, except *what they are not*. Hence, the contrast class for establishing the boundaries of civility or humanity is defined in terms not of self/Other, but in terms of self/*not-self*. Difference is reduced to a question of one's relation to the norms and belief systems of the dominant Christian European society." (Alcoff 2017, 401, original italics)

The image of the "not-self" represents the core of the self-centered model of strangeness; that is, one is strange not because who one is but because who one is *not*, according to a pre-existing set of norms.

For Alcoff, the image of the "not-self" is problematic because it represents the other as a negation of the self, which means that other peoples' particularities are left unacknowledged. In this way, they end up being compared to norms and values which have little or nothing at all to do with them. From another angle, then, this image is in effect a *de facto* negation of the other, as it dismisses the substantive difference of the other and replaces it with a forced relationship to a certain set of norms that have nothing to do with their particularities. This image of the "not-self" defines other people by *a lack*, in the way that the racial categories of "yellow" and "black" indicate a lack of "whiteness," the gendered "woman" is what a man is not, the "immigrant" is what a deeply rooted local is not.

The image of the not-self errs in that it too confidently assumes that "the self" is universal, while "the other" is particular. This arrogant asymmetry renders the self-centered model of strangeness problematic. Like the other, the self represents a particularity as well. However, due to other geopolitical and/or social-historical reasons, this particularity has been exaggerated to be universal. Alcoff bases her analysis of the "not-self" on Walter Mignolo's theo- and ego-politics of knowledge that are characteristic of the colonial mentality. According to Mignolo, the theo-politics of knowledge is the way in which 15th and 16th century Christianity systematically destroyed its competing sign-systems and mapped the world according to its own terms during colonial expansion. To the colonized in Latin America, this meant that they had to "incorporate European languages and frameworks of knowledge into their own," while the colonists "did not have to incorporate the Indigenous language and frameworks of knowledge into their own" (Mignolo 2005, 9). For the colonized, self-decentralization is hence an unavoidable consequence, since accommodating European Christianity into their knowledge framework meant that they had to respond to a different principle of knowledge that had little to do with their own. Additionally, their social positioning determined that they could not respond to that external epistemic system in the same way as the colonists responded to the indigenous one. They must accept it and identify with the way they are defined by the ideology of the colonists, whereas the colonists could easily suppress and dismiss the epistemic framework of the colonized.

In his reflections upon colonialist politics in Latin America, Mignolo notes that for the colonized people, the Enlightenment did not bring about politics that were any better than their religious predecessors'. In its earlier phase, colonialism was accompanied by Christianity while later on, as Christianity began to decline and give way to secularism, it was accompanied by reason. However, this change did not improve the colonists' views of colonized people. At first, they viewed colonized people as possessing the wrong faith, while later, they saw them as uncivilized. Beneath the different appearances, colonialist politics remained the same; that is, it held that there was only one form of rationality, just as there was only one true God. This rationality is, from today's view, far from universal, for it came from a very small group of privileged people. However, material conditions like military power at that time secured the absolute authority of this particular form of rationality. Mignolo refers to this form of colonialist politics accompanied by the Enlightment as "ego-politics" because, like the Cartesian meditation, knowledge was considered to come from the abstraction of inner experience. In this manner, knowledge claims that were different from the inner experience of the self – in this case, different from the colonists

– were dismissed as irrational.[14] Like theo-politics, which recognizes only one God, secularism solely demands the recognition of the ego. So, although the shift to secularism opened a new era in some respects, the marginalized remained excluded. It is in this sense that some scholars problematize the conventional modernity marked by the Renaissance and contrast it with the excluded moderns.[15] They see in conventional modernity the problem of self-centralization: a certain self that is geographically, physically and culturally specific but due to other contingencies has become the norm.

The image of the "not-self" is not the image of "other people" but a representation of other people according to what the self is not and hence according to the image of the self. This negation does not bring knowledge about other people but rather perpetuates the given self-knowledge in an unreflective way and presupposes what qualifies as strange. The asymmetry in this epistemic structure is clear. Being disadvantaged by their social position, colonized peoples are forced to adopt the dominant viewpoint and to decentralize their "selves," while the privileged social position of the colonists affords with the privilege of maintaining their "selves." This is what theo- and ego-politics of knowledge have in common: an imperial epistemology. Alcoff describes this in the following way: "theo-politics proposes a singular historical developmental trajectory of progress and redemption, ego-politics proposes a spatial mastery from a singular nodal point" (Alcoff 2017, 405).

Being ignorant of the particularities of the self and other people, as well as the relational context in which the self is situated fosters a vice, which Alcoff calls the "transcendental delusion"; that is, "a belief that thought can be separated from its specific, embodied, and geo-historical source" (ibid.). In this way, one loses sight of one's social position, thus arrogantly leading one to assume that one's achievement is unaffected by any pre-existing privilege, and thereby perpetuating the self. The outcome of this view, according to Alcoff,

---

14 See Mignolo (2005), *The Idea of Latin America*. For a short summary, see Alcoff (2017), "Philosophy and Philosophical Practice," 397–408. See also Mignolo (2009), "Epistemic Disobedience, Independent Thought and De-Colonial Freedom," *Theory, Culture & Society*, Vol. 26, Issue 7–8, 1–23.
15 For a reference, see Oluífeìòmi Taìíìwoĺ (2017), "Of Problem Moderns and Excluded Moderns: On the Essential Hybridity of Modernity," in Paul C. Taylor, Linda Martín Alcoff, and Luvell Anderson (eds.), *The Routledge Companion to the Philosophy of Race*, 14–27. London: Routledge. Nissim Mannathukkaren (2010), "Postcolonialism and Modernity. A Critical Realist Critique," Journal of Critical Realism, 9:3, 299–327. For Dipesh Chakrabarty, this imagined European modernity is a capitalism modernity, see Chakrabarty (2007), *Provincializing Europe: Postcolonial Thought and Historical Difference*. Princeton: Princeton University Press.

is an inability to learn. Transcendental delusion engenders the misperception of both the self and of the other: the former will be mistakenly exaggerated into universality while the latter confined to an undesirable particularity subject to the former's judgment.

Relationships are sources of self-knowledge. For example, what I know about myself is partly due to my knowledge about my family and friends, what languages I know, things I have learned from playing piano or fencing, and how my travel experiences have opened my eyes, etc. All of these are matters of human interdependence. But relationships can only be sources of knowledge provided that they are genuinely someone's relationships, not just any relationship imposed externally. However strange I may be judged according to Buddhist ethics or how my grandmother thinks one should live, I should not be held accountable for failing their standards nor should I be condemned for being strange in their eyes, provided that others are not harmed by how I live. Insofar as I am not related to either Buddhist ethics or my grandmother's life experience, those two viewpoints do not constitute my self-knowledge. If anyone should be held accountable for explaining "strangeness," it is those who make the judgment that others are strange, since they are responsible for identifying people by that label. I may be condemned for being other things, but being strange is not one of them because being strange does not result from my capacity. This is where the self-centered model of strangeness goes wrong: it is at its best a descriptive account of a particular epistemic relation with a presupposed center that is unrelated to the object of judgment. In practice, however, the self-centered model of strangeness is constantly misused as a normative basis for moral judgments and confuses self-particularity for universality.

I base my analysis of the self-centred model of strangeness on Alcoff's examination of the other in terms of the "not-self." This account helps to outline the framework of a malfunctioning sense of strangeness: it shows that misunderstanding difference can reinforce the injustice of domination and oppression. Looking at the other through the lens of the "not-self" either mistakenly decontextualizes other people by reading them against social structures that do not accommodate how they think or act, or it simplifies their motivations or actions by relying on a single social structure that is mistaken to be the overarching source of their behaviors. There is yet another aspect that needs to be noted herein. I suppose that it is now clear that people should not be understood through the lens of the (not-)self, but how exactly should that be avoided? Put otherwise, what does the self-centered model of strangeness look like in the context of actual reasoning and evaluation? In this respect, some pragmatic suggestions can be found in Martha Nussbaum's work. Nussbaum lists some intellectual vices that are common in our efforts to learn about other people: descriptive chauvinism, romanticism, normative chauvinism, arcadianism and skepticism. I will first attend to the two forms of chauvinism and then to the three other vices. Descriptive chauvinism "recreates the image of other in the image of self, *reading the strange as exactly like what is familiar*" (Nussbaum 1998, 118, my emphasis) while normative chauvinism "believes one's own tradition is the best and that others, insofar that they are different, are either wrong or inferior" (ibid., 131). Chauvinistic readings of other people misread them because they situate the other in the wrong context; that is, they fail to grasp the distinct rationality of others because the wrong context does not allow certain behaviors or thoughts to be understood in an intelligible way.

At times, the wrong context may even cause behaviors or thoughts to be counter rational. One heated topic arising out of the Muhammad cartoon controversy is whether the protest against those cartoons signals self-censorship and therefore threatens freedom of speech. If it is accepted that satire represents the inviolable right of freedom of speech, this logic will indeed lead us to perceive any protest against caricatures of Islam as some form of silencing. However, from the perspective of Muslims, especially those who took to protest, the act of caricature in question was an act of disrespect. For them, critiques of certain aberrant Muslims or religious interpretations of the Qur'an should not culminate in a general stigmatization of Islam. In addition, if I may repeat my own point, satire should not be exaggerated as the only way of exercising the freedom of speech. To the extent that both sides have their own ways of making sense of what is going on in the caricature controversy, all are obviously situated in different contexts. How one side reads the other engages in what Nussbaum calls descriptive chauvinism, i.e. recreating the strange according to what is familiar. Consequently, it is not surprising that both sides draw the conclusion that the other makes a mistake. Whether consciously or unconsciously, both sides do not notice that what they perceive to be the other's mistake is actually to some extent caused by the context in which their respective selves are situated. Decontextualization may make appropriate understanding look pessimistic, since the self is always somehow situated and the epistemic gap between two subjectivities, i.e. the self and the other, seems to be unavoidable. However, I think that an antidote to this problem is nevertheless possible; that is, it is imperative that we strive to know other people on their own terms. Such an idea is behind the ethics of difference in the last chapter, which takes its departure from the point that moral agents and recipients are different people and that a practically meaningful moral relationship can only follow from our knowledge about those involved and us treating them as equal participants in the moral relationship we are about to develop with them. Otherwise, our knowledge, both about the self and about other people, will not be improved.

Three other vices which simplify the actual complexity of other people by reading them against a single social structure are descriptive romanticism, normative arcadianism and skepticism. Nussbaum notes that in Puccini's *Madame Butterfly*, Pinkerton's deep conviction that Japanese culture is so exotic and foreign propels him to believe that a Japanese woman needs not to be treated with the same moral regard he has for his Western wife. Besides, his ignorance of the Japanese moral order makes his false belief even worse, for he is completely incapable of developing an appropriate moral relationship with the Japanese woman. He sees her as a mere plaything.

In analyzing descriptive romanticism, Nussbaum points out the precise danger of this vice. She writes:

"[The young people who were drawn to Indian culture in the 1960s and 1970s] *sought out* mystical versions of Hindu religion because they felt that these supplied what America seemed to lack—spirituality divorced from economic necessity and military aggressiveness. In so doing they, like many people before them, portrayed India as the mystical other, a portrait that distorts the real variety of Indian traditions. *People brought up in one set of habits frequently notice in the foreign only what seems different*; they take the similar things to be evidences of international Westernization (as, of course, in some cases they are) and refuse to acknowledge the authenticity of anything that looks like what they associate with the West." (Nussbaum 1998, 124, my emphasis)

The danger is that, under romanticism, the other becomes so symbolic that it becomes impossible to see them as an actual conversation partner. They simply have nothing in common with us, because their image serves the purpose of compensating for a lack. Unlike chauvinism, the misperception in romanticism does not lead to a hierarchy of superiority and inferiority; instead, it engenders an entirely unbridgeable gap. This makes further evaluation impossible, for there is simply nothing in common that could facilitate any comparison or reflection. So for Nussbaum, romanticism leads to normative arcadianism and skepticism. The former is a mistaken evaluation that simply glorifies the exotic, whereas the latter adopts a "hands-off attitude" that gives up on evaluation of any sort. While chauvinism exaggerates the self's ability, the second group of vices perpetuates the self's inability. The exaggeration of the self's inability results from misreading the other against only one single social structure and dismissing apparent commonalities. Anyhow, although epistemic dislocation can occur differently, the consequence remains the same: that is, it causes the other to be confined in a self-centered model of strangeness and it deludes the self into thinking that there are no other possibilities for interaction besides assimilation or segregation.

"Strangeness" has been perceived in a predominantly negative manner. It is a widely shared belief that, since "strangers" do not *originally* belong, their existence presents a potential threat to the integrity of the extant culture and hence should be controlled or even, when necessary, excluded. Assimilation and segregation, which are commonly used in dealing with such situations, seem to be two different methods, but in terms of purpose they are the same: both mechanisms perceive "strangeness" according to a self-centered model, and aim to undermine the actual influence of "strangers" upon the "local." In this regard, necessary identity and its related structures give the impression that assimilation or segregation is necessary for the sake of self-preservation. Of course, these necessities are often only apparent rather than justified. Moreover, though "strangeness" can be perceived negatively, it does not have to be. In order to appropriately capture the tension between two epistemic structures appropriately, it is important to make sense of "strangeness" in a different way, which is not only enriching but also conducive to reflecting upon problematic structures that persist under the guise of what is normal.

The "Stranger" and the Need for the Third Element

In this part, I shall first introduce Georg Simmel's analysis of the "stranger" as a sociological form of the third element. As I shall show, Simmel captures what is epistemically valuable about "strangers." Then, I will proceed to discuss in what sense a third element is significant for society and solidarity.

Simmel famously provides an account of the sociological form of the "stranger." For him, the construction of the "stranger" presents a distinct existence. He writes:

"If wandering is the liberation from every given point in space, and thus the conceptional opposite to fixation at such a point, the sociological form of the 'stranger' presents the unity, as it were, of these two characteristics. This phenomenon too, however, reveals that spatial relations are only the condition, on the one hand, and the symbol, on the other, of human relations. The stranger is thus being discussed here, not in the sense often touched upon in the past, as the wanderer who comes today and goes tomorrow, but rather as the person who comes today and stays tomorrow. He is, so to speak, the potential wanderer: although he has not moved on, he has not quite overcome the freedom of coming and going. He is fixed within a particular spatial group, or within a group whose boundaries are similar to spatial boundaries. But his position in this group is determined, essentially, by the fact that he has not belonged to it from the beginning, that he imports qualities into it, which do not and cannot stem from the group itself." (Simmel 1950, 402)

According to Simmel, the "stranger" is neither fixed nor ephemeral; he is a third element located between "local" and "wanderer." Locals are fixed, while wanderers are ephemeral. To some extent, they are both located in blind spots: the wanderers cannot reflect upon local life because their ephemeral existence does not allow them to properly grasp it, while the locals' incapacity to reflect results from their taking for granted how they live.

The "stranger," one who comes today and stays tomorrow, shares the quality of coming from elsewhere with the wanderer (or in the case of the immigrant, this can also be interpreted as "having inherited qualities that are from elsewhere") and shares the quality of staying here with the local. This spatial feature enables the "stranger" to make an *effectual* difference that both locals and wanderers are unable to do; namely, to import qualities that do not and cannot stem from the spatial group where the stranger now is. In this sense, the stranger's spatial proximity is epistemically significant. Locals are not in a position to make a difference because they do not know what differences are possible; but wanderers are not in a position to do so either, for they don't know how to import those qualities that could make a difference. Put otherwise, locals lack know-that, while wanderers lack know-how. But the stranger is the one who bears the possibility of bringing together know-that with know-how.

Simmel continues:

"The unity of nearness and remoteness involved in every human relation is organized, in the phenomenon of the stranger, in a way which may be most briefly formulated by saying that in the relationship to him, distance means that he, who is close by, is far, and strangeness means that he, who also is far, is actually near. For, to be a stranger is naturally a very positive relation; it is a specific form of interaction. The inhabitants of Sirius are not really strangers to us, at least not in any social logically relevant sense: they do not exist for us at all; they are beyond far and near. The stranger, like the poor and like sundry 'inner enemies,' is an element of the group itself. His position as a full-fledged member involves both being outside it and confronting it." (Ibid.)

The stranger unites the far with the near, in the sense that the far becomes near and the near becomes far. The far becomes near because strangers import "qualities that cannot stem from here," whereas the near also becomes far because strangers' particular qualities indirectly put what locals take for granted into question. Simmel notes that the "stranger" is actually an internal element to a group, as are notions like the "poor" and the "enemy." Without knowing what or who the "self" is, there can be no such thing as the "stranger."

Concepts such as the "poor" and the "enemy" also require some kind of presupposed standard in order to mean anything at all. In calling something "strange," some standpoints are always presupposed as "normal," as the example of "self/not-self" shows. Simmel remarks that there is no point of talking about the "inhabitants of Sirius" as "strange" because they don't exist in relation to us in any meaningful sense. Insofar as they do not constitute or influence how we understand ourselves in any way, they are beyond the far and the near, meaning that there is no way to describe them as "strangers." As Simmel highlights, "strangeness" reveals more about the self than the other because the reason for the other appearing strange lies in the self. Therefore, it is in fact a mistake to simply focus on *what* is strange without thinking how come *this* is strange, *but not that*. That is to say that the perception of "strangeness" in fact enables us to capture the tension between the two epistemic structures at issue and thereby realizes an opportunity to examine what has been otherwise hidden.

In this regard, Simmel sees more in the figure of the "stranger" than how they have normally been perceived; ultimately, he appreciates "strangers." In comparison to Miller's "stranger," Simmel's "stranger" poses questions to the otherwise legitimately assumed self-standard while Miller's "stranger" simply enhances that self-standard. I do not suggest that Simmel and Miller are equal rivals, and it is not a matter of personal preference to choose either one of them. The self-centered model of strangeness, which Miller's stranger represents, exhibits severe mistakes. It too easily presumes what the self takes to be normal; what's more, such a self-centered model often dismisses how past injustices endure by clinging onto shared conceptions of what is normal. But, just as "strangeness" can be used to reinforce pre-existing structures, it can be emancipatory as well. Simmel considers "strangeness" as the key to overcoming "either/or" binary thinking, according to which there is no third possibility except for choosing between yes or no.[16] For Simmel, this emancipatory function of strangeness can enrich human interactions and offer greater freedom for individual development.[17] Moreover, it is not only conducive to individuals but also to society. Simmel envisions the positive side of this interaction in city life, where individuals acquire the chance to delimit their individuality for something larger and more interesting than what is immediately given. The preference for individuality should not be confined within the narrow interpretation of individual freedom and ignore in which sense individuals and society can contribute to each other mutually rather than remain opposed. Simmel privileged the individual not due to a simplistic preference for individual freedom; contrarily, he recognizes that *individuals can move within different social settings and renegotiate given social bonds.*[18] In that sense, individuals can mitigate what appear to be unbridgeable gaps. Yet for that to happen, strangeness should be perceived in a decentralizing way; that is, acknowledging "strangeness" can also denote the tension between epistemic structures of different conceptions of what is normal.[19]

---

[16] Simmel considers binary thinking to be a severe shortcoming of the philosophy of the 19th and early 20th century. He notes that when philosophy only focuses on the unity and coherence of *Dasein*, this logic in fact generates an incredible narrowness and leaves no room for any life development. For a reference, see Simmel (1997), "The Crisis of Culture" (D. E. Jenkinson), in David Frisby and Mike Featherstone (eds.), *Simmel on Culture: Selected Writings*, 90–100. London: SAGE Publications (Original work published 1916). See also Vince Marotta (2012), "Georg Simmel, The Stranger and The Sociology of Knowledge," *Journal of Intercultural Studies*, Vol. 33, Issue 6, 675–689.

[17] See for reference Simmel (1950), "The Metropolis and Mental Life," translated by Kurt Wolff, in Kurt Wolff (ed.), *The Sociology of Georg Simmel*, 409–424. New York: Free Press. (Original work published 1903)

[18] I want to thank Antonio Calcagno for pointing this out to me.

[19] Christian Neuhäuser pointed out to me that "strangeness" and "stranger" are concepts that are tainted in such a way that they cannot be rescued, or at least not under present conditions. Therefore, it remains a question whether my attempt to advocate the Simmelian understanding of "stranger" and "strangeness" is realistic at all. I agree with his observation. Under present conditions, Miller's use of "stranger" indeed represents how the concept is widely understood today, namely as expressing a negative and even undesirable connotation. However, by revisiting and discussing the Simmelian concepts, I aim not to change how the concept is commonly used today – not because I do not want to, but because it is simply impossible. What I want to achieve primarily is to point out the overlooked emancipatory capacity of "strange" by clarifying the epistemic structure of "strange" and its logical relation to "normal." However closely "stranger" and "strangeness" may be used to express negative meanings under present conditions, that epistemic structure remains the same.

The "stranger" is not as threatening or disadvantageous as Miller depicts. Of course, this is not to deny that there are people who violate the law or who support the oppression of women and homosexuals among those with a migrant background. The problem with Miller's "stranger" is that he uncritically adopts what he claims to be the inevitable perception of "immigrants" and builds on it his unrealistic position of the so-called "weak cosmopolitan." In so doing, he reinforces myths around national identity and misrepresents the political, the economic and the historical role of immigration. Such a notion is not only unjustified but also predetermines that some people can never belong, no matter how hard they try. They will always be "strangers" despite having settled down generations ago. The shared conceptions of nation and national identity can end up impairing not only immigrants' social participation but also the overall solidarity of a society, especially in cases where there are national minorities. National identity, be it based on a supposedly deep rootedness or some shared culture, is at best an apparent rather than a justified necessity. It can be made necessary, but its apparent necessity depends on contingencies, exclusions and the structural process that solidify it into an absolute value.

It is not just that the shared conception of national identity can bear racist or ethnocentric marks. Moreover, the idea that "nation" is necessary to the social solidarity of the receiving society only begs the question of why the idea of the nation *should* be necessary, especially as Fine and Sangiovanni pointed out that there is no empirical evidence supporting the claim that with national identity comes a kind of solidarity that is lacking if one looks just at economic and political relationships (Fine and Sangiovanni 2015, 193–210). Certainly, "nation" can be made necessary, and it can generate some emotional ties, but whether it is morally justified is a different matter. What's more is that prioritizing a specific idea of nation or national identity means promoting solidarity in a particular way, such as in the form of nationalism or populism. This kind of "solidarity" is only illusionary, because it unites some people at the expense of dividing them from other people. Such "solidarity" is only apparent because it perpetuates unjust structures rather than correcting them. Solidarity with those who suffer from gender, race, and class oppression may also require singling out some people who perpetuate gender, race, and class related injustices, but this singling out aims at correcting agential as well as structural wrongs. Hence, this solidarity is not illusionary, for it indeed makes more voices heard and improves the overall understanding of experiences that used to be obscured. However, this is not the case with promoting a version of the nation that is based on a mystifying notion such as deep rootedness. The latter only perpetuates what has been taken for granted rather than re-examining the idea in order to correct wrongs and biases.

The emancipatory capacity that Simmel sees in the "stranger" indicates a self-negotiating model of strangeness. As opposed to the self-centered model, the self-negotiating model of strangeness acknowledges the epistemic value of the "stranger"; namely, by providing a third element that goes beyond "either/or" dualistic thinking. The "stranger" also opens the possibility of reflecting upon structures of normativity. The relational feature that "strange" represents can raise questions about things we were too blind to see. In this manner, "strangeness" is technically speaking similar to Bertolt Brecht's alienation effect (*Verfremdungseffekt*), which distances the audience from un- or subconscious identification and thereby contributes to uncovering invisible conditions that are mistakenly taken as necessary or natural.[20] Uncovering life conditions fosters the capacity to re-include that which had been excluded from the realm of morality due to what appears to be necessary or natural. In this manner, the construction of moral relationships as well as the related norms can be rethought and reevaluated.

The self-centered model of strangeness presumes the self as the standard. It simply depicts as "strange" those who are too different without taking into consideration that the perception of "strange" can also indicate the tension between different epistemic structures about what is normal. In contrast, the self-negotiating model deploys the perception of "strange" as a chance to question or even challenge the self.[21] It does so by taking seriously the tension between different epistemic structures indicated by "strangeness." To the extent that the self-negotiating model does not take the standard of the self for granted, it can effectively facilitate the cultiva-

---

[20] See for reference Bertolt Brecht (1967), *Schriften zum Theater. Gesammelte Werke 15*, 339–379. Frankfurt am Main: Suhrkamp. And Walter Benjamin (1977), "Was ist das epische Theater?," in Rolf Tiedemann and Hermann Schweppenhäuser (eds.), *Walter Benjamin Gesammelte Schriften II·1*, 519–539. Frankfurt am Main: Suhrkamp.

[21] In this regard, consider how the everyday experience of learning challenges what the self is familiar with. Learning languages is a common experience to many people. Translations more or less help in the process of learning, but more importantly, learning a new language requires us to learn to think and express ourselves in that language. The latter practically means to abandon ways of constructing sentences and formulations that we are used to. Translation cannot teach us that. Part of learning new languages means learning new ways of organizing thoughts, which is irreducible and untranslatable.

tion of the self. It takes into consideration that the underlying norm can make moral relationships seem difficult or even impossible (or natural) for certain groups of people. National identity is not lacking as a source of social solidarity to the extent that it can be a source of collective ties; rather, it is lacking to the extent that it should be made necessary. Among all the things that are truly and justifiably necessary for social participation, i.e. expertise, language skills and the willingness to contribute, why does national identity stand out as a necessity? I don't see how the answer can imply anything but some sort of centrism, as in ethnocentrism, be it in racial terms or cultural terms.

Solidarity that is based on given relationships, such as the one based on the shared conception of national identity, is only apparent since it does not really concern actual socialization but only orients people according to an aspiration of the future. Given relationships omit important considerations about actual problems, such as how inequality is embedded within the social infrastructure, income gaps and the way in which social oppression impairs social solidarity. Instead, given relationships presuppose that solidarity would automatically arise once a certain pre-defined relationship is set in motion. In this regard, one may object with examples such as family and friendship, pointing out that they are instances of how a relationship in which people share commonalities can indeed enhance solidarity between its members. Hence, it is not at all wrong to say that implementing and emphasizing the shared notion of national identity can be conducive to social solidarity. However, there are three problems with this.

First, the analogy between the nation and family or friendship does not work as it is supposed because family and friendship are not given relationships. They are made relationships. We make friends; our friends were once strangers (as in "people we don't know") to us. Regarding family, we should not confuse family with kinship. Although there is a common assumption that families are connected by blood relation, blood is neither a sufficient nor a necessary condition for family. Family can very well result from love relationships and adoptions, and not all people who are related to me by blood are part of my family. I shall say more about this in the next chapter. To actually sustain a family relationship or friendship, mutual efforts and care must be involved. Second, the problem with basing social solidarity upon a presupposed idea of the nation is that it determines with whom solidarity is possible entirely on presumptions. This approach requires little actual knowledge about the persons in question and about what social problems in fact impair solidarity in a society. Instead, one simply takes it on assumption that national identity is the crux of solidarity. Third, one may nevertheless insist that enhancing emotional ties can be conducive to social solidarity. This may not be wrong. But in order to avoid the mistakes analyzed in the previous two points, enhancing emotional ties requires a new conception of the nation; one that speaks to all regardless of one's descent or how deep one's rootedness is.

The problem with the notion of a given relationship is that it misleads people's way of seeing the world. This has to do not only with its potentially biased and deficient epistemic capacity but also with its unjust or unjustifiable moral view. Consider the debate regarding "society" (*Gesellschaft*) and "community" (*Gemeinschaft*) between Ferdinand Tönnies and Helmuth Plessner. Tönnies claims that "communitas" (as in community) and "societas" (as in society) are the only forms of interpersonal interaction. And, while the communal interaction is directed by natural elements such as blood (relatives), place (neighbors) and spirit (friendship), the social interaction is instrumental. People that come together via social interaction are not essentially connected; rather, there is an instrumental purpose to be fulfilled, such as in business. This voluntary feature (*Kürwille*) of social interaction determines that social interaction does not serve the common good like communal interaction (*Wesenswille*). What Plessner considers untrue in Tönnies' theory is the supposed notion of a pure form of interaction. For Plessner, there is no such thing as a pure form of communal or social interaction as Tönnies claims; rather, communal and social interactions are intertwined with each other. What's more, Plessner considers Tönnies' preference for communal interaction to be a form of radicalism, which assumes that the Good and the True is only to be found in origins such as blood, place or spirit.

From the perspective of a given relationship, be it based on blood or ancestry, the presence of "strangers" can be interpreted as a sign of danger, for it indicates a loss of touch with what is true and good. In this way, moral panic can divert locals' dissatisfaction towards "strangers," since it seems as if strangers have "destroyed" the very routines locals had been enjoying for so long. But strangers are not necessarily threatening to social solidarity; in contrast, they may contribute to a more inclusive and realistic form of social solidarity by revealing a pretentious one. Miller's strangers are immigrants, people whose presence is considered intrusive because they are not deeply rooted in the receiving society as the locals are. This selective account leaves out important questions such as "How does a diverse country like the UK, which has been receiving people from around the world since at least the 19th century, manage to maintain such a homogenous national imagination?" or "What obstacles prevent some people from being seen as part of UK society even after generations of settlement?" I think that these questions apply not only to the UK but to many other immigration societies as well that have been receiving immigrants for decades or even centuries.

In Chapter Four, I proposed the ethics of difference as the guideline for "knowing people." It is an ethics that is moral recipient oriented and aims at the self-cultivation of moral agents. This ethics seems realistic to me, due to its epistemic premise: it asks moral agents to treat the moral recipient as a concrete other and urges moral agents to know people before they can decide what is moral and appropriate in a certain situation. In so doing, this ethics promotes a more responsible and just cognitive process than identity-based thinking. Nevertheless, virtue ethics is not enough when structural injustices are involved, for there are wrongs that go beyond the behavior of careless agents and are rooted in unjust structures. Among these structures, epistemic practices and circumstances can also uphold unjust structures. They do so via the process of normalization, which enables institutions, discourses and practices to, in one way or another, distinguish the so-called aberrant from the normal. Such epistemic structures can have far reaching distributive implications but, more importantly, they are a matter of domination and oppression, which primarily concern what knowledge is produced and how it is produced.

In this chapter, I analyzed the role of structural injustice and the two structures that are responsible for making "strangers." Based on the discussion about the emancipatory capacity of the "stranger," I argue for a self-negotiating model of making sense of what is strange. I stress the point that "being strange" is primarily a relational, rather than an intrinsic feature because in order to identify that which is strange, one must first assume what it is normal. In that sense, I suggest capturing "strangeness" primarily as the tension between different epistemic structures about what counts as normal. I placed a particular emphasis on the point that the self-centered model and the self-negotiating model are not equal rivals. Put otherwise, it is not a matter of a choice between different models because the self-centered model of strangeness may contain and perpetuate epistemic as well as moral fallibilities. In contrast, the self-negotiating model is supposed to make use of the tension between different epistemic structures in order to better reflect upon what one has been blind to see. As I shall further explore in the next chapter, the epistemic mobility "strangers" realize with their emancipatory capacity is not only horizontal, as in bringing qualities from different places, but also vertical, as in bringing qualities from different pasts. Because ways of reasoning and knowledge are products with historical features: they are produced by different contingencies, power relations and hermeneutical resources.

In the next chapter, I shall continue exploring the making of the notion of the "stranger" from a historical perspective. By examining the relation between history and alienation, I argue for an ethical understanding of history which allows history to be applied as Young's "social connection model of responsibility." As I understand it, immigration history is an important part of a nation's history, although it remains rather obscured and marginalized. One reason why the supposed nation-immigration-dichotomy persists may be that immigration has always been treated as an aberration of nation rather than as a part; immigration has always been considered to be some temporary solution to problems that a nation does not have the resource to deal with at the moment. Since immigration is temporal, immigrants should be gone as soon as those problems are solved. But the problem is that immigrants are never just immigrants. Though the identity of the "immigrant" serves as a convenient tool for the state to manage domestic issues, it also offers an incorrect epistemic basis for thinking about immigration's actual relation to a nation's well-being. Immigration is not an aberrant, but a normal part of a nation.

Six –
History and Structural Transformation

In the last chapter, I analyzed two structures that make "strangers." Apart from pointing out the relevant institutional structures, my focus has been on "normativity"; one of the basic structures of social justice. In this regard, justice primarily concerns the way to handle issues like domination and oppression, although they may also have far-reaching distributive implications. The paradigm of domination and oppression demonstrates that the organization of production conditions can affect justice issues by defining the context in which institutions operate and peoples' social relations are conditioned. Domination and oppression also concern the conditions and the process of knowledge production, such as what reasons have capacity for legitimation, what concepts and discourses are (widely) accepted, how epistemic authority and credibility are thus distributed and so on. Especially regarding normativity, issues of justice primarily concern how the conception of normality can encourage discrimination, exclusion, and violence or fail to discourage these harms.

In this regard, the making of "strangers" is not unrelated to the process of normalization; that is, a shared conception of membership that is unjust could make it difficult for some people to belong in a society, even if they have already been settled in that society for generations. Whether a group of people is "strange" to a place or "should belong" depends less on their contributions and relations to that society than on the extent to which the accustomed sense of membership makes it difficult for them to be accepted as "one of us." As a typical identity of membership, national identity is often seen as a source of solidarity that is lacking when one focuses only on economic and political relations. Among other things, I point out that not only is such an assumption and understanding of national identity mystifying and questionable, but such a conception also often turns out to be the consequence of problematic epistemic processes, such as those with hegemonic premises, discriminative frameworks and severely impoverished hermeneutical resources, as well as those that were themselves products of institutional exclusions and dominations. On the one hand, such problematic epistemic processes concern the racist, ethnocentric or otherwise excluding make-up of national identity; on the other hand, such processes only add to the doubt why national identity, or at least that particular understanding of a national identity, should be made necessary for one's social participation and presence.

In this chapter, I shall first analyze the experience of "being strangers" in the eyes of other people from the angle of Catherine Lu's interaction, structural and existential alienation, though my emphasis will be structural alienation. Then, I will explain why history has a particular role to play in redressing structural alienation, and I will demonstrate herein the ethical role of history. In the third step, I shall argue for the ethical significance of history by analyzing its role as a social connection model of responsibility. After that, I will clarify in what sense exploring history as an ethical discourse does not distort or deny facts about the past. I will then conclude with an analysis of the relationship between history and structural transformation. Structural transformation regarding integration concerns not only changing epistemic processes that are alienating to those who are predetermined to be excluded, it also concerns changing the view about making immigrants feel welcomed, which was mentioned in the first chapter. As previously suggested, this position is not only unclear but more importantly problematic. The issue herein is, to say the least, misleading because it defines the relationship between immigrants and their receiving society first and foremost as a matter of hospitality. Though this may be true of immigrants who come as students or for the purpose of work, especially those from rich or developed countries, this position misses the point when it comes to a migration population whose family first arrived at the receiving society due to colonial activities or who remain marginalized after generations of settling-down due to that society's xenophobic public culture. The latter situation concerns in particular people of color as well as people from poor or developing countries. In cases like these, the relationship between immigrants and the receiving society is above all a matter of justice because their seeming lack of integration partially results from being pushed away by the receiving society in one way or another. The latter situation is the true face of integration immigrants face: for them, integration is more than learning languages and rules, it is also about whether and to what extent they can be accepted according to their receiving society's pre-existing conception of membership. Since such a conception is unjustifiably friendly to some but hostile to others, integration means an extra burden for those who are excluded before they could even begin to try.

Alienation: the Interactional, the Structural and the Existential

The process of normalization can be alienating. Rahel Jaeggi refers to alienation as a relation of relationlessness (*eine Beziehung der Beziehunglosigkeit*). Alienation refers to the agent's failure to make oneself or the world "one's own." Jaeggi defines alienation as a condition marked not by the absence of a relation to oneself or the world but by a deficiency in the relationship that agents have to themselves, to their own actions, and to the social and natural worlds.[1] According to Jaeggi, overcoming alienation does not mean returning to an undifferentiated state of oneness with oneself and the world; rather it too is a relation: a relation of appropriation. The alienated relationships that agents have to themselves and to the world are not independent from their interactions with other people. Those who are constantly discursively demeaned and/or institutionally impaired will undoubtedly experience deficient relationships with other people. And although the symptom of alienation may give the impression that it is an individual failure to appropriate oneself,[2] social structures and interactions with other people are also major causes of alienation.

For example, homosexuals can be alienated from other people as well as from themselves where being normal is defined as being heterosexual or being involved in a relationship that is reproductive. The shared consensus

---

1 See Rahel Jaeggi (2005), *Entfremdung. Zur Aktualität eines sozialphilosophischen Problems*,19–20. Frankfurt am Main: Campus Verlag.
2 Jaeggi's description of alienation gives this impression as well. She writes that "alienation is the inability to relate to other people, to things, to social institutions and therefore, also to oneself. The alienated is, as the early Alasdair MacIntyre puts it, 'a stranger in the world that he himself has made'" (my translation. Original text: Entfremdung ist das Unvermögen, sich zu anderen Menschen, zu Dingen, zu gesellschaftlichen Institutionen und damit auch … zu sich selbst in Beziehung zu setzen. [...] Der Entfremdete ist, so die frühe Alasdair MacIntyre, 'a stranger in the world that he himself has made'." (Jaeggi 2005, 20)

among some that homosexuals are abnormal makes them vulnerable to harassment and violence. The lack of recognition also causes them to feel ashamed of themselves. In order to live a "normal" life, they must hide their sexuality or even become "heterosexual." Women can be alienated from society as well when, on the one hand, the human ideal is defined according to the male experience of being autonomous and independent while, on the other hand, the ideal of femininity is closely associated with the sexual objectification of a woman's body. Such alienation matters to how women are treated as well as to how women view themselves.

Immigrants can also experience alienation. The shared conception of national identity can preclude certain groups of people on the basis of descent, race or cultural background. They are alienated from the society because they do not share the physical and the cultural image of a nation and because accumulated discrimination and microaggression not only push them away but also provoke feelings of anger and displacement that make them question their belonging and their identification with the society where they live. What's more, another layer of the difficulty many immigrants experience in social participation is that they must try harder to justify their presence and to prove that they are the "good" ones. As if their existence alone in the society where they live is a mistake.[3]

For example, one shared experience common among second- or third-generation Asian Americans is that of feeling ashamed of their family background or even trying to deny it. They wanted to be as white as possible, thereby determining what language they speak, how they behave and how they identify. However, despite their efforts their Americanness remains unrecognized due to their descent or family background.[4] On the one hand, be-

---

[3] The body of migration literature is vast, so I will give only some of them as references here. For a diverse reflection on being an immigrant in UK and US, see Nikesh Shuka (ed.)(2017), *The Good Immigrant*. London: Unbound. Nikesh Shuka and Chimeney Suleyman (ed.) (2019), *The Good Immigrant: 26 Writers Reflect on America*. Boston: Little Brown & Co. As well as the famous Paul Gilroy (2002), *There Ain't No Black in the Union Jack*. London and New York: Routledge. For an overview of migration experience in German-speaking regions, see for reference Özkan Ezli and Gisela Staupe (ed.) (2014), *Das Neue Deutschland. Von Migration und Vielfalt*. Konstanz: Konstanz University Press. Lena Gorelik (2012), *"Sie können aber gut Deutsch!": Warum ich nicht mehr dankbar sein will, dass ich hier leben darf, und Toleranz nicht weiterhilft*. Munich: Pantheon Verlag. Aras Ören (2017), *Wir neuen Europäer*. Berlin: Verbrecher Verlag. Stéphane Maffli (2021), *Migrationsliteratur aus der Schweiz*. Bielefeld: Transcript.
[4] Apart from literature already metioned so far, see also Phuc Tran (2020), *Sigh, Gone. A Misfit's Memoir of Great Books, Punk Rock, and the Fight to Fit In*. New York: Macmillan. Helen Zia (2001), *Asian*

ing rejected as part of the nation can weaken their feeling of belonging; on the other hand, this rejection can indirectly motivate or encourage immigrants to identify more with their descent or the cultural background of their family. This is not to say that there is anything wrong with identifying with one's descent or one's family background. The point is simply to say that when it comes to how immigrants identify themselves, the receiving society plays an important role. The less immigrants' relationship to their receiving society is recognized, the more alienated from a sense of belonging they can become. Such alienation can also affect how immigrants identify themselves. They may adopt what they try to deny or may even identify more strongly with another source rather than that of their receiving society.

Based on Jaeggi's analysis, Catherine Lu distinguishes three aspects of alienation, namely the interactional, the structural and the existential. "Interactional alienation" refers to a distorted relationship between agents, when one experiences powerlessness when interacting with another, such as when slaves are alienated as property or when women are alienated as sexual objects. People are alienated when they are forced to take up a role for the sake of social orders, such as in the case of necessary identity, or when their lives are reduced to a version of the not-self. "Structural alienation," which "denotes defects of the social/political structure that hamper the ability of the appropriate agents to engage in reparatory dialogue," "may arise from the social and political institutions [...] that define agents' positional status, rights and agency, and mediate agents' interactions and activities."[5] Being placed within such social/political structure with defects, the alienated are disabled in participating "in the making of meaning in the social world" (Lu 2017, 200). Lu uses the relationship between the colonized and the colonizer as an example to demonstrate that even when the former is incorporated into the sovereign state or similar system, but as long as "their status as peoples or groups who have suffered distinct historical wrongs associated with colonialism and who may require particular forms of accommodation" is not recognized by the latter, structural alienation continues. According to

---

American Dreams: The Emergence of an American People. New York: Farrar, Straus and Giroux. Cathy Park Hong (2020), *Minor Feelings. An Asian American Reckoning*. London: One World. Frank Chin et al. (eds.) (2019), *Aiieeeee!: An Anthology of Asian American Writers*. Seattle: University of Washington Press.

5 Regarding forms of alienation see Catherine Lu (2017), *Justice and Reconciliation in World Politics*, Chapter Six. Cambridge: Cambridge University Press.

Lu, for genuine communication to happen one needs to "ask the question of who the agents are who should participate in such dialogues" (ibid., 194).

As for the relation between interactional and structural alienation, Lu notes that not every interactional form of alienation provokes the agents' structural alienation from the social and political order. Interactional alienation can just as well be contingent, due to, for example, personal ignorance about certain matters. However, structural alienation, I shall argue, is a sufficient condition for provoking interactional alienation. In Lu's example of Syrian refugees being attacked in Vancouver, Canada, the attacker's motivation was personal rather than institutionally conditioned. For Lu, this attack is clearly an interactional form of alienation but not a structural one because the attack was widely condemned by civic officials and the police treated it as a hate crime. In general, there is no evidence showing that the attacker's motivation was triggered by some institutional structure. However, it is not difficult to imagine that in places where social order is designed along the lines of necessary identity, interactional alienation will largely result from structural alienation. For example, when a nation is experienced as white, this race norm encourages people to see people of color as outsiders who do not deserve to belong. On the one hand, this is structural, for it involves practices such as what narratives are told and taught as part of national history, what the racial make-up of officials is, how immigration policies are designed, as well as the media representation of people of color and their chance of political participation. On the other hand, this is also interactional. Living in a racist environment practically means that people of color must endure discrimination and marginalization.

Regarding immigrants, I have already highlighted the fact that not all immigrants are considered undesirable or, as Miller calls them, "strangers." Indeed, this only happens to some of them. What's more is that resentment against immigration also often involves national minorities. Put differently, whatever is done in the name of immigration is not always about de facto immigrants, i.e. people without citizenship, but rather about a racist, ethnocentric or xenophobic understanding of who (should) belong. In this regard, immigration is a way of invoking and provoking the imagination of a nation. Immigration control is often framed in the language of protecting economic prosperity, cultural integrity and self-determination. However, the threat that immigrants pose to a nation is one that is assumed rather than real. The assumption that it is real requires a homogenization of not only immigrants but also citizens, as if the achievements of that nation owe to the similarities shared among citizens and the decline of that nation is due to the presence of those who are all too different. Besides institutional restrictions, structural alienation of immigrants can be facilitated by a problematic conception of national identity, the underrepresentation of national minorities and the misrepresentation of immigrants, as well as the non-cooperation of ordinary citizens in matters regarding immigrants' social participation. Last but not least, if one agrees that national identity cannot justifiably be made into a necessary condition for social belonging and participation, then the process which normalizes the apparent role of national identity should also be examined as potentially upholding unjust structures. Once structural alienation is in place, interactional alienation is likely to follow.

Lu's notion of existential alienation is such that it "denotes an agent's anxiety and uncertainty about what constitutes authentic agency" and "may take the form of inauthentic or alienated agency, a condition precipitated by the disruption and collapse of social and moral frames by which agents were socialized and engaged in the activity of self-realization" (ibid., 184). Ignorance involved in interactional alienation may be accidental, as in the lack of a certain experience or in the case of personal prejudice, but ignorance in structural alienation is facilitated by substantive epistemic practices. For the oppressed as well as the dominant, structural alienation is systematic insofar as they both experience a distorted relation to the self and the world. Neither the dominant nor the oppressed possesses subjective freedom to organize their roles and aspirations in a world in which they participate; rather, they are both manipulated by external powers (though the actual effects are quite different, given that the privileged have apparently more choices than the oppressed). What life they will have has already been predetermined by the identities into which they are born. In this sense, they are both existentially alienated.

Alienation, according to Jaeggi, manifests as a relation of relationlessness, according to which a person experiences powerlessness in his/her relation to him/herself and the world. Alienation, according to Lu, can be interactional, structural and existential. Framed as a "relation of relationlessness," Lu's three forms of alienation can be comprehended as the deficiency with respect to another agent, with respect to a system and with respect to one's own life. The Syrian refugee who was attacked on the street experienced interactional alienation, i.e. by not being treated as an equal person to the attacker. He did not experience structural alienation. For the attacker, however, structural alienation may nevertheless exist; the cause of the attack may very well have been what led to the refugee's interactional alienation. It is certainly possible that the attacker is racist, xenophobic or has a problematic understanding about who should belong to Canada. For the attacker, some people may not deserve to build a relationship with Canadian society, the Canadian nation or both. As part of the social order, necessary identity can cause all three forms of the alienation that Lu identifies. Alienation means more than external coercion; it also involves a process of internalization, which proceeds as follows: "Victims may internalize the morally inferior status they have in the eyes of their aggressors, while violators may come to have a distorted sense of their own moral superiority, furthering the asymmetry in relationship that makes a just relationship impossible."[6]

Structural alienation can provoke interactional alienation and in the long run, can also promote and facilitate existential alienation. The question arises, then, as to how to overcome alienation. Both Jaeggi and Lu suggests "authentic agency," though their definitions are different. Jaeggi stresses that a person should possess – or should be able to regain when deprived – himself or herself at his or her own command (*über-sich-verfügen-können*), generating the capacity to substantively criticize forms of life without needing to refer to some final metaphysical justifications of substantial ethical values, as well as interpreting relations to self and world without needing to presuppose a subject that is unified and in possession of all its power from the beginning.[7] Lu, however, being primarily concerned with decolonization, emphasizes "the idea of individuals being true to themselves rather than the passive inhabitants of roles defined by a prevailing social order" based on her understanding that "authenticity is not the enemy of demands that emanate from beyond the self; it presupposes such demands" when "(the) moral sources outside the subject" "resonate within him or her."[8]

But my take on structural alienation as well as its solution is different. Unlike Jaeggi and Lu, my discussion does not focus on what the alienated victim should do to overcome alienation. Rather, I wonder what may serve as a structural remedy for the alienating structure so that individual agents who unconsciously contribute to it, if not benefit from it, can correct their wrong-

---

6 Cited from Lu (2017), *Justice and World Politics*, 204. See also Kok-Chor Tan (2007), "Colonialism, Reparations, and Global Justice," in J. Miller and R. Kumar (eds.), *Reparations: Interdisciplinary Inquiries*, 280–306. Oxford: Oxford University Press.
7 See Jaeggi (2005), *Entfremdung*, 45–70.
8 See Lu (2017), *Justice and Reconciliation in World Politics*, 182–216.

doings and block discrimination. In Chapters Three and Four, I noted that in the case where agential wrong results from being part of a problematic epistemic environment, individuals may be innocent in the sense that they have no intentions to discriminate or exclude anyone, but the epistemic failures involved in such actions should not be dismissed as innocent because they are nurtured and upheld by unjust epistemic practices. Therefore, structural measures need to be taken in order to change the environment. As I understand it, changing such structures will also contribute to the acquisition of authentic agency both in Jaeggi and Lu's sense since one of the reasons why people become alienated is that their political and social status is demeaned by a set of practices that shape the production and distribution of epistemic and moral authority. So, changing the environment can at least eliminate some background obstacles that prevent the alienated from acquiring authentic agency.

In comparison to Jaeggi's discussion of alienation, Lu's appears to be more useful for my discussion due to the similarity of our topics. By examining historical cases of colonial injustice, Lu aims to show that the international practices of justice and reconciliation have not only historically suffered from, but also continue to reflect bias and produce injustice. Comparably, my discussion regarding integration aims to highlight that in one way or another, problematic understanding of who belongs, as embodied by the discourse of "nation," is not only a historical consequence of exclusions in the past, it also continues to influence how immigrants are viewed and how integration is understood in the present. Due to this reason, many of Lu's observations are more suited to my discussion than Jaeggi's. As the later part of this chapter will show, some of my suggestions about how to the change the epistemically problematic processes also borrow Lu's insights. In the following, I shall elaborate why and how history can be conducive to overcoming alienation and how it works. Then, I will argue that history should be thought of as a model of responsibility due to its socially connecting function, and I will underpin this argument by exploring a different understanding of history, wherein I refer to history as the site of "possibility." Finally, I will conclude by clarifying how history can contribute to structural transformation.

Why History?

History can offer a remedy to alienation. To begin with, I shall address the following questions: Why history? What can history do? Why does focusing on institutional structural injustice, such as in terms of rights, not suffice to solve injustice? The idea of leaving history behind and striving for radical freedom and self-invention is not realistic, since making sense of the present always demands some references to the past. For individuals, one may point out that no one cannot live as if their contemporary lives are not affected by their past. For structural issues, the same applies. As Young argues, though structural injustice is interpreted as contemporary injustice perpetuated and experienced by contemporary agents, it is impossible to "tell this story of the production and reproduction of structures without reference to the past" (Young 2011, 185). For one thing, as structural alienation demonstrates, past injustice is related to forms of alienation that perpetuates the structural injustice some people experience as contemporary; for the other, where past injustice occurs, there will be not only victims but also those who benefit from past injustices.

Structural alienation consists of processes in which many people participate. The structural alienation some immigrants suffer does not result from mere agential wrongs, it is a product of institutional exclusion, political oppression, social marginalization, media misrepresentation, systematic racism or ethnocentrism, and so on and so forth. Due to this reason, knowing people at the individual level will not be effective for addressing the interactional alienation which is structural in nature. In structural alienation, those who participate may simply act according to widely shared conceptions of social identities and the moral views behind them, by means of which they fail to understand the intelligibility of those who are alienated when it comes to their experience of belonging. For example, the structural alienation of race does not only result from ignoring the national minority's experience but also from the fact that a minority's experience as part of a nation cannot be rendered intelligible when a nation is defined and experienced as white. Simply adding what seems to be missing does not solve the alienation of racial minorities; rather, different structures of reasoning as well as different hermeneutical resources are needed. Problematic structures support oppressive practices and so, without structural changes, structural alienation cannot be appropriately rectified. Simply drawing attention to the alienated person may in fact turn out to reinforce the very undesirable impression that was supposed to be eliminated.

Regarding structural injustices, such as that of alienation, I think that the primary problem is the lack of knowledge about problematic epistemic practices: that is, practices that produce ignorance in the form of knowledge. In her discussion of normativity, Young argues that handicapped people will be further disabled in a society whose infrastructures and products are only developed for those with functioning legs, eyes etc. When "normal" is defined according to the attributes and capacities of one group of people, then we may not only fail to perceive the other as equally capable, but even worse, we may disable them. Their incapability will be amplified, thus only reinforcing prevailing perceptions and ignorant beliefs about them as being deviant. Said makes a similar observation about "Orientalism," which is "a mode of discourse with supporting institutions, vocabulary, scholarship, imagery, doctrines, even colonial bureaucracies and colonial styles." For Said, orientalism is "the whole network of interests inevitably brought to bear on (and therefore always involved in) any occasion when that peculiar entity 'the Orient' is in question." The orient is not just there; it is an idea, a systematic discipline by means of which the colonial Europe "gained in strength and identity" (Said 2003, 2–3).

The process of normalization has an innate structure; it has a way in which its concepts, vocabularies, set of beliefs, and its determination of whose experience is and should be adopted cooperate. Therein, discourse produces knowledge as well as ignorance; in Charles Mills' words, in this process, ignorance presents itself "unblushingly as knowledge" (Mills 2007, 13). This ignorance can be put in two different ways: the assumption of necessity or the unconsciousness of contingency. Knowledge is not always produced out of rational necessity. As Foucault argues, power relations can produce knowledge as well. Hence, we are ignorant if we suppose that all we know is only a matter of necessity. When we are ignorant of contingencies, we implicitly accept that there was no other choice than what exists, hence meaning that there is no room for ethical discussions, because the matter in question is altogether necessary. Processes of acquiring knowledge are affected by both contingencies and powers, suggesting that there are indeed other possibilities to think and act.

But then, what about forgetting identities? If gender, skin color, origin and so on can invoke structural injustice, couldn't ignoring people's identities solve structural injustice, or even eliminate potential alienation? Mills offers an answer to this question, as he explains that being color-blind does not solve but, quite contrarily, exacerbates racial discrimination. He says:

"If previously whites were colour demarcated as biologically and/or culturally unequal and superior, now through a strategic 'colour blindness' they are assimilated as putative equals to the status and situation of nonwhites on terms that negate the need for measures to repair the inequities of the past. So white normativity manifests itself in a white refusal to recognize the long history of structural discrimination that has left whites with the differential resources they have today, and all of its consequent advantages in negotiating opportunity structures. *If originally whiteness was race, then now it is racelessness, an equal status and a common history in which all have shared, with white privilege being conceptually erased.*" (Ibid., 28)

Racial segregation seems to be over, but it would be a grave mistake to think that it has no legacy. We still live in its aftermath. Past injustices have changed how various social resources are distributed and the structures of distribution are defined. What's worse is that unjust practices in the past produced biased and misleading knowledge. The epistemic dimension underpins unjust structures by providing and legitimizing problematic descriptions and explanations about the racial appearance of social achievements or failures. Mills is right in pointing out that white privilege best manifests in emphasizing the individualistic efforts of the successful, as if a person in no way benefits from racially imprinted structures. This is like saying that the children of billionaires are *self-made* millionaires whose successes are only individualistic. It is a misleading belief because it entirely ignores how social structures can make life easier for some people while they are harder for others.

Biased knowledge facilitates the endurance of unjust social structures; color or gender blindness makes an existing injustice worse by reinforcing the inability to perceive that injustice. Such blindness may seem to provide unbiased criteria, when in fact it ends up reinforcing ignorance about actual inequality. Historical episodes, such as racial segregation and colonialism, continue to shape the present; the idea or strategy of blindness hence helps to keep structural problems intact. Therefore, it is not at all pointless to turn to history for a remedy; quite contrarily, history becomes even more important, timely and urgent in addressing problems of this nature. The belief that history is useless for addressing structural injustice commits the same mistake as the blindness strategy.

History can be effective in revealing illusions and misleading beliefs. Historical studies, to paraphrase the Foucauldian point, reveal that the development of knowledge and worldviews are random rather than rationally necessary, that there is less inevitability than a knowledge discourse lets on. The point of historical analysis is to demonstrate "the contestability of [the] hegemonic status [of a conceptual framework], revealing it as a selected alternative rather than as a necessary moment in a unilinear history" (Code 1991, 49). Another illusion can often be found in thinking about political membership, such as the illusion of homogeneity manifested by the idea of nation. Neither the assumption that there is a homogenous nation which is based on "long histories and rich cultures" – as Miller puts it – nor the postulation that immigrants pose threats are free from illusions. Such statements are empirically faulty, and they reinforce the fear of economic and political decline by configuring the relationship between locals and immigrants as always having been undesirable and problematic.[9] The impression that "they are takers, and we are givers" is not unrelated to the reinforcement of a highly selective set of past events whose correlation with the present is contestable rather than inevitable.

Philipp Ther suggests that although the current public debate about social integration is constantly related to past events and past-present relations, materials regarding the past rarely receive historical examination (Ther 2017, 303). Historically related "proofs" are frequently heard especially in arguments against immigration or in favor of closed borders, whereas those arguing in favor of open borders mostly rely upon abstract theories and concepts. Although the latter do enjoy wider support among specific audiences, i.e. in universities and among academies, the former are more broadly popular and bear more success in political campaigns. Compared to memories about the past, theories are less accessible and more demanding for people without a background in philosophy, political science, sociology, etc. In order to deal with the "fear of integration" (*Integrationsängste*) more effectively, Ther thinks that we must endeavor to remind people of another potential for immigration, namely, that it has enriched the receiving society. The point is not to say that immigration is only positive, but rather to recall

---

9 This configuration is even more obvious in Plamenatz's 1965 article "Strangers in Our Midst," the title of which Miller borrows for his book. Miller thinks that his book and Plamenatz's article are closely related, both with respect to the background from which they write and that of their political concerns. Although the article is polemical and rhetorically charged, Miller considers it to be a "still instructive" piece for contemporary Europe. See Miller (2016), *Strangers in Our Midst*, 178n37.

how immigration has always been part of many nations, how they have contributed to the societies where they live. Recollecting this past aims to balance the overtly negative and selective representation of immigration. By showing the forgotten side of the past, histories of this kind are indeed unsettling; but more importantly, they provide powerful historical materials that contest the alleged necessity of the dominant narrative and its hegemonic status.[10] These narratives "make visible, intelligible, and consequent the contributions of marginalized and oppressed perspectives" (Lu 2018, 5); in this way, they offer opportunities for changing the background epistemic conditions.

Panikos Panayi, among others,[11] points out the lack of immigration history when it comes to making sense of the British nation. "For the leading historian of Britain, Professor Sir David Cannadine, immigrants simply do not exist, even though he deals with core social history issues such as class" (Panayi 2014, 12). The majority of migration historiography does not come from mainstream historians but from individuals working on the history of their own respective communities. Some such studies appeared as late as the beginning of 2000s, although immigrant groups have been a part of British society since the colonial period, such as the Indian group. Even so, it has only been in recent times (specifically, the beginning of the 21st century) that these studies began to draw wider attention.[12]

The homogenous understanding of political community may be a contingent product; however, the contingent can be very much consequential, especially when it is not corrected in time. In 1986, Professor Sir Geoffrey Elton told a Historical Association lobby in the House of Lords the following: "Schools need more English history, more kings and bishops . . . *the non-existent history of ethnic minorities and women leads to incoherent syllabuses*" (ibid.,

---

10 Apart from the abovementioned *Die Außenseiter* by Philipp Ther, many other historical studies remind us of what is left out by dominant narratives, but what is nevertheless important to understanding social reality, such as James Scott (1985), *Weapons of the Weak*. New Haven and London: Yale University Press. Natalie Zemon Davis (1997), *Women on the Margin*. Cambridge, MA: Harvard University Press. Mae M. Ngai (2014), *Impossible Subjects*. Princeton: Princeton University Press.
11 For a reference, see Tony Kushner and Kenneth Lunn (eds.) (1991), *The Politics of Marginality: Race, the Radical Right and Minorities in Twentieth Century in Britain*. London: Routledge. Robert Winder (2004), *Bloody Foreigners: The Story of Immigration to Britain*. London: Little Brown. Rosina Visram (2002), *Asians in Britain: 400 Years of History*. London: Pluto Press. Michael H. Fisher, Shompa Lahiri and Shinder Thandi (2007), *A South Asian History of Britain: Four Centuries of People from the Indian Sub-Continent*. Westport, Connecticut: Greenwood.
12 See Panayi (2014), Chapter One.

210, my emphasis). When no woman or no person of color has ever appeared in the narrative of a nation, when their stories have never been told, then at least implicitly the nation has already acquired an image of a particular gender, class and race. Therefore, Panayi remarks that "it still proves difficult to argue against Paul Gilroy's assertion that *There Ain't No Black in the Union Jack*" because the ethnic makeup of British historians decides that they "generally encounter members of ethnic minorities as restaurant owners or cleaners of their offices, rather than as their academic colleagues" (ibid., 3). Besides the empirical inaccuracy of these homogenous narratives, another disturbing problem is that their conceptual framework and corresponding epistemic practices will train and encourage the imagination of "strangers" with regard to some groups of people.[13] This consequence only reinforces the alienation of those who are already marginalized.[14] Mills points out that ignorance not only refers to a lack of experience or motivation but could also be a substantive epistemic practice.[15] Especially within oppressive system such as racial and gender order, ignorance persists in the form of knowledge.

History influences how one remembers the past, and how one remembers the past constitutes the reasons that motivate how one thinks and acts in the present. One's capacity as a moral agent is hence related to one's knowledge and beliefs. Misleading or biased knowledge about the past can therefore be highly consequential for affecting one's actions. More importantly, history narratives can shape the collective imagination of political communities, which further affects the notion of membership as well as who deserves to belong. In addition, the imaginative power social identities co-ordinate is also a historical consequence; while some are imagined as naturally compatible with a certain national identity, others are perceived as antagonistic. When the histories being told and repeated are biased and alienating, our ability as present agents to perceive injustices will also be hampered. The above example of the colorblindness strategy shows that ceasing to perceive injustices does not simply make them vanish; and what's worse, this super-

---

[13] I have conducted elsewhere a more detailed discussion about structures that contribute to the imagination of "strangers." See Wang (2021), "Imagine 'Strangers' in Our Midst."
[14] Also in the US, reports about school education show similar problems. In particular, from the perspective of US history, Asian-Amerians and Pacific-Americans simply do not seem to exist. See Stacey J. Lee and Kevin K. Kumashiro (2005), *A Report on the Status of Asian American and Pacific Islanders in Education: Beyond the "Model Minority" Stereotype*. Washington: National Education Association of the United States.
[15] See for reference Mills (1997), *The Racial Contract*. New York: Cornell University Press.

ficial strategy may in fact become a perfect accomplice that hides and perpetuates existing racist structures. In this sense, history can and should be a living force, for it reveals illusions about the coherence, inevitability and homogeneity.

However, one difficulty remains: one cannot return to the past and change what happened. How then should the role of history in correcting structural injustices be understood? According to Young, as agents of the present, we can deal with structural injustice through the way we narrate the past.[16] For one thing, encountering the past is a matter of rediscovering what has been left out and marginalized. For this purpose, new resources may be helpful in generating different perspectives. Moreover, rethinking the narrative of the past involves questioning those structures of domination and oppression which play a role in structural alienation. We don't simply narrate the past, as narratives about the past are always selected according to some standards that reflect certain beliefs and worldviews. More importantly, narratives produce knowledge about the past that can further affect our epistemic and moral capacities as agents of the present. Hence, the way in which the past is narrated and processed matters for justice in the present. In the next part, I shall first introduce the social connection model of responsibility. Then, I will argue in favor of understanding history as a social connection model of responsibility by explaining how history connects.

History as a Social Connection Model of Responsibility

To address structural injustice, Young proposes a social connection model of responsibility. According to this model, "individuals bear responsibility for structural injustice because they contribute by their actions to the processes that produce unjust outcomes" (Young 2006, 119). Unlike the liability model, according to which "responsibility" means being "guilty or at fault for having caused a harm and without valid excuses," the social connection model proposes a sense of "responsibility" according to which "we bear responsibility because we are part of the process" (ibid.).

---

16 See Young (2011), *Responsibility for Justice*.

According to Young, structural injustice is a peculiar kind of injustice since it does not result from any direct harm; rather, it is the consequence of everyone participating in a system by simply doing their jobs. Structural injustice exists even when no one intends to harm anyone else; it is a structural deficiency. Hence, those who participate in the system all bear responsibility because "they contribute by their actions to the processes that produce unjust outcomes" (ibid.,). This means that correcting structural injustice does not lie primarily in identifying a perpetrator or punishing anyone, as there might be no one to identify or punish; rather it is a matter of how the structure can be changed. However, the social connection model does not exclude the liability model. A perpetrator, if there is one, will nevertheless be punished in a society where the social connection model applies. Young concludes that there are five major characteristics of the social connection model: that is, the social connection model (1) *does not seek to isolate* those who are responsible for an injustice, and rather holds that everyone can bear responsibility in different ways such that they may have contributed to an unjust structure differently. In this sense, the responsibility sought by the social connection model is (2) a *shared* and (3) *forward-looking* one that is (4) *discharged only through collective action*. And it concerns primarily what is problematic or unacceptable in the (5) *background conditions*, such as rules and norms, that (re)produce injustice.

The social connection model and the liability model deal with different types of injustice. Structural injustice may, for instance, still involve direct harms, such as hate crimes. However, where the liability model provides the means for stopping a single hate crime, it cannot prevent more hate crimes from happening. Addressing the latter requires the social connection model. The same also applies to historical injustice. First, regarding historical injustices, perpetrators and victims are likely no longer alive, making restitution impossible because neither punishment nor compensation can any longer be carried out. Second, people who are still alive are normally not related to perpetrators or victims in a direct way; rather, they share nationality, kinship and so on by accident. This means that they are inappropriate bearers of liability or compensation. Third, even if it is possible to punish and/or compensate the perpetrators and/or the victims, historical injustice is only partially dealt with in this way. Indeed, the legacy of historical injustice may remain intact in the present-day structure, be it institutional and epistemic. That is to say that the problematic structure may continue affecting agents in the present without them being in any way aware of it. Then, the illusion of having solved injustice will conceal or even solidify the remaining injustice. The homogenous national understanding and the pretentious color-blindness discussed earlier in this chapter are on point examples of this.

What's more, without sufficiently considering the structural complexity of social reality, dealing with injustice often ends up in too simplistic a liability model consisting of perpetrators and victims. This not only fails to address the structural forms of injustice but may also turn the efforts into pointing fingers. At best, this liability model of responsibility can redress interactional alienation but not the unjust structures that cause structural alienation and promote existential alienation due to existing ignorance of structural injustices. Structural injustices are not reducible to agential injustices. Identifying and rectifying problematic structures requires treating issues of justice not only as matters of distribution but also as matters of production. In this regard, there are at least three reasons why history can be seen as a social connection model. First, histories can provide a more comprehensible understanding than the us-versus-them ideology. They can reveal other forms of injustice and problems, and in so doing, provide us access to background conditions that give rise to present problems.

For example, although the Oldham riots of 2001 seem to be what Miller calls "integration failure," a closer look shows that the conflicts between ethnic minority immigrant groups, white people and the police were the result of long-term and deep-seated segregations, for which the government was also responsible. Besides some superficial analysis which attributed the cause of the riots simply to immigrants' failure to integrate, the two official reports, the Cantle Report and the Ritchie Report did take notice of other factors, such as the declining economy and housing segregation. But the two reports nevertheless suggest the lack of a common identity as a cause of the riots, though in this case, the common identity is primarily understood as "being Oldhamer." In contrast, other analyses, especially those from the minority perspective, argue that immigrant groups never lack a common identity. They identify themselves both with the country and with the city they live in. But they keep being rejected due to racist or other reasons that deem them undesirable.[17] Or in the case of Turkish immigrants in Germany, though in the eyes of some people the clock of integration may have begun to count down at the moment of their arrival, the lack of an integration policy and the lack of a possibility for them to acquire citizenship left in limbo many Turkish

---

17 For a detailed discussion see Wang (2021), "Imagine Strangers in Our Midst."

immigrants who came as migrant workers but remained in Germany. For the later generations, many exhibit a defensive nationalism identification with Turkey due to their experience of discrimination and other forms of disadvantage related to their migration background.[18]

However, history cannot be understood according to the social connection model of responsibility unless it incorporates multiple perspectives. As illustrated above, a more comprehensible knowledge often requires including perspectives that have been conventionally ignored or excluded. A socially connecting history must not be confined to dominant narratives, as examining the past should not be confined to the purpose of upholding some presupposed necessity. In that sense, the history to which I am referring, and which can play the role of a social connection model of responsibility, demands a particular understanding of history. In this approach, history is not the discipline or domain of necessity but of possibility. I shall continue my discussion of this matter in the next part of this chapter. The point I am making here is that we don't simply narrate the past; rather, we choose which past we narrate, and we rationalize the way we narrate it. Herein lies the second reason why history can be seen as a social connection model of responsibility. The act of narrating the past is an active choice, hence a normative endeavor. There are other factors at play that concern values and ideals, just like the notion of nation never only contains a descriptive account but also a prescriptive one. Therefore, since our understanding of justice and injustice changes, the narration of the past should be examined as well, for there might be compelling reasons to abandon some outdated principles that have long dominated how we make sense of belonging and membership. By revealing problematic structures, history does not isolate individuals as blameworthy but points out wrong orientations.

So, there are multiple ways to represent and to remember the past, some perhaps more problematic than others. In addition, depending on the purpose of what inquiry we may be conducting, we can have compelling reasons for choosing one narrative rather than another. For instance, the complete absence of the history of immigration is not justified for nations that have a large population with a migrant background. When a conception of a supposedly homogenous national identity dominates – be it in racial, descent or cultural terms – there is an even stronger reason to question whether the exclusion of the history of immigration serves the purpose of upholding an

---

18 Ther (2017), *Die Außenseite r. Flucht, Flüchtlinge und Integration im modernen Europa*, 318–345.

exclusionary understanding of belonging and membership. The importance of immigration history lies not only in showing that a nation's achievements owe much to the contributions of immigrants, such as migrant workers and intellectuals, but also in reflecting those factors that are assumed to be necessary for the conception of that society's membership. In his *Die Außenseiter*, Ther addresses what he considers to be the forgotten side of immigration. The significance of his effort to tell the successful side (*Erfolgsgeschichte*) of immigrants' and refugees' integration in Europe is more than generating positive implications in contemporary debates regarding immigration. More importantly, this history also shows the illusoriness of the belief that things were better when there were no foreigners. "Strangers" have always been a part of the society, and they have contributed to the economic and cultural achievements in which Europe takes pride.

However, the following question remains: besides the reason that different histories should be told, what are the criteria for choosing which to tell or for assessing which perspective is more important? Due to limited space, I will not be able to develop a thorough account of analytically clear criteria on this matter. But I will nevertheless make several points in this regard that I find important. First, telling one history over another cannot simply be based on the criterion of being true. Both the histories of kings and the histories of peasants are true accounts of certain periods of the past in the sense that neither of them is made up. However, in telling one history rather than another, we don't choose simply based on the criterion of whether something happened or not. For why, among all the occurrences, do we tell this history as opposed to another? Second, I emphasized that telling histories from a different perspective can be conducive to reflecting whether concepts and frameworks are oppressive and whether these epistemic structures have contributed to rather invisible forms of injustice along the process of normalization, for example, structural alienation. My point has been to draw attention to the possible epistemic deficiencies of dominant concepts, discourses and hermeneutical recourses. I argued that, in this regard, there may be apparent rather than justified necessities that can only be reflected when examined under a different light.

These two points do not suffice as analytically clear criteria. However, we don't need analytically clear criteria to say that immigrants' history has been excluded from the history of nation, just like we do not need analytically clear criteria to prove that women have been largely written out of the history of science. The almost complete absence of some social groups results not from a minor neglect of details in concepts but from a fundamental exclusion of some people as equal members of that society. I have stressed several times that immigration issues never affect immigrants alone, nor do they affect all immigrants. They only affect immigrants of a certain race, descent or cultural background. And they also affect national minorities who happen to have those same features. It is not that those immigrants and national minorities have not contributed to the society in which they live but rather that they have come to be seen as undesirable due to certain conceptions of national identity. Insofar as national identity is considered necessary for legitimately participating in and being part of a society, those who do not fall into this imagination cannot truly belong. So, leaving out immigration history is not only a matter of leaving out a significant past; it also means that a particularly excluding and biased understanding of social belonging and political membership will be consequentially reinforced.

How the past is narrated, then, involves making choices; that choice of narrative is inevitably based on the purpose or interest, even if unconsciously. Apart from something being true, there are also always some present interests involved in the choice of histories. To the extent that this reason is implicit or not clear, narratives about the past can be misleading because we narrate as if it is only motivated by something being true. Once we stop deluding ourselves into thinking that we narrate the past out of necessity, we will become aware of the hidden injustice which we were too blind to see.

Throughout my discussion, I have argued and emphasized that despite its apparent legitimacy, national identity – be it based on descent, race, cultural background or a mixture of all these factors – is not really necessary for a person's social participation. Nevertheless, it can be made necessary. The making of necessity raises important questions about the responsibilities of agents in the present, for by classifying those who are one of us and those who are not, the making of necessity can determine the scope of ethics. For example, Avishai Margalit argues that we have an obligation to remember those with whom we have thick relations, such as family, friends and fellow countrymen, whereas we have no such obligation to remember strangers or people with whom we have remote or thin relations.[19] For Margalit, memory is a primary concern for ethics because it is constitutive of "care." We remem-

---

19 See Avishai Margalit (2004), *The Ethics of Memory*. Cambridge MA: Harvard University Press.

ber families and friends because we care, and we care due to our shared past. In this regard, Richard Bernstein remarks,

> "The most controversial *ethical* arguments about memory concern those with whom we have *not* had any thick caring relations. [...] We may grant Margalit's point that if we extend care to all human beings, including total strangers, we are debasing the notion of care. But it is a crucial issue for ethics – and for the ethics of memory – to *extend* our caring relations to persons about whom we might initially be quite indifferent – to persons with whom we have not had thick relations. *Ethical education involves enlarging the range of persons and things that we ought to care about.* (This does not mean that we have to extend this to all of humanity.)" (Bernstein 2004, 174, original italics)

Bernstein's point is to say that we don't have thick relations with everyone, but we can potentially develop thick relations with everyone, just as we don't simply have relationships with friends and family but develop relationships with people we initially do not know through friendship and love. And by getting to know new people and developing relationships with them, we extend the initial scope of our care. That is one point.

The other point is that, as I emphasized, since the initial scope of "us" can contain moral problems, an ethics of what to remember and how to remember must necessarily examine the making of "us" in order to be justifiable. The ethics of memory concerns more than Margalit represents. Besides questions such as whether we are obligated to remember and, if we are, who are we obligated to remember, it is also important to examine whether the notion of "us" involves unjustifiable exclusions. As I discussed in Chapter Five, "strangers" can be made, they may not be remote at all. They may have always been part of the society which "we" considered to be "our own," but they remained excluded from the scope of "us" due to racism and segregating policies. Regarding national identity, factors such as descent, cultural background and deep rootedness may in fact result in excluding people who have always been part of society and whose contributions should be more readily acknowledged. The "stranger" will remain a "stranger" if what makes them a "stranger" in the first place remains unexamined. The notion of the "stranger" is especially pertinent to matters of justice if "being strange" results from a prior exclusion.

As it appears to me, the obligation does not lie in the question of whether to remember or what to remember. It lies in reflecting upon our choice of what we have remembered, for we may have dubious or historically limited reasons for justifying what or whose history to adopt and pass on. We have an obligation to reflect upon our choices of history. We recognize some people as "one of us" by sharing memories with them, personally or symbolically, as is the case with the nation. Whether between friends, family, colleagues or fellow countrymen, the process of getting to know each other, sharing, and relating eventually gives rise to thick ethical relations. In this sense, knowing the past enables the kind of "thick" relations that we can call "ethical," and forgetting or systematically excluding the past of some people makes developing "thick relations" extremely difficult, if not impossible. Therein lies the third reason why history can connect: by building or thickening relationships. This is a shared and forward-looking collective act.

The role of history in ethics should not be underestimated. One common fallacy is to assume that thick relations are simply given rather than developed over time. This view thereby ignores the sense in which remembering and narrating a certain past can give rise to relations that we call ethical. First, consider individual examples like friendships and family ties. We make friends with people we initially do not know, and the experiences and memories we share with them give rise to our friendship. It is not the case that we first have friends and then begin to experience things with them together. The same applies to family as well. Although family comes with a stronger sense of givenness than friendship, kinship does not necessarily mean "family," even in the closest biological sense of a "parent." For Margalit, a "father-daughter" relation is a thick ethical relation, but not every "father-daughter" relation is a good one. A daughter may simply not recognize her biological father as her father in the familial sense, and vice versa. The mere fact that children cannot choose to be born makes them passive bearers of their biological parents, but whether the biological parents become their recognized family depends on many other factors, such as whether they spend time together and support each other. Or consider the case of adoption. In this case, parents don't share blood ties with the children, but this does not prevent them from developing familial relations because they accompany and support each other. In a similar vein, love relationships can develop into what we understand as family ties as well. While "kinship" is given, "family" is earned.

Now, consider collective relations like that of co-nationals or compatriots. Such a collective relation is by nature imaginative since we don't know and can never know everyone face-to-face. As Benedict Anderson notes, we have to imagine such large-scale relations via other media like language. Thus, we don't imagine our relationships herein with particular people. It is important to note that the co-national relation is almost never directly connected to a particular person; in fact, we may dislike a person who happens to be our fellow-countryman. We may even feel ashamed by his/her behavior and explain that he/she is only an exception. But our dislike for that individual will not change our national identification overall because, in having compatriots, we develop relations with national memories rather than with particular persons. Our relation to a fellow countryman does not result from us knowing him/her personally but rather from the fact that *our national identification enables us to see certain people as our fellow countrymen* and hence grant them some level of priority. Nevertheless, also regarding fellow countrymen, memory is the premise for developing thick relations, and only based on the fact of having thick relations can we further meaningfully distinguish between relations of friendship, family ties and so on.

Individually, the ethical importance of the thick relation results from choices and efforts exerted by individual agents rather than by some supposedly intrinsic features of its members. This is certainly the case with friendship and family ties. Collectively speaking, the ethical scope of political membership and social belonging is facilitated by concepts and knowledge that depend upon narratives and historical representations. Treating features such as descent, cultural background and deep rootedness as necessary will generate a notion of "us" and a narrow conception of thick relation, but such thick relation cannot convincingly justify one's obligation to remember. Just having a seemingly thick relation with someone does not always mean that that relation triggers one's obligation to remember. Especially for cases like family members and co-nationals that come with a strong sense of givenness, basing the obligation to remember simply on an unreflective acceptance of thick relations can mean reinforcing injustices, be they agential or structural. Regarding collective relations, thick relations can involve past injustices. Some people may be considered "strangers" not because they have never developed a relationship to the society in which they live, but due to other features about them that make them undesirable in the eyes of that society. If "being a stranger" means that some people will not be remembered, then they may be cursed with the "original sin" or "bad luck" that they will never be remembered or known. This will only serve to reinforce existing patterns of exclusion. We will continue to remember the past as it has always been remembered; injustices will remain invisible, and there will be no improvements to social justice. In this way, history is of no use to structural transformation for it does not provide restitution for structural injustice. I will return to this point in the later part of this chapter.

On the one hand, being a "stranger" to someone or to a group of people means not sharing memory with them, but the reason for one seeming to not share any past is equally important, as it may very well concern issues of justice. On the other hand, we are responsible for how we narrate the past, for narratives reflect not only how we connect to the past but also to which past we connect and what notion of "us" such connections generate. As I understand it, memories and a shared past are important conditions for people developing thick relations, and once they have developed such a relation, that thick relation and memory are mutually reinforced. While it may be controversial to say that a justifiable obligation to remember can be founded on the basis of a thick relation, one can at least say that it creates an obligation to reflect upon the epistemic structures that uphold concepts that are vital to thick relations, especially those that facilitate a notion of "us." This draws the discussion back to Bernstein's critique of Margalit: namely, to the crucial question of whether an ethic of memory concerns extending the scope of care to persons who do not seem to belong with "us" in any significant way.

History facilitates forming connections between people, not only by providing a richer understanding of the actual complexity of social reality but also by revealing narration as a normative endeavor and by building and thickening relations. However, as I mentioned earlier, this is not to say that history cannot be abused. While I argue in favor of understanding history as a social connection model of responsibility, I also explicitly emphasize that history can only play this role when it contains multiple perspectives and is not confined to some presumed necessity or continuity. I emphasized that a socially connecting history concerns a particular understanding of history. In the following part, I shall engage with this discussion.

History as the Site of "Possibility"

In this part, I shall address three questions. First, what is the problem with the assumption that history should be impartial or neutral? Besides concerns about the instrumentalization of history, I shall argue that this kind of assumption also disguises actual power structures. Then, I will clarify what it means to understand history as the site of "possibility." There, I will list three kinds of possibility, i.e. possibility of content, value and form. However, how to ensure that this account of "history" does not distort the past? Isn't there a danger of falling into subjectivism or inconsistency if we acknowledge the diversity of different histories and our capacity to choose among them? In the third step, I will explain in what sense understanding history as the site of possibility does not mean denying facts about the past.

I argue that history's potential for forming social connections is greatly limited when "history" is understood in terms of "necessity"; that is, when it is understood according to the view that there is a single truth, an inner coherence, or an inevitable course about the past as well as the past-present relation, and that the task of history is to find it. According to this understanding, historical representations of the same period or the same event cannot be simultaneously true but are at best different versions of a past competing for the crown of truth. When competing, every narrative attempts to show why it is more objective and neutral while the others are too subjective and contaminated by ideologies and other interests. Similar to the questionable ideal of objectivity, this understanding of history presupposes that historical knowledge should be autonomous and unaffected by the knowing subject's social position or attitude. Otherwise, what is known does not qualify as knowledge or it is not true. Earlier, I argued that both subjectivity and objectivity are conditions of knowledge, and that the alleged ideal of objectivity is itself the product of a problematic conception of subjectivity, namely that of patriarchalism and gender oppression.[20] What's more, by predetermining history in terms of what is necessarily true, history will become a handy tool for prioritizing one truth over another and avoiding relevant and important moral discussions. Like this, treating history as the site of "necessity" will perpetuate existing structural injustices, and will also aggravate existing forms of alienation by making a lack of agency look like the necessary consequence of some assumed necessity. In contrast, I argue that we need to understand history as what I call the site of "possibility" to properly grasp its relevance to matters of social justice. To treat it in this way, we need to approach history according to the idea that there are multiple truths about (an event of) the past or that they do not necessarily contradict or compete with each other. As the name suggests, by offering different narratives and by enabling the possibility to make sense of different voices, history will not only

---

20 Feminist critiques offer thorough a discussion on this matter. For a reference, see Miranda Fricker and Jennifer Hornsby (eds.) (2000), *The Cambridge Companion to Feminism in Philosophy*. Cambridge: Cambridge University Press. See also Linda Martín Alcoff and Elizabeth Potter (eds.) (1993), *Feminist Epistemologies*. London: Routledge.

become emancipatory for some people but, more importantly, can function as a social connection model of responsibility.

Foucault, for example, disagrees with the claim that "truth" suggests a (quasi-) transparent form of knowledge free from bias and limitation. He holds that "knowledge" depends upon a "regime of truth" or "a general politics of truth" that includes "the types of discourse which it accepts and makes function as true; the mechanism and instances which enable one to distinguish true and false statements; the means by which each is sanctioned; the techniques and procedures accorded value in the acquisition of truth; the status of those who are charged with saying what counts as true." A statement *functions as truth*, which is to say that, like Williams' idea of a *thick concept*, such statements are ethically loaded and morally meaningful. They not only describe, but they also evaluate. According to Foucault, "truth" is not antithetical to ideology as had previously been supposed, because "truth isn't outside power"; rather, it is "by virtue of multiple forms of constraint" and "linked in a circular relation with systems of power which produce and sustain it." According to this understanding, the mistake of thinking about the battle for truth as being "on behalf of truth" lies in the assumption that there is a transparent form of knowledge to be had. This not only obscures the power structure behind knowledge production, but also prevents one from "detaching the power of truth from the forms of hegemony, social, economic and cultural (systems)." Hence, to paraphrase Foucault, thinking history as the site of "possibility" is a matter of "ascertaining the possibility of constituting a new politics of truth" and "[changing] the political, economics, institutional régime of the production of truth."[21]

As discussed previously, knowledge is both objectively and subjectively conditioned; what's more, due to the historical characters of the knower and the knowing conditions, certain kinds of thinking and knowing can evolve and become effective only until certain processes have run their own courses. So it is not unreasonable to think that knowledge needs to be re-evaluated

---

21 For this discussion see Michel Foucault (1980), "Truth and Knowledge," in Michel Foucault, *Knowledge/Power. Selected Interviews and Other Writings 1972-1977*, 109–133. New York: Patheon. It is important to point out that Foucault does not understand power as juridical and negative, which "identifies power with a law which says no" and thereby carries "the force of prohibition." His definition of power is rather "technical and positive," in the sense that power does not simply function as repression but also produces knowledge. Power is hence also constitutive of reason. Because of this, it is meaningful to speak of "empowering the marginalized." This certainly does not mean to repress them further; rather, it means to help them reclaim their agency.

and updated, for some conditions might not exist or might no longer be legitimate. Changes in knowledge conditions necessarily put knowledge up for contest accordingly, since knowledge may be misleading or completely wrong. Besides "the possibility of content," i.e. what can be told, it is also important to consider the validity of what is told, for example, how true a statement is, whether it is still true or valid. I call this "the possibility of value." Here, the historical character of knowledge is at issue. In a sense, it is impossible to avoid the fact that the world is given in a certain way, but without considering the historical character of knowledge, existing forms of alienation are likely to be perpetrated.

In addition, historians do not simply offer an account of the past; they also try to convince the reader that their accounts are plausible. It is important to note that "history" is not free from verbal structures. In *Metahistory*, Hayden White offers a compelling analysis of how styles of plots, tropes and so on influence the explanatory effect of different historical representations of the past and of the past-present relation. Apart from the "data" provided in historical accounts, every instance of historical writing also possesses an ahistorical core, namely, its poetic and linguistic form. White notes, "considered purely as verbal structures, the works they [master historians of the 19th century such as Ranke or Tocqueville and prominent philosophers of history such as Hegel or Marx] produced appear to have radically different formal characteristics and to dispose the conceptual apparatus used to explain *the same sets of data in fundamentally different ways*" (White 2014, 4, my emphasis). For White, "history" is more than just data; it is a verbal structure in the form of a discourse of narrative prose that "purports to be a model, or icon, of past structures and processes in the interest of *explaining what they were by representing* them" (ibid., 2, original italics). This "linguistic turn" within professional history studies offers an important insight into how one thinks about what one can know about the past and the past-present relation via the body of historical writings. In short, the past cannot be directly observed, for no one can return to the past. Instead, different historical writings are used for indirect observations of the past and for suspecting about what happened and what might be a probable explanation. Hence, as long as we engage with history, we always have to engage with how it is written. In this sense, there is also "the possibility of form."

Natalie Zemon Davis makes the same point. She remarks that "[w]henever I read these royal letters of pardon and remission – and the French archives are full of them – I marvel at the literary qualities of these texts, or, I might say, their fictional qualities, by which I mean the extent to which their authors shape the events of a crime into a story" (Davis 1987, 2). The "fictional" is not only to be found within the available data itself; but, considering that historians do not always have sufficient "data" of what happened to inform their accounts, they always have to *craft* the available data into a story with a beginning, middle and ending, just as Davis did in her *The Return of Martin Guerre*. However, the biggest difference of Davis' work is that instead of guaranteeing any certainty, she shows her vulnerability as a historian, as someone who tries her best to find out what happened but nevertheless cannot know everything. Although historical writing is in a sense fictional, it nevertheless demonstrates a fundamental difference from fictions such as novels. In real fictions (e.g. Harry Potter), one indeed *can know* everything one needs in order to understand the development of the story; no more and no less. However, this is not the case with history, as in this case one pretends to know everything when one in fact can't. One always misses or ignores something, which one either misses forever or may realize later. Hence, "history" is fictional in the sense of possibility whereas real fictions are not. There is only one version of *The Lord of Rings*, no second.

When talking about history, one may expect (or at least we used to) that history will be precise, exact and independent from social positions, ideologies and so on out of the fear that it might otherwise become propaganda. Yet this conception of history is deeply problematic and misleading. Following this line of thinking, we will not be able to detect what is wrong and what may prevent us from making sense of others' experience and obscure the fact of structural injustice. The problem of thinking "history" in terms of necessity is that it is simply too unrealistic. We must assume that there is a determining coherence, essence or inevitability waiting to be found, while we can in no way prove that this is anything more than an assumption. White notes that we should not observe the world under the assumption that it "just present[s] itself to perception in the form of well-made stories, with central subjects, proper beginnings, middles, and ends" because it may simply not be the case.[22] At most, historical studies can offer a possible representation of what happened in the past with the help of limited resources. Not only social context, the particularities of historians, but also, as Davis notes, the choice of language, detail and other elements are all indispensable for pre-

---

22 See Hayden White (1981), "The Value of Narrativity in the Representation of Reality," in W. J. T. Mitchell (ed.), *On Narrative*, 249–254. Chicago: The University of Chicago Press.

senting an account that seems to both writer and reader true, meaningful, and explanatory.[23] Therein lies what I understand to be the value of history: history can function as an ethical discourse, because it offers choices, and in choosing a past, we also choose a future.

Yet as I mentioned, understanding history as an ethical discourse does not mean that history denies facts. History contains more than immediate knowledge about an occurrence, such as descriptions. For example, "two angry men threw a priest out of the window" is the immediate knowledge that I as a witness can directly acquire from an observation, while "the defenestration of Prague in 1618 triggered the Thirty Years' War" is what is normally understood as "historical knowledge." Arthur Danto notes that "historical knowledge" is closely related to, what he calls, "narrative sentences"; that is, sentences that "refer to at least two time-separated events though they only describe (are only about) the earliest event to which they refer" (Danto 2007, 143, original italics). According to Danto, history books are full of narrative sentences, so for him, since the form of "narrative sentences are so peculiarly related to our concept of history [, the] analysis of them must indicate what some of the main features of that concept are" (ibid., 149). So, the idea is that although studying "narrative sentences" cannot tell us everything we might want to know about the concept of history, it at least gives us an account of what qualifies as historical knowledge and what does not.

In comparison to the plain sentences of immediate knowledge, narrative sentences not only identify an *event* (e.g. the defenestration of Prague), but also place the event within the context of a *set of events* (e.g. the process of the Thirty Years' War). But with respect to immediate knowledge, *events* do not really exist. Though something can be witnessed from this perspective, these actions seem chaotic and lack intention. It is also impossible to place these actions into a larger context. What is important is that "narrative sentences" and plain sentences such as those of immediate knowledge are two completely different descriptions about the same occurrence. For one thing, they convey different forms of knowledge about the same occurrence; moreover, the "historical knowledge" conveyed by "narrative sentences" has an additional premise, namely, that we do not simply know about "the defenestration of Prague," rather we know it by first establishing that we are talking about it from the standpoint of the Thirty Years' War. Danto explains as follows:

---

23 See Davies (1987), *Fiction in the Archives*.

"[T]here is a class of descriptions of any event under which the event cannot be witnessed, and these descriptions are necessarily and systematically excluded from the I.C. [ideal chronicle]. The whole truth concerning an event can only be known after, and sometimes only long after the event itself has taken place, and this part of the story historians alone can tell. It is something even the best sort of witness cannot know. What we deliberately neglected to equip the Ideal Chronicler with was knowledge of the future." (Ibid., 151)

Even hypothetical ideal chroniclers who can observe everything here and now cannot have historical knowledge about the event they observe. According to Danto, historical knowledge is fundamentally different from immediate knowledge because the former is by nature a future-oriented form of knowledge; that is, it is specifically conditioned knowledge about an occurrence that can only be known under certain premises. In order to know what *really* happens when we witness two men throwing a priest out of a window, we must first know from what standpoint we are observing. Other standpoints will not reveal this occurrence to us as "the defenestration of Prague" but as something else, such as "the consequence of an unsuccessful religious reform," or indeed as nothing meaningful at all.

Danto acknowledges his debt to G. E. M. Anscombe's insights about "intention"; he says that "G. E. M. Anscombe points out that there are many descriptions of an action, only under some of which is an action intentional" (ibid., 151n1). One of Anscombe's insights is that, although both "intention" and "prediction" indicate a belief that a future state of affairs will occur, they direct the future in two different ways. "Predictions," such as that it will rain tomorrow or that he will not survive such a bad injury, are justified by *evidence*, whereas "intentions," such as I will go swimming in this hot weather or, despite his unsupportive parents, he will not give up on his relationship because he loves her, are justified by *particular reasons*.[24] In other words, "predictions" direct the future based upon what is necessary; that is, the evidence is a sufficient condition for a future state to be true, hence what the evidence predicts is the necessary outcome. Yet the relationship between "intention" and "reason" is altogether different, as we use "reasons" instead of "evidence" to justify intentions because "intentions" are not about the necessary outcomes of certain sufficient conditions but about what is useful, attractive or meaningful. "Reasons" in this case show "why it would be useful or attractive if the description came true" (Anscombe 2000, 6).

---

24 See for reference Julia Driver (2022), "Gertrude Elizabeth Margaret Anscombe," *Stanford Encyclopedia of Philosophy*, May, https://plato.stanford.edu/entries/anscombe/, last accessed March 2023.

"Evidence," such as an archaeological finding, can allow us to *predict* that certain techniques were already available some hundred years ago. "Evidence" is not a matter of whether one wants to believe something; one has to, one cannot argue out of believing. In contrast, "reason" connects the present with the past in *a more discursive way*. There is no evidence showing that those who threw priests out of windows attempted to start the Thirty Years' War in this way, but since the direct aftermath of this occurrence was directly correlated to the outbreak of the Battle of White Mountain, later known as the first battle of the Thirty Years' War, there are *reasons* to believe that this defenestration did indeed trigger the war. However, since it is a reason, it is not necessary, and one can also argue against this description of the Thirty Years' War. But for historians who recognize this description, they must justify their position by explaining what is useful or attractive in thinking like this.

In short, "facts" about the past are not denied when thinking about "history" in terms of "possibility," for past facts are secured by evidence alone. Whether we can know something in terms of fact or believe something out of a particular reason depends on the availability of evidence; that is to say, when we deny or suspect, we deny or suspect a reason (together with its purpose and its function). Telling history from different standpoints and by means of different conceptual frameworks does not mean denying what happened according to the evidence, but it does introduce the question of whether there was indeed a rational necessity (e.g. coherence or essence) behind it as some present positions claim. In this sense, history as the site of "possibility" does indeed function as an ethical discourse, for it contests the reasons, values and choices of agents in the present.

Historians such as Hayden White are concerned that history is falling prey to narrow specialization. White notes that history has become something written by historians for professionals and libraries, which has lost its practical significance. On the one hand, his worry is a reminder about the development of professional historical studies and historians' responsibility for this discipline. On the other hand, I think that White's worry bears wider relevance, for historians' works also have an impact upon what resources are available and acknowledged as relevant for the understanding of a concept, such as the "nation." Historians enjoy (greater) authority compared to non-historians when it comes to historical knowledge. Hence, their unconscious bias, problematic consensus or narrow focus, such as on the ethnic or class make-up of a nation as I discussed earlier in this chapter, can be particularly disturbing. White's concern is that within professional historical studies, historians are predominantly concerned with a dead past, which "is constructed as an end in itself, and possesses little or no value for understanding or explaining the present" (White 2014, 9). White suggests that historians should shift their focus and pay attention to "the practical past," "which all of us carry around with us in our daily lives and which we draw upon, willy-nilly and as best we can, for information, ideas, models, formulas, and strategies for solving all the practical problems – met with in whatever we conceive to be our present 'situation'" (ibid.). The term "the practical past" comes from Michael Oakeshott, who is a rather conservative political philosopher. In contrast to Oakeshott, who thinks that "the practical past" is the wrong focus for historical studies, White has a different understanding about the actual significance of "the practical past" and how it should be used.

Oakeshott believes that the essence or the true meaning of historical studies lies in finding out "the historical past," namely the past "built up by modern professional historians as the corrected and organized version of that part of whole past which has been established as having actually existed on the basis of evidence authenticated by other historians as admissible in history's court of appeal" (White 2014, 9). Apparently, this is what White identifies as "the dead past." White disagrees with Oakeshott's understanding of with what history should be concerned. He holds that such a narrow position as Oakeshott's is not only to some extent responsible for the contemporary obsolete status of history, but it also makes history into something rather arbitrary.[25] It greatly limits what (if anything) can be said about the past and the past-present relation. Clearly, Oakeshott adores what I call "history as the site of necessity." In addition, Oakeshott's position too naively supposes that (historical) knowledge can simply be produced as a purely intellectual result. He seems to forget that historians too can bear the marks of different social structures. And the previous analysis of the literary aspect of historical narratives should not be underestimated either. White advocates that historians shift their focus to the practical past. His suggestion comes from a rather professional concern, i.e. how to again make

---

25 See White (2014). For a contrast between Hayden White and Michael Oakeshott regarding the "historical past" and the "practical past," see Jonas Ahlskog (2016), "Michael Oakeshott and Hayden White on the Practical and the Historical Past," *Rethinking History: The Journal of Theory and Practice*, Vol. 20, Issue 3, 375– 394.

history practically significant. In my view, White's concern and suggestion opens other avenues worthy of exploration as well.

There is a further political implication to thinking about history as the site of "possibility," apart from what I have already indicated in this chapter. Professional historians might overlook the practical past, but politicians certainly do not. Above all, populists and the right have constantly and successfully exploited the practical past to nurture a nostalgic attitude toward a homogenous 'we' in order to serve their political purposes.[26] By instrumentalizing the practical past in a particular way, they have successfully provoked certain memories to evoke the practical past they need. And by telling narratives that stimulate the preference for a homogenous "we," they enhance how agents of the present perceive the existence of immigrants as the undesirable other. As Ther points out, the fear of integration comes from rather diffuse and vague feelings that parallel societies (*Parallelgesellschaft*) and ghettos are being built, and that the state has lost control.[27] The negative narratives of migration correspond to the ignorance established by a homogenous understanding of a nation. These narratives might not even intend to explain anything but only to reinforce the memory of good old times when there were no "foreigners", with this enhanced memory completing the rest of the work.

So in order to adjust this imbalance, those who disagree should evoke other memories and enhance other connections. They must and should remind the public of a different past or different pasts. Simply describing a fair future by using abstract theories does not work very well, for the future is not here yet and no one can guarantee that it will come. However, competing narratives can be effective because they show that there is no necessity and that there were choices in the past, so that there will also be choices for the future. Unlike history as the site of "necessity," history as the site of "possibility" concerns not only the past but also the future.

---

26 See, for example, Jason Stanley (2018), *How Fascism Works*. New York: Random House.
27 "Die Integrationsängste [...] sind von dem diffusen Gefühl getragen, dass sich die heutigen Migranten und ihre Nachfahren nicht mehr integrieren, dass sich Parallelgesellschaften und Ghettos gebildet haben, die der Staat nicht mehr unter Kontrolle hat." Ther (2017), *Die Außenseiter*, 305.

Structural Transformation

Earlier, I argued that when the past continues to be remembered as it has always been remembered, injustices are likely to continue, for structures of normativity, especially those concerning conditions of norm and value production, remain intact. In this way, history becomes the accomplice of structural injustice. In terms of "necessity," history disguises existing knowledge and social structures as necessary and inevitable. Problematic frameworks of existing marginalization and ignorance are solidified and concealed, thereby betraying the possibility of structural transformation. In emphasizing the role of history in detecting and correcting structural injustice, I argue in favor of thinking of "history" as the site of possibility, which can allow history to function as the social connection model of responsibility. As it seems to me, these suggestions can help redress the epistemically alienating structures.

Based on Young's theory of structural injustice, Lu provides a more thorough account of how structural transformation works, by refining Young's account of the social connection model of responsibility. She argues that if structural injustices "have played a causal or conditioning role in producing or reproducing objectionable social positions, conducts, or outcomes," then the responsibility to rectify or correct such structural injustices has "both backward-looking and forward-looking functions" (Lu 2017, 19). Its backward-looking function "[repudiates] the wrongs they enabled or generated" while its forward-looking function "is to eliminate any continuing unjust effects that structural injustices may produce or reproduce" (ibid.). Differently from Young, who stresses the forward-looking function of the social connection model of responsibility as a contrast to the liability model, Lu adds that in order to transform problematic structures it is absolutely essential to correct the wrongs. Young focuses on the forward-looking function because she is primarily concerned with the collective feature of structural injustice, namely that we often cannot find any direct perpetrator and that the wrong results primarily from everyone following the rules. From Lu's perspective, there is more to redressing structural injustice than understanding how structures work and acknowledging what can be done to change the structural background.

As a response to alienation, especially that produced by systematic exclusion resulting from political catastrophe such as colonialism and racism, Lu talks about the project of reconciliation. According to her, the contemporary strategies of reconciliation are inappropriate because, among other things, they tend to deal with alienation primarily as a series of individual cases; therefore, "they depoliticize the project of reconciliation" and treat alienation as a psychological problem. In this way, they fail to see the "deeper structural sources of alienation" (ibid., 183). Certainly, personal knowledge is helpful, but it may work only for cases of interactional alienation that are not structurally provoked. What personal knowledge can do is very limited if problematic discourses and its accompanying framework of knowledge are not corrected at the same time.

At an individual level, creating human voices requires other people to be seen as many-faceted persons that reason and choose without first assuming a single or an overarching identity. Collectively, creating human voices requires reexamining what structures and what practices constitute shared conceptions of political membership and social belonging. The exclusions of immigrants from national history have played a causal or constitutive role in producing and reproducing a certain understanding of a nation that, on the one hand, makes it easier to perceive some people as "strangers in our midst" and, on the other hand, makes what are in fact unnecessary identities necessary for a person's social participation and presence. Only when we recognize that backward-looking is essential to correct wrongs, we are able to reassess our capacities as agents and transform social structures in a nonalienating way.

As should be clear from my discussion so far, my standard to determine whether some structures are alienating is based on whether the norm of these structures presupposes unjustified exclusion. One may point out that for such evaluations I need concepts that are sufficiently universal, like dignity or self-respect, to show why certain social structures are alienating. But I think this view has a different interest from mine. I have no doubt that the explanation of alienating structures can be eventually plausibly related to the violation of dignity or self-respect. But as I said earlier in this chapter, my goal is not to clarify how victims of alienation can re-acquire authentic agency, like Jaeggi and Lu originally do; rather, my purpose is more technical. I am interested in demonstrating how distorted knowledge about the past nurtures problematic public environments and prevents the receiving society from realizing its epistemic responsibility, hence preventing it from becoming more epistemically just. This is the collective or the structural aspect of mutual integration. In this regard, as long as I can prove that the knowledge which supports exclusivist understandings of who belongs is wrong or severely biased, it suffices as a standard to show why a certain structure is alienating, or so I think. Put otherwise, such knowledge is not as realistic as it purports to be.

To some extent, I believe that some histories are indeed more suitable today than others. For example, histories of kings, queens or bishops can indeed still be considered a part of national history; however, while they might be interesting for professional historians studying royal or church history, they do not seem to be more suitable for school curricula than immigration history. How can they help children make sense of the diverse society they live in? I shall leave this question for professionals from history and pedagogy to answer. As argued, the need to introduce immigration history is not because that immigration history is somehow magic and can make racist, or otherwise excluding, understandings of belonging and membership vanish. Rather, by taking into consideration the historically excluded perspectives, the hope of change lies in the enrichment of hermeneutical resources. The feminist project has shown that the enriched women perspective amounts to more than just some epistemic material as it can also little by little correct unjust concepts and thinking frames as well as reveal probably more unjust and unexpected structures. What's more, another purpose of introducing better hermeneutical resources to the greatest extent possible is that this changed epistemic environment can help individual agents to notice the otherwise tacit forms of discriminations. Regarding improving the overall epistemic circumstances, there are also other thinkable measures, such as establishing an immigrant heritage month and changing misleading categories in policy-making.

Given that alienated experience is an experience of relationlessness – that is, an alienated experience of a deficiency in the relationship one has to oneself, others and the world – in order to overcome the alienated experience, those who are alienated precisely need to be able to rebuild their relations. But their ability to rebuild non-alienating relations largely depends on those privileged to stop perpetrating alienating structures and interactions. In this sense, one possible way to rebuild relations, as I argued in Chapter Four, is through cultivating virtuous agents who are capable of building morally adequate personal relations; the other way is through history as a social connection model of responsibility, which diversifies perspectives, enriches resources, breaks illusions of necessity and thickens relations.

Conclusion – Integration as Integration of People

Without clearly knowing what we are talking about when we talk about integration, discussions about integration lack a clear way forward. The notion of integration seems alarmingly similar to that of assimilation. Apart from the name, there seems to be nothing substantially different between how integration and assimilation are understood. Like assimilation, integration also seems to refer to a one-way process that is solely the responsibility of immigrants: they should integrate and so they are the ones to blame when integration fails. But when do they fail and when do they succeed? If breaking the law is the standard of failing to integrate, do citizens who break the law also fail to integrate? Or, if following social customs, having local friends or adopting a lifestyle typical of the receiving society counts as the standard, then how to measure that? How often should I adhere to given customs or how many local friends should I have in order to be considered successfully integrated? If some citizens – especially those without a migration background – happen to dislike a given custom and have many international friends, do they become disintegrated members of that society? This goes to show that there are many aspects of social life that cannot be rigidly measured, and this also points out something particular in the expectation of immigrants' integration: namely, many assumed and widely accepted standards are arbitrary and problematic, for they either only apply to immigrants or they measure the failure or success of immigrants' integration against whether and to what the degree they have assimilated themselves.

Integration may not be as strongly enforced as assimilation, but this does not mean that expectations of assimilation, such as what immigrants should do and how they should identify, cannot be carried out implicitly. Of course, this is not to say that all expectations are unjustified. Throughout the discussion, I have acknowledged that expectations such as obeying the law and learning the language (or one of the languages) of the receiving society are reasonable expectations. I am concerned, however, about those unnecessary elements that are deemed necessary for a person's social participation and presence. This not only generates unjustifiable expectations for immigrants to integrate into the receiving society but also obstructs their capacity to participate in the receiving society. As Carens noted, some of pre-existing contexts in a receiving society may very well be problematic and disadvantageous to immigrants' integration. I have focused on the role of knowledge, especially knowledge conveyed by identities and identification, such as the case of national identity. The idea is that the shared conceptions of identities not only affect one's attitudes towards immigrants, they also inform one's expectations about who belongs and who does not. This aspect of identity and identification also extends the issue of the integration of immigrants to national minorities and shows that the tension between locals and immigrants in fact resembles the tension between those who are considered part of the nation and those who are not. Resentment against immigrants never affects all immigrants but only those who do not fit into the imagination of "us."

Understanding integration as a one-way process supposes that problems can only come from outside of a society, but not from the inside. If something goes wrong, it must be the outsiders' fault. Hence, outsiders are supposed to be incorporated in such a way that their influence is minimized at the utmost in order to preserve a status quo. Yet, problems may also exist on the inside of a society, and they are likely to be ignored if integration is treated solely as the responsibility of immigrants. For example, an unequal infrastructure, the income gap between the rich and the poor, a declining economy, racism, xenophobia and so on can all contribute to social problems that impair solidarity. Considering that immigrants struggle to find jobs due to restrictions and racism, their overall social participation will therefore be negatively affected because they cannot afford anything; then, what seems to be their lack of integration could in fact be traced back to other causes rather than their being immigrants or having certain descents or cultural backgrounds. In comparison, it is also possible that immigrants from rich countries and who are not racial minorities don't even need to try hard to integrate because it is likely that the diplomatic relationship between the receiving society and where they come from determines that they face less or almost no restrictions regarding things such as getting a work permit or job hunting; moreover, not being part of a racial or cultural minority means that, in a more or less racist society, they in general face fewer obstacles than those who are racial minorities. Situations like this are common in many immigration societies among developed countries. Apart from racism, there are also hostility, resentment or discrimination based on religion, cultural background or ethnicity. Sometimes they are combined with each other, sometimes one of them is more dominant than others. But in any case, situations like this demonstrate that immigrants' integration also depends on many factors that are not under their control. Whether they can participate in their receiving society equally and successfully and in the end identify themselves with that place depends just as much on the receiving society as on themselves.

Throughout my discussion, I have stressed some unrealistic expectations exhibited by receiving societies, such as supposing that minority communities are a sign of their failure to integrate or that immigrants' different identification with certain social practices means that they have not tried hard enough to integrate. I hope to emphasize that some expectations will become too demanding to be reasonable when they are guided by the desire for homogeneity. Moreover, I wish to indicate that unrealistic expectations can also lead us to overreact to social conflicts. Not every social conflict that involves people with a migrant background signals their failure to integrate. It is unrealistic to hope for a society without conflicts, nor is it reasonable to jump too quickly to conclusions about immigrants' having failed to integrate simply because they have different opinions or because those who have different opinions do not fit into the imagination of "us." Conflict is an inevitable part of any society. It would be absurd to assume that integration should bring about a conflict-free society in which everyone is alike and identify with the same ideal in similar ways. In that case, what we hope for is assimilation.

Prevailing social orders can make salient specific ways of perceiving social reality that do not say much about what is actually going on. For example, the demand of self-preservation and cultural protection assumes that people of a certain descent and cultural background are necessarily threatening. Such an assumption glosses over the fact that not only people of different descent and cultural backgrounds have always been part of that society, but the self or the culture such demands purport to protect or preserve is the product of mixed sources.[1] The careless conclusion that immigrants fail to

---

1 As Ther argues, a closer look at immigration history within contemporary Europe shows their presence to have made enormous contributions to receiving societies. Such a conclusion does not mean denying that there have indeed been problems; rather, it is supposed to balance the

integrate risks, on the one hand, perpetuating the prevailing social orders that are responsible for misconceptions of social conflicts and, on the other hand, nurturing what Ther calls "fear of integration" (*Integrationsängste*), i.e. the vague and confused feeling that the state is losing control due to the arrival of immigrants. Perceiving immigrants exclusively as "strangers" who threaten "our" well-being means turning a blind eye to how structural failures have contributed or even caused social problems that "we" perceive to be the fault of immigrants. As Bauman remarks, we can divert our anger to the messenger for delivering a hateful message, but this does not in any way reach near the roots of the problem.

It is not wrong to insist that people should learn about the laws and the language of a receiving society. Nevertheless, there is also a limit to what immigrants can do and what can be reasonably expected from them. The one-sided and biased views about both citizens and immigrants have much to do with the all too simplistic opposition between these two groups. In assuming such an opposition, both groups are reduced in such a way as if only one identity counts for the members of these respective groups. Sacrificing in-group diversity may be convenient, but its misrepresentation of the reality can have far reaching implications. For example, an examination of the in-group diversity of the Chinese immigrants in Ireland shows that their different levels of social participation are better accounted for by studying their education background, family relations and financial situations. Although the label of "Chinese" may be the most obvious way to make sense of who they are, the old paradigm of studying immigrants based on differences in descent and cultural background misses immigrants' actual motivations in real life. Identifying as Chinese still matters to them, but that identification is not necessary for them to decide how they participate in their day-to-day life in Ireland. However, the old paradigm that relies on descent, ethnicity and cultural identities not only leaves out important information about the immigration population, it also reinforces the perception that immigrants are the cultural, historical and political other.

By focusing on integration as the "integration of people," I want to highlight the aspect that debates about integration focus overtly on the issue of rights and have not looked at immigrants as multi-faceted people. While

---

dominant view about immigrants' participation within the receiving society. There are both positive contributions and problems related to matters of immigration, just as there are challenges as well as achievements regarding integration.

questions about the (re)distribution of rights concern the institutional foundation of immigrants' participation in society and are indeed important, actual people cannot be reduced to rights holders as if rights alone matter. Concerning immigrants' participation in their receiving society there are also many rather invisible areas that improving immigrants' rights alone cannot reach. As the real experience of people with a migration background demonstrates, rights remain ineffective unless officials and ordinary citizens of the receiving society cooperate. If the public culture is xenophobic, rights will only reinforce undeserved impressions of immigrants. Xenophobia does not have to be expressed through overtly aggressive attitudes; they can be expressed in subtle ways as well. For example, if "being a foreigner" or "being an immigrant" is the only identity the media amplifies when reporting on social problems, the media effectively misleads the public into associating being a foreigner or being an immigrant with being the cause of problems. Regarding immigrants' integration in their receiving society, pre-existing contexts beyond rights can also be disadvantageous; therefore, they should be reflected upon and examined as well. However, since the debate about integration has always placed its primary focus upon rights, issues that are beyond rights but nevertheless relevant to immigrants' participation and integration remain underexplored.

Another related issue is that integration does not seem to be sufficiently distinguishable from assimilation. Among others, Parekh bluntly points out that integration is all too often considered to be a one-way process that is not altogether different from assimilation. He points out that integrationists suggest that integration means incorporating outsiders into the prevailing social structure by placing the "onus to integrate" only on immigrants, much like assimilationists. So, it follows that immigrants are to blame when they fail to be incorporated as expected in the prevailing social structures. In the Muhammad cartoon controversy, those who defended satire as a Danish tradition associated immigrants' failure to accept satire with a failure to integrate. According to them, it is only a matter of course to accept satire if one has been or has become a member of Denmark or liberal democracy. This assimilation-like approach to integration leaves no room to consider whether and to what extent the requirements to be incorporated in the prevailing structures can be too demanding to be reasonable. It also leaves no room to reflect upon whether prevailing social structures consist of anything too arbitrary. Rather, it assumes that the beliefs and forms of identification in the prevailing structures are not in any way fallible or biased but that they are to be accepted and obeyed.

This conceptual obscurity of integration also raises several practical difficulties. Without a clear and workable concept, it is hard to differentiate practices of integration from those of assimilation. When integration conceptually overlaps with assimilation, integration effectively serves as a perfect disguise for assimilation. On the one hand, an obscured understanding of integration disguises assimilation; on the other hand, insofar as this obscured understanding perpetuates alienating and exclusionary structures, it also bears the effect of segregation. In this respect, I refer to the phenomenon of the "perpetual foreigner" to explain the kind of structural foreignness or alienation that urgently needs to be dealt with. Yet, without a concept of integration that is sufficiently distinguishable from assimilation, we remain wholly handicapped in attending to those issues.

My attempt to expand the inquiry of integration beyond formal equality requires asking questions about another important aspect of everyday life, i.e. identity. I identify identity-based thinking as one pre-existing context that affects people's lives but lies beyond the realm of formal equality, such as rights. Identity-based thinking concerns how necessary identity contributes to epistemic domination and oppression, and how it impoverishes the hermeneutical resources for making sense of social experience and political membership. Necessary identity does not refer to just any group-based identity, but as Bernard Williams defines, it refers to identities that are necessary to social orders rather to their bearers. I went on to argue that it is important to distinguish justified necessities from apparent ones. Justified necessities refer to what is justifiably necessary for social participation; for example, for a legal order, it is necessary to identify behaviors that are harmful, whereas for activities requiring expertise it is necessary that participants possess professional skills. In contrast, apparent necessities are not really necessary but are rather made necessary for otherwise unjustifiable purposes, such as divide-and-rule and oppression. Not only do apparent necessities have nothing to do with the actual process of socialization, they also reduce actual people to what corresponding social orders need them to be. As apparent necessities, necessary identities are supposed to designate specific functions that primarily serve the needs of certain given social oders rather than the needs of social life. Necessary identities yield more than mere life constraints, such as those concerning social status or distributive justice, they also yield epistemic consequences. By arranging people's lives, they also generate specific circumstances that then reproduce certain perceived regularities. Regularities such as gender roles produce misleading knowledge claims, for instance that women are submissive. And such epistemic circumstances will become part of the reproduction of gender roles that keep women in submissive roles.

I argued that resentment against immigrants never affects all immigrants equally. Those who happen to share features of the imagination of the nation will not be considered threatening and undesirable. So, the guise of a "migration crisis," for instance, also allows for the resurgence of social ills like xenophobia, racism, ethnocentrism and other forms of self-serving superiority. In this regard, national minorities, i.e. people who are citizens but not considered as (equal) members of a nation, can be affected by resentment against immigrants as well. Identities such as race, descent and culture have all played a significant role in the formation of the nation. Put differently, they have come to be treated as necessary features for being a member of a nation, even though they neither result from an actual process of socialization nor can be made justifiably necessary for a person's social participation or belonging. This conception persists as part of the social imagination of who should belong and who should not. It affects how one views the presence of those who are physically and culturally different. As a necessary identity, "immigrant" no doubt offers a convenient tool for a state's control over matters such as welfare and citizenship. Yet at the same time, it offers a convenient tool to reintroduce and deepen different kinds of social division. When prevailing social orders makes certain ways of perceiving a person especially salient, that person's other identities may very easily be ignored. An immigrant may be at the same time poor, a member of a sexual minority and suffer from chronological disease. While "being an immigrant" is something that social orders alone can make it salient to perceive (such as via race and religion), we will not be able to know the latter conditions unless we get to know that person. Although the latter conditions can also constitute motivations to act (or not), our ignorance drives us to draw conclusions simply on the basis of someone's more salient identity, like their being an immigrant. The same happens not only with individuals, but also with groups. Past injustices involve exclusions and suppressions that bar certain groups of people from various social practices, including epistemic ones. These injustices not only cut off those groups' relationships with the broader political community or society, but they also impoverish the hermeneutical resources one can use to make sense of the presence of oneself and other people. What's worse is that this hermeneutical difficulty means that historically excluded people's claims to belong go treated as unintelligible.

The mutual integration for which I argue can be considered mutual in two ways. The first is that locals should reflect upon what they have taken for granted in their encounters with immigrants. These matters of course include ideals, values, and ways of identifications that may function as the basis of unjust structures inherited from the past. Under the misleading conception of one-way integration, locals are exempted completely from any responsibility. Such a concept of integration assumes that there is nothing unreasonable or alienating in the pre-existing structures. Insofar as locals can contribute to or impede immigrants' participation and the effectiveness of their formal equality, locals should integrate as well. Locals' integration is here understood as rectifying structural injustices and constructing new structures, such as new ways to make sense of national identities[2] and to narrate the past.[3]

Although mutual integration may sound counter intuitive, I maintain that locals can integrate as well. By stressing the responsibility of locals in integration, I aim to draw attention to the significance of learning and its relationship with self-decentralization. Both immigrants and locals engage in the process of learning, as they learn from new contexts, and they learn from each other. These learning opportunities would not arise if it were not for the presence of something "strange." In comparison to immigrants, whose

---

[2] In this sense, sociologist Anette Treibel argues for what she calls the "new German." She maintains that Germany should become self-conscious about its immigration history and how this process has enriched and changed Germany. Though "being German" can still be understood in close relation to a remote past and some traditional ideals, that old version of "being German" has little to do with how people live in the present. Concerning the identity of the "new German," she maintains that Germans should integrate as well. See Treibel (2015), *Integriert Euch! Plädoyer für ein selbstbewusstes Einwanderungsland*. Frankfurt, New York: Campus Verlag.

[3] In this regard, historical studies of the invented traditions demonstrates that many traditions are not only recent in their origins, but they are also highly relevant to the historical innovation of "nation" and its associated phenomena. These inventions are sometimes constructed from ancient materials but in novel ways and sometimes result from modified customs. Such efforts, as Eric Hobsbawm concludes, either seek to establish or symbolize social cohesion or the membership of groups, or attempt to legitimize relations of authority, or aim to inculcate beliefs and values. As it appears to me, these efforts amount to new narrations about the past-present relation. See Eric Hobsbawm and Terence Ranger (2012) (eds.), *The Invention of Tradition*. Cambridge: Cambridge University Press.

responsibility may primarily lie in learning the language(s) of the receiving society and learning its laws, locals are in a better place to reflect upon the prevailing structures and rectify them when necessary. Necessary identities, both in the past and in the present, have created and maintained complex social structures and have supported their allied epistemology and morality. This network of necessary identities and the social orders they preserve have realized specific ways of seeing the world, the self and other people. If we have learned to see the world in a certain way, why can't we also learn otherwise, especially when our accustomed ways contain dubious premises and oppressive structures? This necessarily involves challenging the self. For that reason, I introduced the ethics of difference, which proposes an altogether different paradigm from standard moral theory. Such an ethics stresses the moral importance of self-cultivation instead of searching for a moral principle that is supposed to apply universally. The attitude involved in learning contains more than personal interest as well, as it indicates that I acknowledge myself as incomplete and as needing to be improved. This inner condition prepares a basis for self-decentralization and for realizing the moral significance of self-cultivation.

The second meaning of "mutual" refers to the significance of building relationships. Unjust practices intrinsic to some prevailing structures lead to an alienating relationlessness of certain groups to the society where they live or to the political membership that they in fact share. It is "alienating" because although those groups have been part of the society where they live for generations or even centuries, and even though they have contributed to society, they remain outside of the scope of the shared understanding of "us." On the one hand, they have developed relationships by contributing to society in various ways; on the other hand, their contributions remain unseen due to factors such as racism, xenophobia or incorrect conceptual frameworks which reduce them to nothing more than economic units, cultural threats or political enemies. Their actual presence is either effaced or greatly simplified. This not only affects their actual participation; more importantly, such simplification or forgetfulness reinforces the homogenous understanding of "us" which excluded them in the first place.

The meaning of "mutual" with respect to developing relations is twofold, i.e. individual and collective. Regarding individual relationships, I stress the point that it simply is not the case that every immigrant one knows just happens to be the exception to what otherwise is assumed to be a homogenous group. Rather, by getting to know them better and eventually develop a relationship such as friendship, a work relationship or a love relationship, one acquires richer knowledge about who they are. Put otherwise, as knowers we cease to see them as simply an "immigrant." This not only changes their image, it changes our image, too. Relationships, such as those of friendship and love relationship, enrich self-knowledge. It may be too exaggerated to say that the old self is entirely replaced by a new one. Yet, we are no longer identical to the old self. Insofar as having friendships and love relationships change our views about many things, we evolve. Hence, in terms of building individual relationships, the process of integration is a mutual rather than a one-way process.

The individual aspect is not unrelated to the collective aspect of integration. Individual efforts reflect the cooperation of ordinary citizenry. What's more, they are also conducive to a (more) equal and respectful atmosphere, in which they are seen as a multi-faceted person just like how we see ourselves. With the help of various examples and theories I argued that non-institutional and imaginative contexts which involve integration should be taken seriously. Individually speaking, virtuous citizens, who are aware of reductionist identity-based thinking and of the significance of contexts such as social positions, are important. Although limited, individual efforts can be beneficial to mutual integration. The case for building collective relationships primarily concerns restoring excluded or suppressed relationships. Put otherwise, certain relationships and connections between people do not seem to exist because the conceptual framework does not account for them. Therefore, building collective relationships consists of both correction and construction. While the former deals with correcting existing structures that are in one way or another problematic, the latter mainly concerns structures that are socially connecting and inclusive. Since my primary focus in the discussion is how tacit knowledge can affect immigrants' integration, the structures that I am especially interested in are epistemic in nature.

Integration is the integration of people, who are more than right holders and whose social lives cannot be reduced to their institutional status. An important aspect of people's life is imaginative, it involves who they are, how they belong, what those relations mean and so on. That is to say, only attending to the institutional dimensions of immigrants' lives in a receiving society is far from enough, as their integration also partly depends on the non-institutional contexts, such as that of identity. Among others, the shared conception of national identity can affect immigrants' integration by shaping the attitudes of ordinary citizens. This is especially true against the background of immigration control, which has been consistently framed in the language of crises and protection. The more homogenous the shared conception of national identity is, the easier it is to perceive immigrants' participation in society as threatening and their presence as undeserved. In this regard, I addressed what appears to me to be an underexplored aspect of integration: namely, the question of whether the receiving society at its individual and collective level can strive for integration as well? If they can, how should their integration be understood and what responsibilities do they have? By focusing on the epistemic dimension of integration, I argued that locals' responsibility can be understood as the responsibility to know the person they engage with in a non-reductionist way, which is precisely the individual remedy for identity-based thinking. Virtuous knowers are important, although they are not enough to correct identity-based thinking. In addition, the receiving society can contribute to immigrants' integration by dealing with the existing epistemic practices and structures that are problematic, such as those concerning the imagination of a nation. One way to do this is to consider the significance of immigration history, to see that history as narration is always made up of "our" active choices, hence "our" normative endeavor of inclusion and exclusion.

I am not opposed to the idea of the nation, but I do believe that it can be misleading, depending on how it is understood and used. I think that national identity matters to many people, but I do not think it must be made into a necessary condition for social solidarity. Though my discussion has been largely theoretical, some practical measures are imaginable, such as changing or diversifying the criteria for measuring and evaluating migration and many social issues and reforming school curricula. I hope that my attempt has been successful so far. At least when it comes to integration, I hope that I have convincingly shown that integration depends not only on immigrants, but the receiving society at large. There is a limit to what immigrants can do and to what can be reasonably expected from them. The assumption of an us-against-them complex only deepens, rather than heals, social divisions. Identifying strangers or outsiders is not conducive to solving social problems or to easing the fear of integration. Instead, it only aggravates the feeling of losing control and of being threatened. Identities matter, but they do not always have to be necessary. Focusing on actual problems and rectifying injustices – agential and structural – are far more important than enhancing national identification.

In retrospect of the eleven years I have so far spent as an immigrant in Europe, I know clearly that my life would be much harder if I had not met anyone who was willing to know me, understand me and accept me as who I am. Occasionally I have experienced unpleasant things when looking for apartment, looking for job or just having random conversations with acquaintances. In comparison to the discrimination and marginalization some immigrants have experienced (or have been experiencing for generations), they were nothing. But I still noticed how such minor aggression and contempt frustrated me. And for that reason, I know how valuable and encouraging it is to receive help and to talk with an understanding and open-minded person. I could not have integrated if I had not met those who were willing to listen and to change for our mutual relationship. While writing, I am deeply aware that part of my discussion delivers a suggestion as opposed to making a normative point. This may render some of my arguments weak. But I at least hope that these suggestions fit well into the picture that I have illustrated in the name of mutual integration.

Works Cited

Adam, Asvi Warman. 2003. "The Chinese in the Collective Memory in the Indonesian Nation." *Kyoto Review of Southeast Asia* (3): Nations and Other Stories.
Ahlskog, Jonas. 2016. "Michael Oakeshott and Hayden White on the Practical and the Historical Past." *Rethinking History: The Journal of Theory and Practice* 20 (3): 375–394.
Alcoff, Linda Martín, and Elizabeth Potter (eds.). 1993. *Feminist Epistemologies*. London: Routledge.
– 2007. "Epistemologies of Ignorance. Three Types." In Shannon Sullivan and Nancy Tuana (eds.), *Race and Epistemologies of Ignorance*, 39–58. New York: State University of New York Press.
– 2017. "Philosophy and Philosophical Practice." In James Kidd, José Medina and Gaile Pohlhaus (eds.), *The Routledge Handbook of Epistemic Injustice*, 397–408. London: Routledge.
Amin, Ash. 2001. "Unruly Strangers? The 2001 Urban Riots in Britain." *Internaltional Journal of Urban and Regional Research* 27 (2): 460–463.
Anderson, Bridget, and Scott Blinder. 2019. "Who Counts as a Migrant? Definitions and their Consequences." *The Migration Observatory*. July. Accessed March 2023. https://migrationobservatory.ox.ac.uk/resources/briefings/who-counts-as-a-migrant-definitions-and-their-consequences/.
Anderson, Elizabeth. 2012. "Epistemic Justice as a Virtue of Social Institution." *Social Epistemology* 26 (2): 163–173.
– 2013. *The Imperative of Integration*. Princeton: Princeton University Press.
– 2014. "Reply to Critics of Imperative of Integration." *Political Studies Review* 12 (3): 376–382.
Anscombe, G. E. M. 2000. *Intention*. Cambridge MA: Harvard University Press.
Antony, Louise, and Charlotte Witt. 1993. *A Mind of One's Own: Feminist Essays on Reason and Objectivity*. Boulder, CO: Westview Press.
Bauman, Zygmunt. 1993. *Postmodern Ethics*. Oxord: Blackwell.
Benhabib, Seyla. 1987. "The Generalized and the Concrete Other." In Seyla Benhabib and Drucilla Cornell (eds.), *Feminism as Critique: Essays on the Politics of Gender in Late-Capitalist Society*, 77–95. Cambridge: Polity Press.

- 2002. The Claims of Culture: Equality and Diversity in the Global Era. Princeton: Princeton University Press.
- 2004. The Rights of Others: Aliens, Residents, and Citizens. Cambridge: Cambridge University Press.

Benjamin, Walter. 1977. "Was ist das epische Theater?" In Rolf Tiedemann and Hermann Schweppenhäuser (eds.), *Walter Benjamin Gesammelte Schriften II·1*, 519–539. Frankfurt am Main: Suhrkamp.
- 2006. "The Storyteller. Reflections on the Works of Nikolai Leskov." In Dorothy J. Hale (ed.), *The Novel: An Anthology of Critism and Theory 1900–2000*, 61–378. Oxford: Blackwell.

Bernat, Frances. 2019. "Immigration and Crime." *Oxford Research Encyclopedias*. August. Accessed March 2023. https://oxfordre.com/criminology/display/10.1093/acrefore/9780190264079.001.0001/acrefore-9780190264079-e-93.

Bernstein, Richard. 2004. "The Culture of Memory." *History and Theory* 43 (4): 165–178.

Blake, Michael. 2005. "Immigration." In R. G. Frey and Christopher Heath Wellman (eds.), *A Companion to Applied Ethics*, 224–237. Oxford: Blackwell.

Bol, Peter K. 2008. *Neo-Confucianism in History*. Cambridge MA: Harvard University Asian Center.

Brecht, Brecht. 1967. *Schriften zum Theater. Gesammelte Werke 15*. Frankfurt am Main: Suhrkamp.

Brubaker, Rogers. 1998. *Citizenship and Nationhood in France and Germany*. Cambridge MA: Harvard University Press.

Calhoun, Craig, Mark Juergensmeyer, and Jonathan VanAntwerpen. 2011. *Rethinking Secularism*. Oxford: Oxford University Press.

Carens, Joseph. 2005. "The Integration of Immigrants" *Journal of Moral Philosophy* 2 (1): 29–46.

Celikates, Robin. 2017. "Lesenotitz: Weder gerecht noch realistisch – David Millers Plädoyer für das Staatliche Recht auf Ausschluss." *theorieblog.de*. December. Accessed March 2023. https://www.theorieblog.de/index.php/2017/12/lesenotiz-weder-gerecht-noch-realistisch-david-millers-plaedoyer-fuer-das-staatliche-recht-auf-ausschluss/.

Chakrabarty, Dipesh. 2007. Provincializing Europe: Postcolonial Thought and Historical Difference. Princeton: Princeton University Press.

Chan, Wing-tsit. 1963. *A Source Book in Chinese Philosophy*. Princeton: Princeton University Press.

Chin, Frank, Jeffery Paul Chan, Lawson Fusao Inada, and Shawn Wong. 2019. *Aiieeeee!: An Anthology of Asian American Writers*. Seattle: University of Washington Press.

Choy, Philip P. 2012. San Francisco Chinatown: A Guide to its History and Architecture. San Francisco: City Lights.

Chua, Christian. 2004. "Defining Indonesian Chineseness under the New Order." *Journal of Contemporary Asia* 34 (4): 465–479.

Ci, Jiwei. 2014. *Moral China in the Age of Reform*. Cambridge: Cambridge University Press.

Code, Lorraine. 1982. "The Importance of Historicism for a Theory of Knowledge." *International Philosophical Quarterly* 22 (2): 157–174.

- 1984. "Towards a 'Responsibilist' Epistemology." *Philosophy and Phennomenological Research* 45 (1): 29–50.
- 1987. *Epistemic Responsibility.* Hanover and London: University Press of New England.
- 1988. "Experience, Knowledge and Responsibility." In Morwenna Griffiths and Margaret Whitford (eds.), *Feminist Perspectives in Philosophy*, 187–204. Bloomington and Indianapolis: Indiana University Press.
- 1991. *What Can She Know? Feminst Theory and the Construction of Knowledge.* Ithaca: Cornell University Press.
- 2008. "Review: Epistemic Injustice: Power and Ethics of Knowing." *Notre Dame Philosophical Reviews.* March. Accessed March 2023. https://ndpr.nd.edu/reviews/epistemic-injustice-power-and-the-ethics-of-knowing/.
- 2017. "Epistemic Responsibility." In Ian James Kidd, José Medina and Gaile Pohlhaus (eds.), *The Routledge Handbook of Epistemic Injustice*, 89–99. London: Routledge.

Cook, Ian G., and Phil G. Cubbin. 2011. "Changing Symbolism and Identity in Liverpool and Manchester Chinatowns." In Mike Jackson-Benbough and Sam Davies (eds.), *Merseyside: Culture and Place*, 37–60. Newcastle: Cambridge Scholars Publishing.

Coppel, Charles A. 2002. *Studying Ethnic Chinese in Indonesia. Asian Studies Monograph Series.* Singapore: Singapore Society of Asian Studies.

Coughlan, Sean. 2018. "Overseas students should 'stay in migration target.'" *BBC.* September. Accessed March 2023. https://www.bbc.com/news/education-45483366.

Dancy, Jonathan. 2004. *Ethics Without Principles.* Oxford: Oxford University Press.
- 2017. "Moral Particularism." *Stanford Encyclopedia of Philosophy.* September. Accessed March 2023. https://plato.stanford.edu/entries/moral-particularism/.

Danto, Arthur. 2007. *Narration and Knowledge.* New York: Columbia University Press.

Davis, Natalie Zemon. 1987. Fiction in the Archives. Pardon Tales and Their Tellers in Sixteenth-Century France. Stanford: Stanford University Press.

Dennis, Elizabeth. 2018. "Exploring the Model Minority: Deconstructing Whiteness Through the Asian American Example." In George J. Sefa and Shukri Hilowle (eds.), *Cartographies of Race and Social Difference*, 33–48. New York: Springer.

Dhawan, Nikita. 2013. "Coercive Cosmopolitanism and Impossible Solidarities." *Qui Parle* 22 (1): 139–166.
- 2021. "Die Aufklärung vor den Europäer*innen retten." In Rainer Forst and Klaus Günther (eds.), *Normative Ordnungen*, 191–208. Frankfurt am Main: Suhrkamp.
- forthcoming. Rescuing the Enlightenment from the Europeans: Critical Theories of Decolonization.

Driver, Julia. 2022. "Gertrude Elizabeth Margaret Anscombe." *Stanford Encyclopedia of Philosophy.* May. Accessed March 2023. https://plato.stanford.edu/entries/anscombe/.

Dummett, Michael. 2001. *On Immigration and Refugees.* London: Routledge.

El-Mafaalani, Aladin. 2018. Das Integrationsparadox. Warum gelungene Integration zu mehr Konflikten führt. Cologne: Kiepenheuer & Witsch.

Emerson, Michael O. 2011. "Book Review: The Imperative of Integration by Anderson." *American Journal of Sociology* 117 (1): 317–319.

Espejo, Paulina Ochoa. 2017. "Strangers in Our Midst: The Political Philosophy of Immigration. By David Miller." *Migration Studies* 5 (3): 465–469.
Ezli, Özkan, and Gisela Staupe (eds.). 2014. *Das neue Deutschland. Von Migration und Vielfalt.* Konstanz: Konstanz University Press.
Fine, Sarah, and Andrea Sangiovanni. 2019. "Immigration." In Darrel Moellendorf and Heather Widdows (eds.), *The Routledge Handbook of Global Ethics*, 193–210. London: Routledge.
Fine, Sarah. 2016. "Immigration and Discrimination." In Sarah Fine and Lea Ypi (eds.), *Migration in Political Theory*, 125–150. Oxford: Oxford University Press.
Fisher, Michael H., Shompa Lahiri, and Shinder Thandi. 2007. *A South Asian History of Britain: Four Centuries of People from the Indian Sub-Continent.* Westport, Connecticut: Greenwood.
Fitzgerald, David. 2017. "The History of Racialized Citizenship." In Ayelet Shahar, Rainer Bauböck, Irene Bloemraad and Maarten Vink (eds.), *The Oxford Handbook of Citizenship*, 129–152. Oxford: Oxford University Press.
Foucault, Michel. 1980. "Truth and Knowledge." In Michel Foucault, *Knowledge/Power. Selected Interviews and Other Writings 1972–1977*, 109–133. New York: Pantheon.
– 2006. Madness and Civilization: A History of Insanity in the Age of Reason. London: Vintage.
Fricker, Miranda, and Jennifer Hornsby (eds.). 2000. *The Cambridge Companion to Feminism in Philosophy.* Cambridge: Cambridge University Press.
Fricker, Miranda. 2007. *Epistemic Injustice: Power and the Ethics of Knowing.* Oxford: Oxford University Press.
Gentleman, Amelia. 2022. "Windrush scandal caused by '30 years of racist immigration laws' – report." *The Guardian*. May. Accessed March 2023. https://www.theguardian.com/uk-news/2022/may/29/windrush-scandal-caused-by-30-years-of-racist-immigration-laws-report.
Gerbner, Katharine. 2018. *Christian Slavery: Conversion and Race in the Protestant Atlantic World.* Philadelphia: University of Pennsylvania Press.
Ghandi, Leela. 2019. *Postcolonial Theory. A Critical Introduction.* New York: Columbia University Press.
Gilroy, Paul. 2002. *There ain't no Black in the Union Jack.* London: Routledge.
Gorelik, Lena. 2012. *"Sie können aber gut Deutsch!": Warum ich nicht mehr dankbar sein will, dass ich hier leben darf, und Toleranz nicht weiterhilft.* Munich: Pantheon Verlag.
Grunert, Johannes. 2018. "Der Abend, an dem der Rechtsstaat aufgab." *Die Zeit*. August. Accessed March 8, 2023. https://www.zeit.de/gesellschaft/zeitgeschehen/2018-08/chemnitz-rechte-demonstration-ausschreitungen-polizei?utm_referrer=https%3A%2F%2Fwww.google.com%2F.
Harding, Sandra. 1991. *Whose Science? Whose Knowledge? Thinking from Women's Lives.* Ithaca: Cornell University Press.
Hare, R. M. 1963. *Freedom and Reason.* Oxford: Oxford University Press.

Haslanger, Sally. 2012. "On Being Objective and Being Objectified." In Sally Haslanger, *Resisting Reality: Social Construction and Social Critique*, 35–82. Oxford: Oxford University Press.

Hayter, Teresa. 2000. *Open Borders: The Case Against Immigration Controls*. London: Pluto Press.

Hobsbawm, Eric, and Terence Ranger (eds.). 2012. *The Invention of Tradition*. Cambridge: Cambridge University Press.

Hogan, Sophie. 2022. "Remove international student numbers from migration figures, say MPs." *The Pie News*. November. Accessed March 2023. https://thepienews.com/news/intl-student-numbers-removal-net-migration/.

Hong, Cathy Park. 2020. *Minor Feelings. An Asian American Reckoning*. London: One World.

Huang, Yong. 2010. "The Ethics of Difference in the Zhuangzi." *Journal of American Academy of Religion* 78 (1): 65–99.

– 2014. *Why be Moral? Learning From the Neo-Confucian Cheng Brothers*. New York: SUNY Press.

– 2018. "Patient Moral Relativism in the Zhuangzi." *Philosophia* 46 (4): 877–894.

– n.d. "Cheng Hao." *Internet Encyclopedia of Philosophy*. Accessed March 2023. https://iep.utm.edu/cjemg-omgdap-cheng-hao-neo-confucian/.

Huynh, Q. L., and L. Smalarz. 2011. "Perpetual Foreigner in One's Own Land: Potential Implications for Identity and Psychological Adjustment." *Journal of Social and Clinical Psychology* 30 (2): 133–162.

Jacquemond, Louis-Pascal. 2020. "Women of science. 19th – 21st centuries." *Digital Encyclopedia of European History*. June. Accessed March 2023. https://ehne.fr/en/encyclopedia/themes/gender-and-europe/educating-europeans/women-science.

Jaeggi, Rahel. 2005. *Entfremdung: Zur Aktualität eines soziaphilosophischen Problems*. Frankfurt am Main: Campus Verlag.

Jones, C. G., A. E. Martin, and A. Wolf (eds.). 2022. *The Palgrave Handbook of Women in Science since 1660*. London: Palgrave Macmillan.

Jones, Claire. 2018. "Women have been written out of science history – time to put them back." *The Conversation*. December. Accessed March 2023. https://theconversation.com/women-have-been-written-out-of-science-history-time-to-put-them-back-107752.

Joppke, Christian. 2005. *Selecting by Origin: Ethnic Migration in the Liberal State*. Cambridge MA: Harvard University Press.

Keevak, Michael. 2011. *Becoming Yellow: A Short History of Racial Thinking*. Princeton: Princeton University Press.

King, Desmond. 1999. *In the Name of Liberalism: Illiberal Social Policy in the USA and Britain*. Oxford: Oxford University Press.

Kukathas, Chandran. 2005. "Immigration." In Hugh LaFollette (ed), *The Oxford Handbook of Practical Ethics*, 567–590. Oxford: Oxford University Press.

- 2017. "Controlling Immigrants Means Controlling Citizens." *F. A. Hayek Lecture*. April. Accessed March 2023. https://www.mercatus.org/hayekprogram/economic-insights/features/chandran-kukathas-controlling-immigration-means-controlling.
Kundnani, Arun. 2001. "From Oldham to Bradford: the Violence of the Violated." *Race & Class* 43 (2): 105–110.
Kushner, Tony, and Kenneth Lunn (eds.). 1991. *The Politics of Marginality: Race, the Radical Right and Minorities in Twentieth Century in Britain.* London: Routledge.
Lake, Marilyn, and Henry Reynolds. 2008. *Drawing the Global Color Line: White Men's Countries and the Internaltional Challenge of Racial Equality.* Cambridge: Cambridge University Press.
Lee, Stacey J., and Kevin K. Kumashiro. 2005. *A Report on the Status of Asian American and Pacific Islanders in Education: Beyond the "Model Minority" Stereotype.* National Education Association of the United States. Washington.
Lin, A. I., K. L. Nadal, G. C. Torino, J. Bucceri, and D. W. Sue. 2007. "Racial Microaggressions and the Asian American Experience." *Cultural Diversity and Ethnic Minority Psychology* 13 (1): 72–81.
Lu, Catharine. 2018. "Redressing and Addressing Colonial Injustice." *Ethics & Global Politics* 11 (1): 1–5.
- 2017. *Justice and Reconsiliation in World Politics.* Cambridge: Cambridge University Press.
Lu, Zhouxiang, and Weiyi Wu. 2017. "Rethinking Integration and Identity: Chinese Migrants in the Republic of Ireland." *International Review of Sociology* 27 (3): 475–490.
MacIntyre, Alasdair. 2013. *After Virtue: A Study in Moral Theory.* London: Bloomsbury Academic.
Maffli, Stéphane. 2021. *Migrationsliteratur aus der Schweiz.* Bielefeld: Transcript.
Mannathukkaren, Nissim. 2010. "Postcolonialism and Modernity. A Critical Realist Critique." *Journal of Critical Realism* 9 (3): 299–327.
Margalit, Avishai. 2004. *The Ethics of Memory.* Cambridge MA: Harvard University Press.
Marotta, Vince. 2012. "Georg Simmel, the Stranger and the Sociology of Knowledge." *Journal of Intercultural Studies* 33 (6): 675–689.
McClain, Charles J. 1994. *In Search of Equality: The Chinese Struggle Against Discrimination in the Nineteeth-Century America.* Berkeley: University of California Press.
Meade, Amanda. 2016. "Charlie Hebdo Cartoon Depicting Crowned Child Alan Kurdi Sparks Racism Debate." *The Guardian.* January. Accessed March 2023. https://www.theguardian.com/media/2016/jan/14/charlie-hebdo-cartoon-depicting-drowned-child-alan-kurdi-sparks-racism-debate.
Medina, José. 2012. *The Epistemology of Resistance: Gender and Racial Oppression, Epistemic Injustice and the Social Imagination.* New York: Oxford University Press.
Merry, Michael S. 2013. "Book Review: The Imperative of Integration." *Theory and Research in Education* 11 (1): 101–106.
Mignolo, Walter. 2005. *The Idea of Latin America.* Oxford: Blackwell.
- 2009. "Epistemic Disobedience, Independent Thought and De-Colonial Freedom." *Theory, Culture & Society* 26 (7–8): 1–23.
Miller, David. 2016. *Strangers in Our Midst.* Cambridge MA: Harvard University Press.

Mills, Charles W. 1997. *The Racial Contract*. New York: Corell University Press.
- 2005. "'Ideal Theory as Ideology.'" *Hypatia* 20 (3): 165–183.
- 2007. "White Ignorance." In Shanno Sullican and Nancy Tuana (eds.), *Race and Epistemologies of Ignorance*, 13–38. New York: State University Of New York Press.

Ngai, Mae M. 2014. *Impossible Subjects: Illegal Aliens and the Making of Modern America*. Princeton: Princeton University Press.

Nikesh, Shuka. 2019. *The Good Immigrant: 26 Writers Reflect on America*. Boston: Little Brown & Co.

Nussbaum, Martha. 1998. *Cultivating Humanity: A Classical Defense of Reform in Liberal Education*. Cambridge MA: Harvard University Press.

Nwabuzo, Ojeaku, and Lisa Schaeder. 2017. "Racism and discrimination in the context of migration in Europe. ENAR Shadow Report 2015–2016." *European Commission*. March. Accessed March 2023. https://ec.europa.eu/migrant-integration/library-document/racism-and-discrimination-context-migration-europe_en.

O'Connor, Paul. 2019. "Ethnic Minorities and Ethnicity in Hong Kong." In Tai-lok Lui, Stephen W. K. Chiu and Ray Yep (eds.), *Routledge Handbook of Contemporary Hong Kong*, 259–274. London: Routledge.

Okin, Susan Moller (ed.). 1999. *Is Multiculturalism Bad for Women?* Princeton: Princeton University Press.
- 1979. *Women in Western Political Thought*. Princeton: Princeton University Press.

Ören, Aras. 2017. *Wir neuen Europäer*. Berlin: Verbrecher Verlag.

Osborne, Louise. 2018. "In Chemnitz, anti-fascists stand up to the Nazi salute of Germany's far right." *The Guardian*. September. Accessed March 8, 2023. https://www.theguardian.com/world/2018/sep/01/chemnitz-protests-germany-migration.

Panayi, Panikos. 2014. *An Immigration History of Britain: Multicultural Racism since 1880*. London: Routledge.

Parekh, Bhikhu. 2006. *Rethinking Multiculturalism: Cultural Diversity and Political Theory*. London: Palgrave Macmillan.
- 2008. *A New Politics of Identity: Political Principles for An Independent World*. London: Palgrave Macmillan.

Phoa, Liong Gie. 1992. "The Changing Economic Position of the Chinese in Netherlands India." In M. R. Fernando and David Bullbeck (eds), *Chinese Economic Activity in Netherlands India: Selected Translations from the Dutch*, 5–18. Singapore: Institute of South East Asian Studies.

Plamenatz, John. 1965. "Strangers in Our Midst." *Race* 7 (1): 1–16.

Ridge, Michael, and Sean McKeever. 2016. "Moral Particularism and Moral Generalism." *Stanford Encyclopedia of Philosophy*. November. Accessed March 2023. https://plato.stanford.edu/entries/moral-particularism-generalism/.

Roberts, Leith Daniel. 2017. *Liverpool Sectarianism: The Rise and Demise*. Liverpool: Liverpool University Press.

Rose, Flemming. 2006a. "Why I Published Those Cartoons." *The Washington Post*. February. Accessed March 2023. https://www.washingtonpost.com/archive/

opinions/2006/02/19/why-i-published-those-cartoons/f9a67368-4641-4fa7-b71f-843ea44814ef/.
- 2006b. "Why I published the Muhammad Cartoons." *Spiegel International.* May. Accessed March 2023. https://www.spiegel.de/international/spiegel/opinion-why-i-published-the-muhammad-cartoons-a-418930.html.

Rossiter, Margaret W. 1993. "The Mathew Matilda Effect in Science." *Social Studies of Science* 23 (2): 325–341.

Sager, Alex. 2016. "Book Review: Strangers in Our Midst: The Political Philosophy of Immigration by David Miller." *LSE Review of Books.* September. Accessed March 2023. https://blogs.lse.ac.uk/lsereviewofbooks/2016/09/06/book-review-strangers-in-our-midst-the-political-philosophy-of-immigration-by-david-miller/.

Said, Edward. 2001. "The Clash of Ignorance." *The Nation.* October. Accessed March 14, 2023. https://www.thenation.com/article/archive/clash-ignorance/.
- 2003. *Orientalism.* London: Penguine.

Sen, Amartya. 2007. Identity and Violence: The Illusion of Destiny. London: Penguin.

Shklar, Judith. 1980. *The Faces of Injustice.* New Haven: Yale University Press.

Simmel, Georg. 1950. "The Metropolis and Mental Life. Translated by Kurt Wolff." In Kurt Wolff (ed.), *The Sociology of Georg Simmel*, 409–424. New York: Free Press. Original work published 1903.
- 1950. "The Stranger. Translated by Kurt Wolff." In Kurt Wolff (ed.), *The Sociology of Georg Simmel*, 402–408. New York: Free Press. Original work published 1908.
- 1997. "The Crisis of Culture. Translated by D. E. Jenkinson." In David Frisby and Mike Featherstone (eds.), *Simmel on Culture: Selected Writings*, 90–100. London: SAGE Publications. Original work published 1916.

Song, Sarah. 2019. *Immigration and Democracy.* Oxford: Oxford University Press.

Stanford University. 2020. *Chinese Railroad Workers in North America Project.* August. Accessed March 2023. https://web.stanford.edu/group/chineserailroad/cgi-bin/website/.

Stanley, Jason. 2013. *Know How.* Oxford: Oxford University Press.
- 2018. *How Fascism Works.* New York: Random House.

Su, Xiaochen. 2018. "Racism and Apartment Hunting in East Asia." *The Diplomat.* August. Accessed March 2023. https://thediplomat.com/2018/08/racism-and-apartment-hunting-in-east-asia/.

Suryadinata, Leo. 1999. *Political Thinking of the Indonesian Chinese, 1900–1995.* Singapore: Singapore University Press.

Taìiiwoì, Oluìfeìòmi. 2017. "Of Problem Moderns and Excluded Moderns: On the Essential Hybridity of Modernity." In Paul C. Taylor, Linda Martín Alcoff and Luvell Anderson (eds.), *The Routledge Companion to the Philosophy of Race*, 14–27. London: Routledge.

Tan, Kok-Chor. 2007. "Colonialism, Reparations, and Global Justice." In J. Miller and R. Kumar (eds.), *Reparations: Interdisciplinary Inquiries*, 280–306. Oxford: Oxford University Press.

Tchen, John Kuo Wei. 2001. New York before Chinatown: Orientalism and the Shaping of American Culture, 1776–1882. Baltimore: Johns Hopkins University Press.

Ther, Philipp. 2017. Die Außenseiter: Flucht, Flüchtlinge und Integration im modernen Europa. Frankfurt am Main: Suhrkamp.

Tiwald, Justin. 2020. "Song-Ming Confucianism." *Stanford Encyclopedia of Philosophy*. March. Accessed March 2023. https://plato.stanford.edu/entries/song-ming-confucianism/#HistContBuddDaoiNeoConf.

Tran, Phuc. 2020. Sigh, Gone. A Misfit's Memoir of Great Books, Punk Rock and the Fight to Fit In. New York: Macmillan.

Treibel, Annette. 2015. Integriert Euch! Plädoyer für ein selbstbewusstes Einwanderungsland. Frankfurt am Main: Campus.

Tsai, Shih-Shan Henry. 1986. *The Chinese Experience in America*. Bloomington: Indiana University Press.

U.S. Congress.House. 2019. "Recognizing Chinese railroad workers who worked on the Transcontinental Railroad from 1865 to 1869, and their important contribution to the growth of the United States (H. Res. 165)." *Congress.gov*. February. Accessed March 2023. https://www.congress.gov/bill/116th-congress/house-resolution/165/text.

Urban, Gregory S. 2013. "The Eternal Newcomer: Chinese Indonesian Identity." *LUX: A Journal of Transdisciplinary Writing and Research from Claremont Graduate University* 3 (1): Article 19.

Visram, Rosina. 2002. *Asians in Britain: 400 Years of History*. London: Pluto Press.

Walker, Margaret U. 2007. *Moral Understanding: A Feminist Study in Ethics*. New York: Oxford University Press.

Wang, Bodi. 2021. "Imagine Strangers in Our Midst." In Corinna Mieth and Wolfram Cremer (eds.), *Migration, Stability and Solidarity*, 59–80. Baden-Baden: Nomos.

White, Hayden. 2014. Metahistory: The Historical Imagination in Nineteenth-Century Europe. Baltimore: The Johns Hopkins University Press.

— 2014. *The Practical Past*. Evanston: Northwestern University Press.

Williams, Bernard. 1993. *Shame and Necessity*. Berkeley: University of California Press.

Winder, Robert. 2004. Bloody Foreigners: The Story of Immigration to Britain. London: Little Brown.

Wittgenstein, Ludwig. 1958. *Philosophical Investigations*. New York: Macmillan.

Wong, Cara. 2014. "Would We Know 'Integration' If We Were to see It? Measurement and The Imperative of Integration." *Political Studies Review* 12 (3): 353–360.

Wong, Wai-ying. n.d. "Cheng Yi." *Internet Encyclopedia of Philosophy*. Accessed March 2023. https://iep.utm.edu/chengyi/.

Wu, Frank H. 2003. Yellow: Race in America. Beyond Black and White. New York: Basic Books.

Young, Iris. 2003. "Political Responsibility and Structural Injustice." *The Lindley Lecture*. Kansas: University of Kansas.

— 2006. "Responsibility and Global Justice: A Social Connection Model." *Social Philosophy and Policy* 23 (1): 102–130.

— 2006. "Taking Basic Strucrues Seriously." *Symposium* 91–97.

— 2011. *Justice and the Politics of Difference*. Princeton: Princeton University Press.

— 2011. *Responsibility for Justice*. Oxford: Oxford University Press.

Zia, Helen. 2001. *Asian American Dreams: The Emergence of an American People.* New York: Farrar, Straus and Giroux.

Index

agential 14, 17, 77, 98, 104, 105, 107, 171, 185, 186, 194, 200, 225
  non- 98
Alcoff, Linda Martín 160–164
alien 44
  citizen 44
  illegal 44
alienation 176, 179–187, 191, 202, 204, 211, 212, 220
  effect (Verfremdungseffekt) 172
  existential 178, 183, 184, 194
  interactional 181–184, 186, 194, 212
  structural 18, 114, 178, 181–184, 186, 192, 194, 196
Anderson, Benedict 65, 199
Anderson, Elizabeth 46–52, 107, 118
Anscombe, G. E. M. 207
aperspectivity 85
  absolute 84, 85
  aperspectival 85
  assumed 85
Asian 44, 46, 57, 59, 74, 88, 101, 102, 105, 106, 124, 134, 151
  Asian American 44–46, 64, 88, 180
  Asianness 88, 113
assimilation 12, 16, 21–27, 34, 39, 42, 43, 49, 57, 62, 70, 97, 111, 119, 127, 128, 167, 215, 217, 219, 220

bad luck 57, 153, 200
  circumstantial 104, 106
  epistemic 104, 106
Bauman, Zygmunt 41, 71, 127, 130, 218
Benhabib, Seyla 32–34, 36–38, 117
Benjamin, Walter 124–127
Bernstein, Richard 198, 201
Bhikhu, Parekh 22
Blake, Michael 64, 69
Bourdieu, Pierre 57
Brecht, Berthold 172
Britain
  British 12, 148, 149, 151, 190, 191
  UK 147, 149, 174, 175

Cantle Report 12, 194
Carens, Joseph 15, 23, 24, 26, 47, 146, 216
censorship 41, 102
  self- 28, 29, 31, 165
Centrism
  centralization 163
  decentralization 34, 162, 222, 223
  self- 34, 42
Charlie Hebdo 77
Chemnitz 13
Chengs 135, 136, 138–140
  Cheng Hao 135
  Cheng Yi 135
Chinatown 12, 154
Chinese
  China Problem 62, 70

Index

Chinese Exclusion Act 154
Chinese immigrants 59, 115–117, 128, 155, 218
Chinese Indonesian 61, 62, 70
Ci, Jiwei 119, 120
citizenship 11, 15, 19, 43–45, 63, 64, 100–102, 182, 194, 221
civilization 59, 74, 75, 79, 101, 118
   clash of 74, 75
co-ordination
   imaginative 99, 100, 105
   practical 100
   social 99, 100
Code, Lorraine 17, 89–95, 106, 107, 112, 119, 129, 130
colonialism 16, 27, 65, 88, 162, 181, 188, 211
   colonial dominance 60
   colonized 162, 163, 181
   colonizer 60, 181
conditions of production 157, 158
Confucianism 136, 140
cultivation
   self- 18, 136, 140, 142, 175, 223
cultural limbo 47

Danish 28, 30–33, 38, 57, 87
   Dane 38
   Denmark 29, 31, 33, 35, 38, 39, 138, 219
   Prime Minister 28
Danto, Arthur 206, 207
Davis, Natalie Zemon 204, 205
democracy 11, 29, 30, 32, 33, 35, 46, 52, 102, 138, 219
determination
   self- 68, 69, 79, 114, 182
disputability 119, 120, 122, 126
   disputable 120, 121, 124
   indisputable 119–121, 123
   nondisputable 119–122
distribution 64, 97, 134, 157, 185, 188, 194
   distributive 157–160, 175, 177
diversity 79, 119, 142, 202

in-group 61, 114–117, 128, 139, 145, 155, 218
   personal 117
   racial 48, 50, 51, 118, 119
divide-and-rule policy 60, 61
Dutch 61, 62
Dutch East India Company 61

ego-politics 162, 163
Emerson, Michael O. 50
enlightment 162
epistemic
   autority 81, 105, 106, 108, 134, 141, 177
   capacity 70, 106, 112, 121, 135, 137, 140, 142, 145, 174
   circumstances 70, 73, 78, 82, 89, 90, 94, 96, 104, 106, 109, 111, 118, 119, 123, 126, 129, 134, 146, 213, 221
   community 106, 107
   inferiority 99, 102, 106
   location 94, 95
   poverty 122
   proceeding 90–92, 94–97, 127
   structures 14, 17, 19, 80, 81, 104, 105, 152, 156, 159–161, 163, 167, 169, 170, 172, 175, 196, 201
   superiority 83, 103, 166, 184, 221
epistemology 66, 82, 89, 91, 129, 223
   imperial 163
   reliabilism 91–93
   responsibilism 91, 93, 94, 109
   responsibilist 89, 91, 129
equality 48, 67, 78, 122
   inequality 46, 52, 78, 122, 147, 173, 188
ethics of difference 18, 112, 133, 135, 137, 139–142, 145, 166, 175, 223
ethnocentrism 64, 173, 186, 221
   ethnocentric 171, 178, 182
exclusion 18, 21, 27, 28, 43, 44, 46–48, 62, 64, 69, 79, 83, 87, 96, 104–106, 159, 171, 177, 178, 185, 186, 195, 197, 198, 200, 211, 212, 221, 225
   epistemic 43

of women 46
unjustified 212

fallibility 82, 104
  epistemic 27, 90
feminism 112, 129
  feminist 83, 85, 87, 94, 139, 213
Fine, Sarah 63, 171
freedom of speech 29-32, 39, 41, 77, 101, 102, 121, 165
  experience to speak 41
  expertise to speak 41
  freedom to speak 41
Fricker, Miranda 17, 98-100, 102-107, 122

Geary Act 101
generalism 16, 43, 49
  moral 35, 40, 43, 135, 137, 140
Germany 77, 194, 195
Greeks 57, 58, 66
  ethical ideas of Antiquity 57
  free 58

Harding, Sandra 132
Hare, R. M. 32
Haslanger, Sally 17, 83-85
hermeneutical resources 14, 79, 89, 98, 103, 107-109, 122, 143, 155, 176, 178, 186, 213, 220, 221
Hindu 60, 61, 67, 74, 76, 78, 79, 85, 87
Hindu-Muslim riots 60, 76
history 19, 45, 63, 66, 75, 79, 92, 98, 149, 156, 176, 178, 185, 186, 188-192, 194-196, 198-206, 208-211, 213, 225
homogeneity 24, 25, 43, 45, 69, 79, 119, 148, 156, 189, 192, 217
  homogenous 24, 25, 116, 128, 133, 145, 151, 156, 175, 189-191, 194, 195, 210, 223, 225
Huang, Yong 40, 135-137, 139
humiliation 30, 36, 38
Huntington, Samuel 68, 74-76, 79

ideal theory 24, 25
  non-ideal theory 24, 40
identitarian 51-53, 64, 97
  criteria 47, 48
  framework 55, 81
identity
  cultural background 13, 42, 56, 59, 63, 72, 78, 94, 105, 115, 117, 150, 155, 157, 159, 180, 181, 197, 198, 200, 216-218
  descent 56, 63-65, 78, 85, 88, 94, 100, 101, 115-117, 147, 155-157, 159, 174, 180, 181, 195, 197, 198, 200, 216-218, 221
  necessary 16, 55-61, 65, 66, 70, 71, 73, 75-77, 80-82, 85, 86, 88, 118, 143, 167, 181, 182, 184, 220, 221, 223
  polititcs 48
  racial 45, 48
  religious 46, 60, 61
  social 60, 99, 102, 105, 106
identity-based thinking 17, 18, 52-54, 56, 66, 73, 74, 76-79, 81-83, 88-90, 97, 109, 110, 112, 117, 118, 123, 126, 128, 130-133, 135, 140, 142, 143, 145, 152, 175, 220, 224, 225
  qualitative 56, 73, 74, 78, 82, 92
  quantitative 56, 73, 74, 82, 92
ignorance 17, 25, 35, 43, 55, 87, 103, 104, 106, 119, 166, 182, 183, 187, 188, 191, 194, 210, 211, 221
imagination 64, 65, 99-101, 105, 106, 108, 159, 175, 182, 191, 197, 216, 217, 221, 225
immigrant
  equal members 14, 26, 28, 39, 43, 53, 70, 138, 150, 197
  generations 45, 64, 88, 111, 115, 149, 171, 175, 177, 178, 180, 195, 223, 226
  identity 69
  outsider 15, 18, 22, 44, 46, 47, 55, 85, 100, 101, 128, 146, 182, 216, 219, 225
  undesirable 14, 18, 43, 44, 64, 72, 88, 100, 118, 130, 135, 147, 160, 164, 182, 187, 189, 194, 197, 200, 210, 221
immigration

control 63–65, 68, 78, 182, 225
  history 64, 176, 190, 195–197, 213, 222, 225
  policy 64, 117, 182
  restriction 43, 64
  society 14, 21, 27, 175, 217
  studies 15, 115, 116
impartiality 32, 34, 39, 40, 126, 145
India 60, 64, 74, 147, 190
  British India 60
Indonesia
  Indonesian 61, 62, 67, 78, 85, 87, 113
injustice
  distributive 103
  epistemic 17, 82, 88, 98, 99, 102–107, 109, 110, 122
  hermeneutical 99, 104, 106–108
  past 27, 65, 68, 72, 96, 110, 111, 114, 169, 186, 188, 200, 221
  structural 17, 89, 96, 152–154, 159, 175, 186–188, 192–194, 200, 202, 205, 211, 222
  testimonial 99, 106, 108
integration
  assimilation-like 22–27
  failure 12, 24, 26, 27, 39, 68, 80, 88, 194, 217, 219
  gesture of 29–31
  lack of interest 88
  mutual 9, 16, 19, 22, 26, 53, 54, 72, 81, 82, 97, 110, 112, 142, 143, 145, 212, 222, 224, 226
  one-way process 15, 16, 22, 23, 35, 49, 53, 111, 215, 216, 219, 222, 224
  success 12
Ireland 115, 116, 128, 155, 218
irresponsibility
  epistemic 17, 82, 88, 89, 91, 95, 97, 98, 109, 110, 126

Jaeggi, Rahel 179, 181, 183–185, 212
Japan 59
  Japanese 44, 59, 166

justice 25, 44, 58, 89, 157, 158, 177, 178, 185, 192, 194, 195, 198, 200–202
  distributive 99, 220
  epistemic 142
  transactional 107
Jyllands Posten 28

Kantian 40, 41
Keevak, Michael 59
Khan, Genghis 59
know-how 18, 137–139, 168
know-that 137, 168
knower
  irresponsible 95–97, 104
  reliable 91
  responsible 97
  virtuous 17, 82, 89, 107, 109, 225
  would-be 90, 117, 122
knowing people 92, 93, 111–143, 145, 175, 186
  zhi ren 139
knowledge
  about people 92
  about things 92
  degrees of 92
  end-product 91, 92
  historical 202, 206–208
  human 91, 92, 96, 98, 129
  narrative 18, 112, 127–130, 133
  practice 17, 90, 91, 95, 99, 102, 103, 106, 109
  production 93, 95, 103, 106, 109, 112, 158, 159, 177, 203
  seekers 90
  seeking process 82, 89, 91, 93–96, 110
  self- 103, 145, 163, 164, 224
Kohlberg, Lawrence 32
Korsgaard, Christine 40
Kukathas, Chandran 68, 69, 114
Kurdi, Alan 77

Latin America 162
listen 41, 42, 98, 102–104, 106, 110, 134, 226
  inability 103

logical 33, 38, 41, 66, 87, 93, 119
  certainty 66, 67, 92
  coherence 33, 66, 67, 121
  mistake 94
love 136, 139, 173, 198, 199, 207, 224
  ren 136
  with distinction 136, 139
Lu, Catherine 19, 178, 181–185, 211, 212
Lu, Zhouxiang 115, 116

MacIntyre, Alasdair 38
Margalit, Avishai 197–199, 201
marginalization 27, 42, 64, 123, 156, 182, 186, 211, 226
  epistemic 98
  hermeneutical 99
Marx, Karl 157, 204
Mead, George Herbert 33
Medina, José 25, 103
Metzger, Thomas 120
Mia, Kader 60, 73–77
middlemen 61
Mignolo, Walter 162
migration
  background 11, 12, 24, 64, 68, 70, 78, 132, 143, 146, 151, 171, 195, 215, 217, 219
  migrants 27, 160, 195, 196
Mill, John Stuart 41
Miller, David 12, 18, 146, 147, 149–151, 159, 169, 171, 174, 182, 189, 194
Mills, Charles W. 24, 187, 188, 191
minority 11, 46, 48, 50, 51, 67, 128, 138, 147, 194, 216, 217, 221
  communities 48, 50, 118, 217
  ethnic 48, 64, 186, 191, 194, 216, 217
  national 101, 171, 182, 183, 186, 197, 216, 221
  shelters 48
Mongolianness 59
  Mongolian 59
moral
  agent 18, 33–35, 40, 41, 117, 130, 133, 135–137, 139–143, 145, 166, 175, 191

legitimacy 70, 75, 78, 80
  recipient 18, 35, 40, 41, 117, 130, 133, 135, 137, 139–142, 145, 175
  relationship 18, 58, 71, 73, 133, 139, 140, 166, 172, 173
Muhammad
  Muhammad cartoon controversy 13, 27, 30, 33, 87, 101, 116, 120, 138, 165, 219
Muslim 28, 30, 31, 35, 57, 60, 61, 67, 74, 76, 78, 79, 85, 87, 165

narrative sentences 206
nation 44, 45, 62, 65, 85, 88, 96, 101, 102, 105, 109, 110, 114, 149, 150, 159, 160, 171–173, 176, 180–186, 189–191, 195, 196, 199, 208, 210, 212, 216, 221, 222, 225
  narrative 191
  state 15, 24, 32, 44, 45, 47, 88, 129, 149, 157, 181, 210, 218, 221
national 28, 29, 45, 64, 65, 68, 100, 101, 114, 115, 118, 194, 200
  culture 68, 69, 79, 114, 159
  history 147, 182, 212, 213
  identity 19, 44–46, 69, 78, 100, 101, 146, 147, 149, 150, 156, 159, 160, 171, 173, 174, 177, 178, 180, 183, 191, 195, 197, 198, 200, 216, 224, 225
nature 40, 57, 67, 71, 74, 79, 83–88, 91, 95, 96, 102, 109–111, 118, 123, 127, 128, 145, 159, 186, 188, 199, 207, 224
naturalizing 44, 71, 86, 104, 109
necessity
  apparent 17, 56, 67, 72, 73, 75, 76, 78, 105, 114, 145, 167, 171, 220
  economic 58
  epistemic 17, 56, 70–73, 75, 76, 79–82, 89, 97, 98, 114, 121
  justifiable 16, 56, 66, 67, 69, 70, 72, 73, 75, 105, 114, 171, 196, 220
  social 66, 67, 70, 173
neutrality
  epistemic 84, 85
  practical 84, 85

Ngai, Mae 43
norm 14, 16, 17, 21, 24, 34, 37, 49, 52, 55, 58, 67, 70, 72, 76, 79–86, 89, 93, 94, 97, 109, 143, 148, 161, 172, 173, 182, 193, 211, 212
  normalization 18, 25, 100, 146, 152, 157, 175, 177, 179, 187, 196
  normativity 157, 158, 160, 172, 177, 187, 211
not-self 160–164, 169, 181
Nussbaum, Martha 165, 166

Oakeshott, Michael 209
objectification 83, 85, 86, 92–94, 180
  objectifier 83, 85, 86
  objectify 77, 83, 86, 93, 99, 123
objectivity 66, 84, 112, 119, 123, 125, 131, 202
  absolute 84, 87
  assumed 17, 83–87, 90, 91, 93, 104, 110, 117, 128, 141
Oldham 12, 194
  Oldhamer 12, 194
opinionated mind 140
other
  concrete 34, 130, 133, 175
  generalized 33–35, 135

Panayi, Panikos 190, 191
particularism
  defeating factor 36, 134
  enabling factor 36, 134
  moral 35, 39
past
  historical 209
  practical 209, 210
people of color 44, 50, 101, 178, 182
Plessner, Helmuth 174
political membership 13, 68, 72, 89, 146, 189, 197, 200, 212, 220, 223
  nationality 115, 193
power 41, 44, 83, 85, 100, 102, 103, 105, 107, 110, 157, 162, 183, 184, 187, 203
  distribution 16, 81, 103, 105, 110
  identity 99, 100, 102, 105, 107, 109
  imaginative 100–102, 191
  relations 84, 92, 95, 96, 104, 119, 128, 176, 187
  social 99
  structures 66, 67, 201, 203
prejudice 28, 55, 65, 88, 94, 99, 103, 105, 106, 118, 128, 183
  identity 99, 103, 104, 106, 142
public culture 15, 23, 26, 80, 88, 89, 131, 178, 219

race 13, 16, 43, 44, 46, 47, 51, 55, 56, 59, 63–65, 71, 75, 78, 93, 100, 101, 106, 110, 114, 118, 122, 156, 157, 159, 171, 180, 182, 186, 191, 197, 221
  black 46, 51, 58, 59, 63, 64, 102, 105, 106, 122, 128, 151, 161, 180
  non-whiteness 59
  racial equality 48, 50, 51
  racialized 43, 44, 156, 159
  racism 51, 64, 65, 77, 88, 156, 186, 198, 211, 216, 217, 221, 223
  white 44, 48, 51, 66, 101, 102, 105, 122, 128, 132, 161, 180, 182, 186, 188, 194
  yellow 58, 59, 128, 161
Rasmussen, Anders Fogh 28
receiving society 11–15, 21, 23, 26, 27, 42, 53, 55, 63–65, 67–69, 71, 72, 80, 81, 88, 89, 94, 97, 98, 111, 115, 116, 122, 131, 134, 143, 156, 160, 171, 174, 178, 179, 181, 189, 212, 215–219, 223–225
  co-existence 14, 49, 121, 160
  locals 13, 14, 19, 21–23, 26, 27, 43, 49, 53, 55, 69–71, 78, 94, 98, 111, 112, 119, 128, 132, 134, 143, 146, 150, 151, 154, 161, 167–169, 174, 189, 215, 216, 222, 223, 225
  pre-existing contexts 15, 23, 26, 27, 34, 49, 52, 53, 64, 81, 118, 216, 219, 220
reductionist 53, 56, 73, 75, 76, 82, 112, 126, 131, 135, 145, 224, 225
regularity
  genuine 84, 85
  observed 84–87, 89, 91, 94, 96, 126

Index

relationship
  given 173, 174
  made 173
religion 16, 28–30, 32, 33, 35, 38, 45, 46, 48,
  55, 64, 100, 101, 120, 121, 217, 221
  Buddhism 28
  Christianity 28, 33, 35, 36, 121, 138, 162
  Hinduism 28
  Islam 28
responsibility 16, 17, 19, 23, 40, 53, 55, 87,
  89, 95, 97, 134, 176, 178, 185, 192–201,
  203, 208, 211, 213, 215, 216, 222, 223, 225
  epistemic 17, 89–91, 93, 95, 97, 98, 142,
  212
  social connection model 19, 176, 178,
  192–195, 201, 203, 211, 213
responsible 12, 22, 87, 90, 92, 95, 97, 98, 118,
  127, 139, 152, 154, 155, 159, 164, 175, 193,
  194, 201, 209, 218
  epistemic 90, 91, 96, 97, 141
rights 11–13, 15, 21, 23, 24, 26, 27, 31, 33, 39,
  44, 52, 53, 58, 64, 77, 80, 81, 89, 132, 138,
  165, 181, 186, 210, 218–220
  distribution of 11, 25, 26, 111, 219
  formal equality 9, 11, 15, 23, 25, 26, 34,
  52, 64, 131, 145, 220, 222
Ritchie Report 12, 194
Rose, Flemming 28–33, 36, 38, 39, 116

Said, Edward 75, 76, 187
satire 28–31, 33–36, 38, 39, 41, 42, 87, 101,
  102, 116, 120, 121, 134, 138, 165, 219
  Danish tradition 28, 29, 31, 32, 36, 38,
  39, 101, 219
  European values 31
segregation 12, 43, 46–48, 50, 51, 53, 57, 118,
  119, 127, 167, 194, 220
  epistemological 46
  foreignness 16, 42–45, 62, 88, 220
  perpetual foreigners 44, 46, 67, 101, 113
  racial 46–51, 118, 188
  residential 46, 47, 51

Sen, Armartya 16, 56–58, 60, 72–75, 79, 81,
  113
sexism 52
Shklar, Judith 25
Simmel, Georg 152, 167–170, 172
situatedness 90, 91, 93–95, 109, 114
slavery 57, 58, 66
  chattel 57
slaves 57–59, 66, 181
social
  belonging 72, 183, 197, 200, 212
  order 14, 16–18, 52, 53, 55–63, 65–67,
  70–84, 86, 87, 94, 105, 107, 109, 113, 114,
  118, 119, 123, 127, 128, 130–132, 143, 181,
  182, 184, 217, 218, 220, 221, 223
  participation 13, 15, 16, 21, 22, 56, 65, 72,
  94, 114–116, 123, 154, 155, 160, 171, 173,
  178, 180, 183, 197, 212, 216, 218, 220, 221
  position 15, 17, 84, 85, 89, 93, 94, 96, 115,
  116, 124, 126, 128, 152, 155, 162, 163, 202,
  205, 211, 224
  practice 217, 221
  presence 52, 55, 78, 81, 97, 159
  structure 46, 58, 76, 77, 82, 83, 87, 88,
  91, 92, 98, 104, 109, 112, 117, 151, 154, 155,
  157, 158, 160, 164, 166, 167, 179, 188, 209,
  211, 212, 219, 223
solidarity 11, 14, 24, 56, 80, 147, 167, 171, 173,
  174, 177, 216, 225
Song, Sarah 44, 101
Sosa, Ernest 91–93
sovereignty 43–46, 59, 88, 102, 118
stereotypes 18, 21, 30, 41, 42, 44, 45, 88, 94,
  133
strange
  self-negotiating model 18, 172, 175
  strangeness 18, 152, 160, 161, 164, 165,
  167, 169, 170, 172, 175
  stranger 18, 28, 80, 146–152, 155–157,
  159, 160, 167–169, 171–178, 182, 191,
  196–198, 200, 201, 212, 218, 225
structural transformation 19, 82, 178, 185,
  200, 211

subjectivism 112, 126, 202
subjectivity 17, 112, 113, 119, 120, 125, 129–131, 134, 202
syllogism 33, 66, 67, 92

the Hun, Attila 59
the veiling controversy 37
    laïcité 38
theo-politics 162, 163
Ther, Philipp 189, 196, 210, 218
thick 67, 68, 120
    concept 65, 203
    notion 69, 114
    parameter 120
    relation 197–201, 213
thin
    category 72
    concept 65, 68, 72
    definition 67
    notion 69, 114
    parameter 120
    relation 197
Tönnies, Ferdinand 174

universalizability 32
    procedure of 33
    reversibility 32–36, 41

US 44–46, 88, 101, 156
    America 64, 77
    American 43, 44, 57, 64, 88, 113, 141, 154
    Americanness 46, 68, 88, 180
us versus them 18, 21, 78
    friend-and-foe 61
    good and evil 75, 77, 82

vice 89, 163, 165–167
virtue
    epistemic 90, 107, 108
    ethics 135, 138, 140, 175
    intellectual 91

Walker, Margaret U. 56, 70, 73, 81
White, Hayden 204, 205, 208–210
Williams, Bernhard 16, 55, 57, 58, 65, 66, 81, 203, 220
Wittgenstein, Ludwig 148
Wu, Frank H. 45
Wu, Weiyi 115, 116

Yellow Peril 59
Young, Iris 19, 96, 152, 153, 157, 158, 160, 176, 186, 187, 192, 193, 211